WINFIELD SCOTT STRATTON

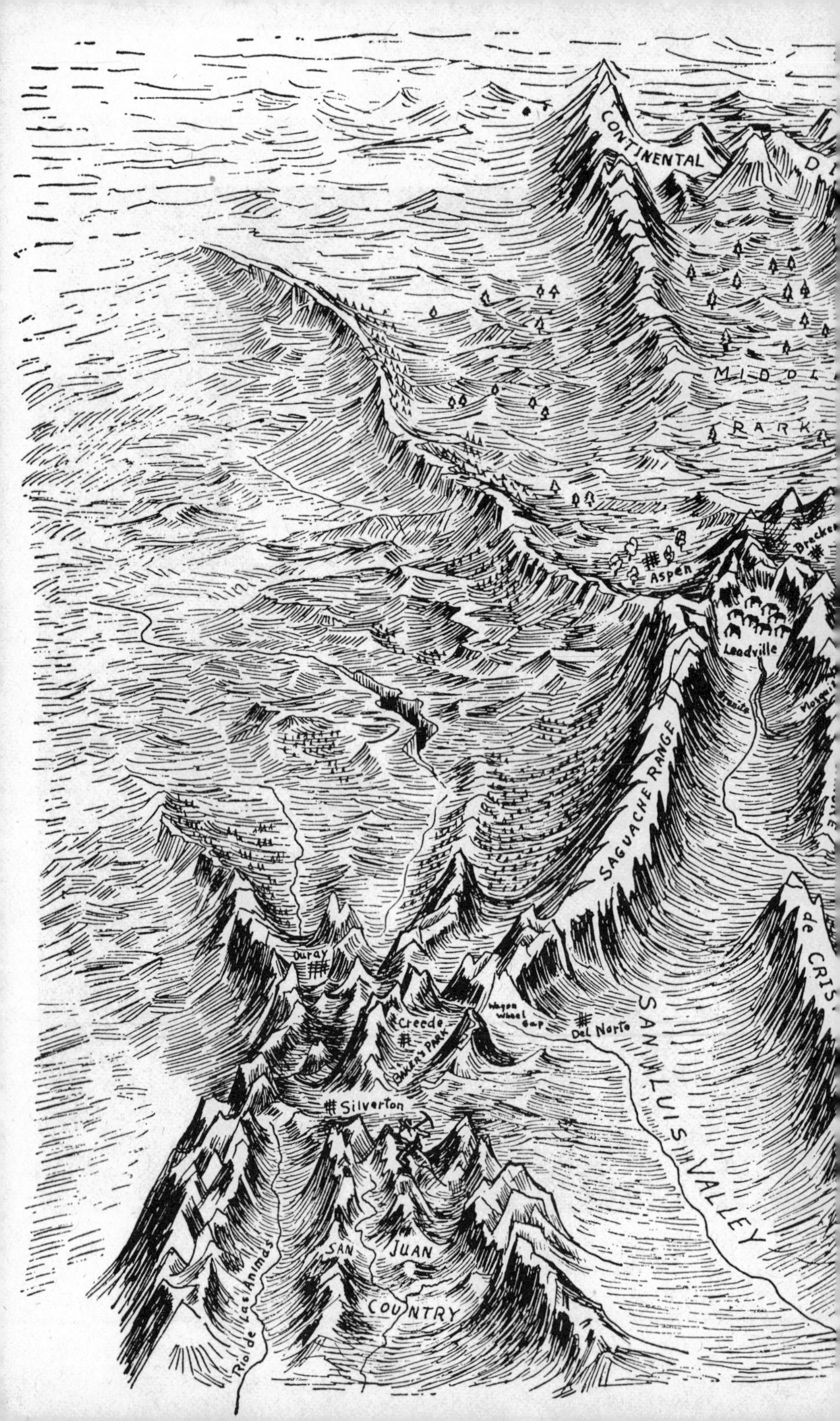
CONTINENTAL
D
MIDDL
PARK
Aspen
Brecken
Leadville
Granite
Mosqui
SAGUACHE RANGE
de CRIS
Ouray
Creede
BAKER'S PARK
Wagon wheel Gap
Del Norte
SAN LUIS VALLEY
Silverton
SAN JUAN
COUNTRY
Rio de Las Animas

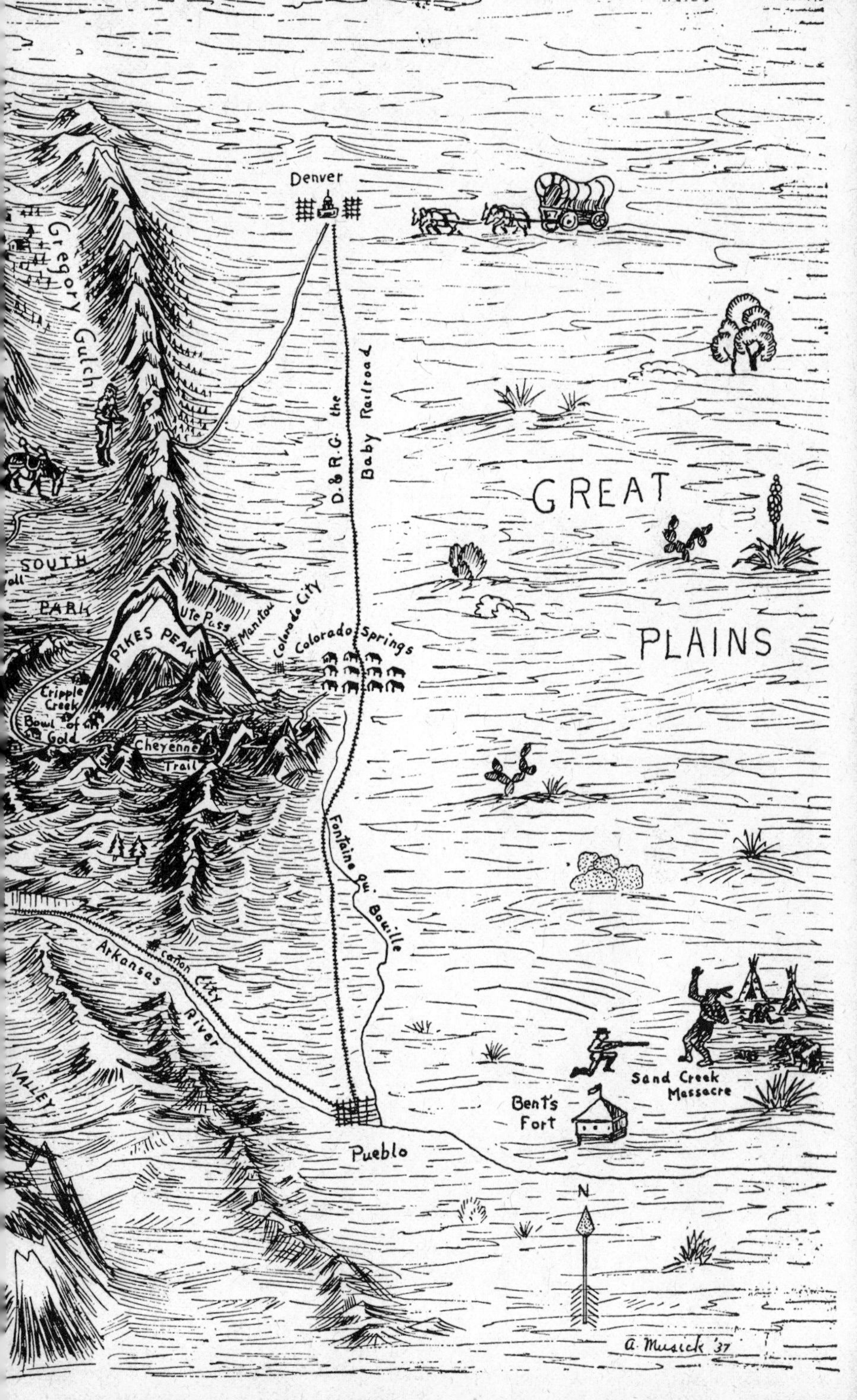
Denver
Gregory Gulch
D.&R.G. the Baby Railroad
GREAT
PLAINS
SOUTH
PARK
Ute Pass
Manitou
Colorado City
Colorado Springs
PIKES PEAK
Cripple Creek
Bowl of Gold
Cheyenne Trail
Fontaine qui Bouille
Cañon City
Arkansas River
VALLEY
Sand Creek Massacre
Bent's Fort
Pueblo
N
A. Musick '37

MIDAS OF THE ROCKIES

OTHER BOOKS BY FRANK WATERS

People of the Valley (1941)
The Man Who Killed the Deer (1942)
The Colorado (1964)
The Yogi of Cockroach Court (1947)
Masked Gods: Navajo and Pueblo Ceremonialism (1950)
The Earp Brothers of Tombstone (1960)
Book of the Hopi (1963)
Leon Gaspard (1964)
The Woman at Otowi Crossing (1966)
Pumpkin Seed Point (1969)
Pike's Peak (1971)

MIDAS OF THE ROCKIES

The Story of Stratton and Cripple Creek

BY FRANK WATERS

SAGE BOOKS

THE SWALLOW PRESS INC.
CHICAGO

Printed in the United States of America

Third Edition
First Printing

Sage Books are published by
The Swallow Press Incorporated
1139 South Wabash Avenue
Chicago, Illinois 60605

This book is printed on 100% recycled paper

Midas of the Rockies was first published by Covici • Friede, New York, 1937. The Stratton Centennial Edition was published by the University of Denver Press, Denver, 1949.

The original edition of this book was dedicated to H. K. Ellingson of the *Colorado Springs Gazette*. The dedication of the Stratton Centennial Edition was to David P. Strickler, Trustee and President of the Myron Stratton Home.

ISBN (CLOTHBOUND EDITION) 0-8040-0554-0
ISBN (PAPERBOUND EDITION) 0-8040-0591-5
LIBRARY OF CONGRESS CATALOG CARD NUMBER 73-163716

CONTENTS

ILLUSTRATIONS

INTRODUCTION

A DIRT ROAD along the creek leads a mile or so through the red willows from the village of Arroyo Seco near Taos to the home of the man who wrote *Midas of the Rockies.* The narrow road, usually golden with sunlight, passes the garden plots and homes of the writer's beloved Spanish-American neighbors, plots alive with their movement and sounds and that of their dogs, horses, cattle and cats. Beyond the plots are sage pastures and then the forested mountains that shelter them. You can't quite see the granite summit of New Mexico's highest, Wheeler Peak, but it is only nine miles away as the magpie flies, and so is the sacred Blue Lake that Frank Waters helped to save for its immemorial owners, the Taos Pueblo Indians.

The Waters house is a brown L-shaped adobe with a long shed on the creek side stacked full of piñon to heat the house. Part of the house, built by the Martinez family, is more than a century old. Two small furry horses, Tommy and Betsy, stand in the courtyard near the woodshed munching hay. They greet the visitor benignly, if with no great show of interest. And then the writer steps from his red-pepper-draped doorway, hand outstretched, head bent a little and smiling. The heart of the visitor lifts. It is that kind of greeting.

Frank Waters is a tall, slender man with a lanky sort of grace and an air of serene, careless composure. He may be in his late sixties, but he lacks any mark of age. His hair is more darkish than gray, reasonably kempt in front but falling behind in straggles over the collar of his plaid shirt and tweed jacket. The cowboy breeches are cuffless and held up by a belt with a big silver buckle. His ears are large. His ruddy face is softly, not harshly, craggy. His voice, low and clear, is full of affection and concern.

He leads you into a living room as cheerful and reassuring as his welcome. Chunks of piñon flair in the corner fireplace and throw out their fragrance. Navajo rugs brighten the pine floor. Hundreds of books line the white walls. There is a shelf of Kachina dolls and a Sioux buffalo-hide shield hanging from the rafters. A coffee table of inlaid potsherds holds a scrabble of little black cheroots and a meerschaum pipe. An absurdly small Olivetti typewriter stands on Waters' big oblong writing desk. He has sat at that desk three hours a day for thousands of days during the past quarter-century punching out with one typing finger of each hand the compassionate novels and perceptive studies of Pueblo culture which have won for him his place in the top rank of western writers.

Midas of the Rockies was not written at the desk. That book belongs to Waters' early period at Pikes Peak and Colorado Springs where he was born and raised. His Grandfather Dozier was a Springs pioneer and one of the first arrivals at the great gold camp of Cripple Creek on the other side of the peak. Waters studied engineering at Colorado College and worked for the phone company in the southwest for some years. During that time, he wrote a novel called *Lizard Lady* and legend has it that he wrote the book high in the air while stringing lines on telephone poles. That is not true. His work involved no pole climbing. He submitted *Lizard Lady* to the publisher Horace Liveright who described it as "the worst manuscript we have ever received." But the merciless critic found glints of vibrancy in it and published it with the plea to Waters, "For God's sake learn how to spell!"

For the budding author that was encouragement enough. He quit the phone company and retired to a tar-paper shack near Colorado Springs where he could live virtually without money. He starved his way through the writing of a novel about Cripple Creek called *The Wild Earth's Nobility*. He was cheered on by a number of bibulous male and female companions who were subsisting in *their* tar-paper shacks on handouts from Roosevelt's New Deal art and writers programs. One of his chief cheer-leaders was the painter, Archie Musick.

Liveright's advance for *The Wild Earth's Nobility* was minuscule. When the famished Waters finished the book he needed money for food right away but he was too worn out emotionally to start a second novel. He had picked up a lot of stories about the Cripple Creek mining king, Winfield Scott Stratton, and so he turned to writing Stratton's biography as a measure of therapy. Liveright did not want a biography but Waters stumbled onto a man in Greenwich Village who claimed to be a literary agent and who delighted him by collecting an advance of $150 from the distinguished firm of Covici·Friede. But Waters never saw the advance. The agent absconded with it in the deeps of Washington Square and the writer had to starve for eight months more in his shack until he finished writing *Midas of the Rockies*.

He had bad moments with *Midas*. A key source of information about Stratton was Henry McAllister, Jr., general counsel for the Denver and Rio Grande Railroad and the state's most awesomely powerful lawyer. McAllister was absorbed at the time with concocting a charitable trust for the Springs magnate Spencer Penrose that would save the Penrose estate from the greedy clutches of Roosevelt's New Deal tax collectors. Waters recalled that McAllister's father had been a neighbor of his Grandfather Dozier in the earliest days of Colorado Springs. But when he went to see the lawyer he found him to be rudely uncooperative and disapproving as though he had heard tell about Waters' association with all those crackpot New Deal companions of his in their tar-paper shacks. Within minutes, McAllister ended the interview and began edging the would-be biographer out the door of his office.

Desperately, Waters dredged up a fugitive memory. "I used to hear a lot about you, Mr. McAllister," he said, "from my Grandfather Dozier. You were the bandy-legged kid who used to herd the neighborhood cattle, including a mean hook-nosed cow of my grandfather's named Grace. Do you remember Grace, Mr. McAllister?"

The crusty barrister burst out laughing, gave Waters a hug and melted full away. He remembered Grace far better than many of his legal triumphs, and with deep pride in his brave conquest of her hook-nosed meanness. From then on he could not do enough for Waters in the matter of digging up priceless inside data on Stratton.

It turned out to be an incredible story. Stratton was a good three-dollar-a-day carpenter who spent his winters building houses in Colorado Springs and his summers chasing the will-o-the-wisp of a rich gold strike all over the Colorado mountains. For twenty summers he searched and found nothing and then suddenly, at Cripple Creek practically in his own backyard, he hit pay dirt. Within months he was a millionaire. Six years later he sold his Independence Mine for eleven million dollars—to this day the highest price ever paid to an individual for a single mine. Thereafter, for three hectic years until his death in 1902, Stratton was the most powerful, influential and envied of the world's mining elite.

The strange tale suited not only Frank Waters' sense of the dramatic but his emerging philosophy as well. He wrote *Midas of the Rockies* in the descending discords of tragedy, for the gold king discovered that his fantastic wealth brought him nothing but despair and death. As a prospector roaming the hills he had found fulfillment and peace in his struggle with "the wild earth's nobility." But his millions snatched him out of this meaningful reality into a false world of vanity and degradation. When the book appeared it was praised highly by the nation's reviewers. Covici·Friede began paying the author royalties on sales that have continued briskly through the years right up to the present new Swallow Press edition.

Looking back, Frank Waters has only one regret about *Midas*. Through some mix-up, his faithful painter friend, Archie Musick, never received a cent from the publisher for creating the book's fine end-paper map of the Pikes Peak region.

MARSHALL SPRAGUE
Colorado Springs, 1972

FOREWORD*

THE YEAR 1948 marks the one-hundredth anniversary of Winfield Scott Stratton's birth, and lends an appropriate excuse for the timely reissuance of this book in a Stratton Centennial Edition.

It offers a better excuse to completely revise the text. Reread after a decade, the book's faults are readily apparent. There is too much "history" in it, too many "statistics" and "local anecdotes," too honest an attempt at bald factual truth. It lacks the streamlined speed, the cellophane smoothness and conclusive patness of the novelized biography to which, in 1949, we are now accustomed. "Why, if you'd whip this thing into fictional shape now," one of its critics keeps insisting, "Stratton would hit a bigger jack-pot in Hollywood than in Cripple Creek,"

Yet after thinking it over, I have decided to let Stratton stand in his own boots and the book remain unaltered. Stratton was never a grandstand player. He refuses to be glamorized. Year by year he keeps growing on us with the slow insistence of his own contradictions and irascible shyness. Melodrama will discover him soon enough.

The book too, with all its own faults, seems to have a stubborn life of its own. It has been long enough out of print to be decently buried and forgotten. Yet someone is always writing in about it: an old miner hidden away in a tuck of the Colorado Rockies, a bank president retired

*1949 Stratton Centennial Edition

to a Park Avenue penthouse, a college research student, librarians, inquisitive tourists. And after an eleven-year lapse it is being serialized in a small Colorado weekly newspaper, *The Independent*, to meet the demand for information about the region.

It is impossible to tell what keeps the book so stubbornly alive. To be sure, it is the only biography of Stratton yet written, and probably the only one that will ever be written with any authenticity. For the people who wrote it were Stratton's contemporaries. Miners, muckers, housemaids, coachmen, carpenters, lawyers with roll-top desks, my grandfather—nearly fifty collaborators. Their testimony was of the man, not the legend they were oblivious of creating; and when they spoke they were mindful of the voices of their consciences. They were simple people. They were impressed by a million dollars. They did not pop a champagne cork without reason, and they knew what it meant to give a dollar to the poor. Now they are gone; and their yellowed newspapers, their old letters, reports and receipts are gone with them. But their homely incidents and confusing contradictions, even the statistics which seem so outmoded nowadays, yet render the flavor of a life irretrievably beyond fictional recapture.

Perhaps, naively enough, it is the story itself that supersedes the manner in which it is told. For it is more than a regional history and the tale of a carpenter who made good in his own home town. It is at once the story of a mountain, a mine and a man. A story so fabulously impossible and yet so excruciatingly true that it commends itself to the whole of America, the only earth, the only people who could have created it.

In all America there has never been a mountain with

the inexpressible fascination of Pike's Peak. From the day its twenty-two-year-old discoverer first glimpsed it hovering on the horizon like a white cloud, it has been a snowy beacon for all travellers. It is as well a symbol of our national unrest, our never-ending search for the elusive and mysterious. With "Pike's Peak or Bust" emblazoned on our wagon canvas and engraved on our hearts, we have perpetually sought the end of the rainbow trail.

It would have been amazing, a national calamity, had the pot of gold not been found buried in Pike's Peak. The joke is that it was found there only after the search for it was given up and disappointed heads were nodding the moral that mere gold was the least worthy of men's desires. But discovered it was. On the south slope of the Peak. Beside a crooked stream called Cripple Creek. Just one mile straight up and eighteen miles due west of the conservative resort of Little London.

"Gold! Gold! Gold! Gold!
"Bright and yellow, hard and cold!"

What a potful there was! Stratton's Independence. "The most noteworthy gold mine of the Western Hemisphere if not of the world." A mine that embraced fourteen claims, whose underground workings aggregated eighteen miles, whose principal veins were named like other complete mines. Gold so pure a man could carry out a fortune in his pants pocket. Stopes so rich they were locked with bank vault doors. A treasure box that sold for $10,000,000 cash, that produced over $27,000,000.

A mine that overnight made the Cripple Creek cow pasture the greatest gold camp on earth. A mere 6 square miles, 11,000 feet high, it supported 175 shipping mines,

11 gold reduction mills and 9 samplers; gave rise to the highest incorporated town in the world, 3 cities of the second class, and a population of 46,000; led the world in gold production; and produced over $450,000,000 in gold.

Of all this timberline domain Stratton, the obscure carpenter and handy-man, was its undisputed sovereign: "The Croesus of Cripple Creek," "Colorado's Count of Monte Cristo," "The Midas of the Rockies," "America's Greatest Mining King."

This of course provides the happy ending of the traditional American success story. Sired by Rugged Individualism out of the Period of Exploitation, it already had given birth to such robust and pathetic mining heroes as H. A. W. Tabor and Thomas Walsh. Rich from the Matchless at Leadville and the Camp Bird at Ouray, they rivalled each other in childish spending.

Senator Tabor, in flowered waistcoat and flaring mustaches, buying mahogany forests in the Honduras and importing peacocks for his front lawn; building his Opera House with cherry logs brought from Japan, carpets from Belgium, tapestries from France; scattering solid silver bricks with the unshaken assurance that there was enough silver coming up the shaft to erect a wall of it forty feet high clear across Colorado.

"Monsieur Tom" Walsh, not to be outdone, took over the Elysée Palace Hotel and began dazzling Parisians with his dinners: four hundred guests at a whack, the Czar's own band from St. Petersburg, songs by Mary Garden and Madam Nordica. After visiting King Leopold of Belgium in a special train of five coaches attended by retinues of servants, he returned to America. In Washington he built a house of sixty rooms, the reception hall of green-veined marble columns rising four stories to a glass dome. This was augmented by a lease of "Beaulieu," the residence of Cornelius Vanderbilt, Jr. at Newport, a summer house at "Manchester-by-the-Sea," Massachusetts, and his "Wolhurst" estate neat Littleton, Colorado. Nor did his daughter fail to keep stride when she bought the Hope Diamond for a decoration to wear while visiting Moscow night clubs.

Today after two World Wars these happy endings and their tragic anti-climaxes seem distinctly old-fashioned. The stories are period pieces. Their heroes are almost forgotten.

The story of Stratton is made of sterner stuff. His legend begins at the very point where the others end. Nearly fifty years after his death it keeps on growing with a mounting significance.

Why? How does it differ from those of his time?

The answer lies hidden in Stratton himself. Elusive, subtle and confounding, he was a man no one knew. Eccentric and unpredictable, he was always an enigma. Even his appearance was unprepossessing: neither short nor tall, never fat nor too thin, dressed well but unobtrusively in trousers neatly pressed without creases, and always in boots hand-made by an old cobbler from Switzerland—his closest friend. His expression was mildly inquiring and a little melancholy; his white hair, eyebrows and mustache were thin and carefully combed.

Mild mannered and diffident, he yet gave rise to the written report that "he had no morals, no trust, no faith and apparently no hope. His debaucheries were said to be not alone bad but positively Satanic. His numerous affairs cost him great sums of money. He was capricious, irascible and absolutely unstable. To be your friend in the morning was no guarantee that he would not be your bitterest enemy by night." Yet nothing of this affected his fundamental austerity. He lived simply and trusted as friends only working people, day laborers and boarding-house keepers.

Everything about him built up a gigantic paradox.

Shy as he was, he saw to it that the names of Winfield, Scott, Winfield Scott, Stratton and Strattonia were amply sprinkled on the map. He was an excellent carpenter and cabinet maker, and read theology. He was addicted to whiskey and kindness, and known equally for his furious rages and unparalleled generosity. In a time when men prospected with picks and mined with shovels, he was going after the newest machinery and finest mining brains. Yet he always held to the belief that ore was worth more in the ground than above it, and treated his great Independence as a vast underground bank, drawing from it only as he needed funds. The very people who considered him colorless and unimportant yet trembled at what he might do next, like a gray ghostly wolf slinking down the mountains into town.

Carpenter, prospector, mining king, multimillionaire, man of affairs, financier, philanthropist, eccentric, neurotic, hermit—this was the enigmatic personality that today has outworn the boisterous antics of his predecessors and contemporaries, whose vision thrusts forward into the future.

What was the key to his character? We only know that he was always the solitary outcast who for seventeen years had plodded the Rockies with his burro. It was in his blood to stay, that strange malady which made him kin to the thousands who swarmed gulch and peak to leave their whitened bones on undiscovered hillsides. What were they seeking behind the convenient symbol men called gold? Stratton knew when he found it in Pike's Peak. It was his one weak moment of utter disillusionment, and his one great moment of fulfillment. Henceforth he knew the strange destiny to which he, as all of us, are inexorably confirmed. That is what made him seem queer to his neighbors. That is the heritage he leaves behind him, the legend that is ours to decipher.

F. W.

PART ONE: PRAIRIES

"Our citizens being so prone to rambling and extending themselves on the frontier will, through necessity, be constrained to limit their extent on the west to the borders of the Missouri and Mississippi, while they leave the prairies incapable of cultivation to the wandering and uncivilized aborigines of the country."

1. PRAIRIES

LATE one afternoon in July, 1848, one of the prominent citizens of Jeffersonville, Indiana, carefully closed the front door of his house, and with a relieved smile strutted proudly enough down the board walks to his boat-building yards on the river.

The firm, Logan and Stratton, of which he was now a partner after following his trade as ship's carpenter, was doing well to nicely; their boats plied up and down the Ohio and the Mississippi. He belonged to the Masonic Order and the Jeffersonville Lodge of Odd Fellows. Too, he had just been elected to the Town Council which he was to serve for twenty-one years, and was soon to become a school trustee for seven years. He was devoutly conscious that the Lord ever stood at his brawny right hand. For despite Henry Ward Beecher's boast that "We have given Indianapolis a deep-blue Presbyterian tinge which should last for several generations to keep her straight," and his hope to do likewise for the neighboring towns, he had devoted himself to the Christian Church and remained a member for forty-six years.

An imposing beginning for one who had settled in town just thirteen years before.

But Myron Stratton was not a man to make a vulgar display of pride on the street. What kept the faintest trace of a smirk on his face and the bounce in his usually measured stride was the arrival of a son. This birth was neither unexpected nor unusual. In the ten years he had been married there had been five others. But two of them were boys who had died in infancy, and the other three were mere girls. Now, with a new son—a little puny perhaps, but robust enough to pull through with care—Myron Stratton knew his luck was on the rise.

One sees him, then, striding proudly down toward the river, well dressed in a long-tailed broadcloth, high beaver, white shirt and black bow tie—an erect but stolid figure thirty-six years old, with a firm indomitable face that his new son was never to reflect, however faintly.

Jeffersonville, Clark County, lies on the Indiana-Kentucky border just across the Ohio River from Louisville. It is a small quiet town that today has gained little in population, but lost much of its importance. Any good Hoosier will tell you that when General de Lafayette was making his tour of America it was at Jeffersonville that he was welcomed to Indiana soil. Indianapolis had just been established on a new site sixty miles from civilization and without roads, so the governor rode horseback to Jeffersonville to greet Lafayette. In the forest adjoining the village a feast was spread to which the general was conducted, children strewing flowers in his path. At the head of the long two hundred and fifty foot table was an arch bearing the inscription: "Indiana welcomes Lafayette, the champion of liberty in both Hemispheres." Lafayette perhaps needed cheering. The steamboat *Mechanic* on which he was riding had struck a snag in the Ohio River and sunk. General Lafayette fell overboard, was almost drowned, and lost all his effects and $8,000 in money.

Twenty-two years later the first railroad entered Indianapolis, making it accessible, but Jeffersonville was still an important town on the Ohio.

In the adjoining forests, game was then plentiful at all times. Chickens could be bought for six cents and turkeys for twenty-five cents. Young ladies were educated at the Academy or sent to St. Mary's Convent to learn to make wax flowers and "do" the old masters in cross-stitch. Guitar lessons were twenty-five cents each, and vocal music lessons could be had for ten. Women wore stiff brocades and cotton prints. For the stately silks eighty bushels of corn had been bartered in New Orleans for a single yard, and eight bushels a yard for the prints. Barter was still universal. No gold coins were in circulation, and the common specie along the Ohio was still British and Spanish silver. For small change Spanish dollars were often cut into quarters, eighths and sixteenths. These were known as "bits," "two-bits," or "fo-pence" pieces. A "fip" was equal to five cents and it was common to hear quoted a price of "a fip-and-a-bit."

Men in their Sunday best affected claw-hammer coats and bell-crowned beaver hats, swearing and b'godding for emphasis. The arrival of a steamboat was the day's most important event. Between times they concerned themselves over President Polk's campaign against Great Britain's claim to Oregon, and joined in the cry of their own State Senator Edward Hannegan: "Fifty-four forty or fight!" And already the Fugitive Slave Law, which made it a crime to aid escaping slaves across the river, was causing trouble to "black abolitionists" in the community.

But the one engrossing topic that held men on their cracker boxes and in the saloons past which Myron Stratton took his sprightly way, revolved around the five Indiana regiments which had been to the Mexican War. They were returning home not entirely heroes. Members of the Second Regiment particularly were embittered by the unjust reports of General Taylor regarding their engagement at Buena

Vista. There, fighting a force of eighteen to one, they had been called upon to retreat, leaving a fourth of their men dead on the field. The sentiment of Jeffersonville, indeed of all loyal Hoosiers, turned solidly against General Taylor. When he was elected President it was without the electoral vote of Indiana. Their hero, instead, was General Winfield Scott, who had steamed down the coast of Mexico to storm Vera Cruz and march into Mexico City—the quiet, unassuming and gentlemanly soldier who conducted himself so decorously among the politicians that he was dubbed "Old Fuss and Feathers."

Myron Stratton, befitting his position, justly condemned General Taylor and enthusiastically acclaimed his rival. It was not surprising then that on July 22, 1848, this leading citizen of Jeffersonville hesitated not a moment over a name for his newborn son: he was promptly, decisively, christened Winfield Scott Stratton.

To be sure it was not only in the fashion of the time but consistent with family tradition to name a son after a national hero. A Stratton then living in Nelson County, Virginia, who had given his native town a "Stratton Free Library" had been named George Washington.

But Little Fuss and Feathers was well named: he always lived up to the mild aloof manner of the general. But he needed a soldier's constitution. The family, tragically, was not a long-lived one.

Only Myron, God-fearing, successful and respected, lived sturdily to take another wife and outlive her. Retiring early from ship-building with a comfortable fortune, he died on November 10, 1885, from a stroke of paralysis. A monument was erected to his memory on the Stratton lot in Eastern Cemetery, Jeffersonville, and his trustees were given $500, the interest to be used in keeping up the lot. Today, a half century later, he has to his memory another monument costing $1,041,825, the yearly upkeep of which is possibly 5,000 times greater than the first; not a cemetery lot, but an estate of over 5,000 acres; not a stone tablet, but an institution of 40 buildings dedicated to "poor persons who are without means of support," which has rendered to them 3,200 years of equivalent life service.

Stolid, solid Myron Stratton little suspected as much of his new and puny little son that July day of 1848. To him children were hardly a novelty. He himself was the eighth child of ten. There was also in his family the record of a Solomon Stratton in Virginia, commonly called "King Solomon," who had ten sons. And that same year, 1848, a Mark Stratton was settling Hopewell Farm in Wayne County, Indiana, with twelve children, the youngest of which, Gene Stratton, was to become widely known as Gene Stratton Porter with the publication of her Indiana novels, *Freckles* and *The Girl of the Limberlost*.

Myron, in fact, looked backward as well as forward on the theory that "Those who do not treasure up the memory of their ancestors, do not deserve to be remembered by posterity." So because he did have a great deal to look backward to, it is of interest to inspect those "dry branches of genealogical trees" which may "bear many pleasant and curious fruits for those who know how to search for them."

2

The Strattons originated in Great Britain. The name is a place name derived from the Anglo-Saxon words *stræt* for paved road and *tûn* for home or village, thus denoting those whose homes lay along the old paved Roman roads in Great Britain. Perhaps the first record of a Stratton is that of Alexander in Kincardineshire, Scotland, who in 1124 was granted the "lands of Straton" by David I of Ledland who introduced feudalism into Scotland. He took the name of Alexander de Straton, later dropping the "de."

There were three lines of Strattons in Great Britain. The Stratons of Lauriston have a family record complete from 1124 to 1904 and Lauriston Castle has been their home for over four hundred years. The Strattons of Shotley, seventy-five miles east of London, centered around Kirkton Manor, the original seat of the Suffolk Strattons whose records date back to 1392. In Shrivenham, seventy miles west of London, the third branch of Strattons are recorded in Burke's "Landed Gentry" with the burial of Thomas Stratton in the churchyard in April, 1587.

In England today there are more than forty places named Stratton. They include Stratton-on-the-Foss, County Somerset; Stratton, a township in parish Tilston; and Stratton St. Andrew, a market town and parish including the small seaport of Bude in Cornwall. There is also a Stratton Park in Hampshire, eight miles from Winchester, where the old Roman road may be seen. It is now the seat of the Earl of Northbrook.

It is probable that many Strattons were among the early arrivals in America, though the first record is of John Stratton of Shotley arriving in New England and Joseph Stratton of Harwick arriving in James City, Virginia, in 1628. They spread rapidly. By the time of the Revolutionary War there were 112 Strattons enlisted, their names posted in the rolls of 9 of the original 13 States. There was also a Charles Creighton Stratton born in Stratton Hall, Swedesboro, New Jersey, on March 6, 1796. He was elected to the State Legislature, was twice a member of Congress, and Governor of New Jersey from 1844 to 1848.

Myron Stratton was a descendant of one of the eleven Colonial lines whose record is fairly complete. That he might be forgiven for a possible stiff-necked appearance among the less successful Jeffersonvilleites, a casual review of his four forebears will show. He came of a line of hustlers that did not end until the death of his son, Winfield Scott.

William Stratton of Winsor, Connecticut, and of the first generation, was one of the company sent to invade Canada during Queen Anne's War and died in service October, 1709.

His son, Serajah, moved to the adjoining town of Simsbury, enlisted in the French and Indian War, and also died in service on July 30, 1758.

Of Martin, born in 1730 in Simsbury, Hartford County, family tradition says only that he was a "Revolutionary patriot who bankrupted himself to supply the army with flour." The successful and frugal Strattons did not have a habit of going bankrupt. It is more probable that he was amply rewarded for his service with a land grant in Pennsylvania; for his son Cephas, born on May 13, 1769, went with his family to Bradford County, Pennsylvania. It was the last of the family in Connecticut, but five miles from Simsbury there is a small village still bearing the name "Stratton-Brook."

Cephas Stratton, Winfield Scott's grandfather, operated and was owner of a saw and gristmill in Bradford County, Pennsylvania. In 1769 he married Hannah Adams and lived near Towanda until 1813. The family then moved to Tioga County and lived five years near Canoe Camp. On October 12, 1818, he left Pennsylvania for Hamilton County, Ohio, settling at Cumminsville on Mill Creek, a few miles north of Cincinnati. There he died on October 28, 1833. In section 35, lot 94 of the old Cumminsville Cemetery back of Cincinnati, once part of the Stratton farm, may be seen the last resting place of Cephas and Hannah Stratton with three of their ten children.

Myron was the eighth. He had been born in North Towanda in 1812 and at the age of six had accompanied his family to Cumminsville, Ohio, moving to Jeffersonville, Indiana, in 1835.

It appears that the family, whatever its faults, could boast of members who used both head and hands. They were hard workers like most men of their times, with the knack of making money and the more unusual one of keeping it. Their history is one of continual moves, yet they left their mark on the country wherever they went. It seems to be the one distinguishing feature about them—a passion for leaving monuments and places marked by the name.

In addition to those in England, there are Stratton, Maine, and Stratton Island off the coast; Stratton and Stratton Mountain, Vermont; and others in Virginia, Pennsylvania and New York.

To these, consistent with the family habit, Winfield Scott was to add more: a Stratton Park in Colorado to match that in England; the towns of Winfield and Strattonia. He too moved westward; was industrious, frugal and successful; erected monuments; left his name inscribed upon the maps. His life abounds with coincidences which link him to his past.

And there, paradoxically, the resemblance ceases. Born at the crossroads of both time and place, he takes on a character that refutes his lineage. The sixth child of twelve, of a father who was the eighth of ten, he had but one and denied him. His wealthy associates of English extraction he abhorred, preferring as friends boarding-house keepers and laborers. Of square-jawed, sturdy folk like his father, he was a "modest, slender, frail-looking man, quiet, unassuming, unassertive in manner and wholly inconspicuous in appearance." To them he indeed would have seemed a strange ghost strayed into the family fold.

3

The Jeffersonville Strattons lived a few blocks up from the river in a large, double, two-story frame house on Chestnut Street. One half of the house was occupied by a family named Parker, whose boy, James, was about Winfield Scott's age. The Stratton half was better filled most of the time. Preceding Winfield there had been two boys, James Augustus and William Riley, who had died in infancy. His three older sisters, still living, were Diantha Jane, nine years older; Harriet Newell, seven years older; and Anna Augusta, his favorite, just two years older than he. By the time he was five and starting to school there were two more sisters, Mary Anne and Hannah Virginia.

Myron, the prominent and successful school trustee, provided for his only boy the best education the town afforded. Winfield went to the public school and thence to the C. Leonhard private school of Jeffersonville. The mild little chap trotting docilely back and forth from home lived up to his name of Little Fuss and Feathers. He was sensitive and almost abnormally tidy, quiet and retiring. In school he showed a remarkable talent for drawing, being "exceptionally gifted" at composing pencil sketches. At home his one absorption was in reading the Bible. He once offered his two younger sisters a small gift of money to persuade them to read the New Testament, and his first earnings from helping his father at the shipyard he used to buy his mother a new Bible. It is probable that he had worn the family one out.

An observer prejudiced against Jeffersonville once remarked that in "a town of tumble-down buildings, notoriously shiftless citizens whose most pressing occupation always had to give way when the whistle of an Ohio river steamboat was heard, it is almost a miracle young Stratton should have imbibed lessons of thrift and perseverance there. The only imposing structure in the place was the grim old Prison South whose frowning battlements confirmed in the mind's eye the terrible tortures carried on in the worst penitentiary in the United States." But despite his background at the worst, thrift and perseverance were the two virtues which little Fuss and Feathers acquired as a boy and which remained with him throughout his life. Some of the others he was to lose very soon.

Jeffersonville, throughout his school-days, was swept by unrest. Like all river towns, it was in a continuous flux. Abolitionists persisted in running escaping slaves across from Kentucky; the Civil War emptied into it its quota of derelict men; steamboats kept puffing up-river with men and tales from the newly opened West. This excitement and continual parade was more than matched in the Stratton house.

The household echoed to a perpetual wail and moan. Following his two younger sisters, three more girls and a boy were born; Luella, Jesse Eliza, Ada Carman and Frank Myron. All of them died before reaching the age of six. Winfield might have stood by with his Bible opened to the text, "The Lord giveth and the Lord taketh away," and confirmed its truth: in eight years, four births and four deaths. Then, on March 10, 1865, his oldest sister, Diantha Jane, died. She was twenty-six and unmarried. With her help removed, Winfield's mother, Mary Halstead Stratton, collapsed under the strain. In November of the same year

Colorado Springs in the early 1870's.

she died at the age of forty-five, almost unknown while alive and never afterwards spoken of by her son. She had been too busy to be noticed: in twenty-three years giving birth to twelve children and burying seven.

The boy, rent by the clamor and distress of such a household, fled naturally to the river-front. It was a breeding-ground of legend, the birthplace of a gigantic phenomenon. Hs was caught in its travail and became a part of the myriad-headed monster. It is impossible to separate him from it. . . .

The year 1848 during which Stratton was born was the hinge upon which swung open the door of America to a flow of westward moving people that has no equal in the world—a vast exodus of a glamor and significance not paralleled since Marco Polo's trip to China and the Crusades to the Holy Land.

The few years preceding were marked by signs of growing unrest. In the little towns along the Ohio River, in Indiana, Kentucky, Ohio, one tasted the flavor of life still fresh and pungent from settlement. It had a curious aspect of cosmopolitan provincialism. Mississippi steamboats puffed up river with cargoes, manners, speech and dress from the Old South. From the Atlantic seaboard to the east, from cities humming with trade, from factories and mills, leapt wood-burning locomotives bringing wallpaper, bathtubs, books, and politics. But to the west a bit where the Missouri makes its turn, one came to a sudden halt. Illinois, Iowa and Missouri were the new frontier. The river marked its abrupt boundary. Set foot on its west bank and it was as if you were immediately adrift on a tawny sea more desolate than any one of blue. It was a wilderness that gradually changed from immense prairies of grass waving high as a man on a horse to short grass plains dotted with vast and countless herds of buffalo, to brazen burning deserts and slow red rivers, and finally to mysterious mountains floating like clouds above the horizon.

It still seemed likely to bear out Zebulon Pike's prophecy:

> A barren soil, parched and dried for eight months of the year, presents neither moisture nor nutrition sufficient to nourish timber. These vast plains of the Western Hemisphere may become in time as celebrated as the sandy deserts of Africa. . . . Our citizens being so prone to rambling and extending themselves on the frontier will, through necessity, be constrained to limit their extent on the west to the borders of the Missouri and Mississippi, while they leave the prairies incapable of cultivation to the wandering and uncivilized aborigines of the country.

Yet fifteen years later, Captain William Becknell had made the first crossing in wagons to Santa Fe. Each year thereafter long straggling lines of Conestoga or Pittsburg wagons followed the old trace. Beginning usually from Franklin or Independence, Missouri, they set out for Council Grove where the hardwood trees thinned out to sparse clumps of cottonwoods growing in the river bottoms, the only wood to be found henceforth to the base of the Rockies. Around the Great Bend the tall prairie grass dwindled to the "short grass" of the plains, the gramma or buffalo grass. Up the Arkansas the trail divided at Bent's Fort, the most famous rendezvous of trappers, prairie and mountain-men in the West. Thence the wagons crawled over Raton Pass at the rate of three or four miles a day and down to Santa Fe, or took the Cimarron Cut-Off. On this stretch of desert between the Arkansas and the Cimarron men might travel for days without water and like Becknell's party have to "cut off the ears of their mules and suck the blood." The Santa Fe Trail was never a rigid, well marked route; it wandered, swinging right or left with the seasons, with Indian raids, heavy rains or passing buffalo herds. Nor was it only a mere geographic trace. It was still an adventure into the unknown. In the summer of 1848 a young man named Gilpin, later Governor of Colorado, counted three thousand prarie schooners crawling past Fort Mann. And that same summer, a government freighting company lost about nine hundred head of cattle and had to abandon its wagons along the way. But on August 10, 1848, the first outfit of a man named Majors left Independence for Santa Fe. It was the first of many scheduled trips by a company later known as that of Russell, Majors and Waddell. The Santa Fe Trail, so long almost legendary, had at last cut into the virgin prairie sod a path deeper than any worn by buffalo, and it was never to be erased.

The second and longest of the three great overland trails, the Oregon Trail, followed up the Platte across Nebraska to Fort Laramie, went through South Pass, and struck north into the disputed Oregon Territory. Unlike the first, mainly a path of commerce to a culture and civilization already old, the Oregon Trail was the pathway of a people moving westward for conquest alone. It too was arduous and dangerous, necessarily slow; the first conducted emigration train had made the trip only six years before.

The third trail, branching off from it, was the route of a people driven from within by a different motive—religion. It had its inception when the Mormon prophet, Joseph Smith, and his brother Hyrum were assassinated in the jail at Carthage, Illinois. The Mormons, driven out of Missouri, had established Zion in Illinois, prospered and built their temple at Nauvoo. With the assassination of Prophet and Patriarch persecution was renewed. At Lima, Illinois, a mob burned 175 houses and forced the Mormon inhabitants to flee to Nauvoo. There, faced with a Mormon massacre or a Mormon exodus, Brigham Young, who had assumed leadership, received a revelation commanding them to seek a new refuge. Where this would be they did not know. California was part of Mexico and the Oregon Territory was disputed by the United States and Great Britain. But somewhere they knew God would reveal the spot and make the wilderness blossom as a rose.

The trek began in the dead of winter. Brigham Young and two thousand Saints crossed the frozen Mississippi River and headed west. It was twenty degrees below zero. Oxen and horses had to live on bark and limbs of trees, becoming so weak they never made more than six miles a day. By summer they reached the Missouri. On the east bank, the site of Council Bluffs, and across the river on the site of Florence, Nebraska, they established winter quarters. Leaving his people to grow grain for seed and to rebuild wagons, Brigham Young and 148 of his people set out on April 7, 1847, for the spot which God would reveal to him as the place to plant the stakes of Zion. The train consisted of "72 prairie schooners, 93 horses, 52 mules, 66 oxen, and there were also 19 cows, 17 dogs, a few cats and some chickens."

After suffering unbelievable hardships and mountain sickness, the train crawled down into a great valley surrounded by snow-capped mountains. "And there on that hill an angel of the Lord stood, and pointed down this valley and said 'Stay there.'" After a journey of 102 days, over 1,031 miles of desert, plain and mountain, they had reached the Promised Land. And here on the site of Salt Lake were planted the stakes of Zion. Leaving his party to lay out a city that never deviated from the original plan, Brigham Young returned to lead the rest of his people out of bondage. The second exodus consisted of 2,417 people, together with all animals and supplies. They left Winter Quarters in May and arrived on September 20, 1848, establishing the third great overland trail. Thereafter, for twenty years, the procession never ceased. The wilderness indeed blossomed as a rose into Deseret, the land of the honey-bee, and the Mormon Empire.

Meanwhile, there took place other events. The first was that which had given little Stratton his name. The second was not only to utilize and make more widely known the three great trails, but was to start the rush which caught up Stratton, to color his life and thought, to make him one of its great emblematic figures.

The United States Congress, after a fiery message from President Polk, had declared war on Mexico. General Winfield Scott and his soldiers set out down the coast, captured Vera Cruz and marched triumphant into Mexico City to storm Chapultepec. General Taylor marched into Mexico across the Rio Grande, and General John C. Fremont marched overland through New Mexico into California and induced the Mexicans of California to revolt. While the Mormons were still encamped at Winter Quarters, Captain James Allen of the U.S. Army arrived and asked for five hundred Mormons to serve in the war, offering $42 allowance per man for clothing in advance. This sum of $21,000 could not be resisted; Brigham Young ordered his men to leave and "to take their Bibles and Books of Mormon, and if they had any playing cards to burn them," promising that in the name of Israel's God not a man would fall in battle. The Mormon Battalion marched to Fort Leavenworth, were outfitted and armed, and set forth over the

Santa Fe Trail to Santa Fe and thence to California. After the Treaty of Hidalgo with Mexico was signed on February 2, 1848, they were discharged and began working their way back from California over the mountains to rejoin the Mormon colony in Utah.

Early that spring a group of them were working as laborers under James W. Marshall, digging a mill race for Captain Sutter near Sacramento. The small yellow specks turned up in the soft dirt by their shovels proved to be the greatest single discovery of gold ever known. Within a year the news had spread over all the country and the great rush of Forty-niners had begun. By July of '49 it was estimated that there were forty thousand Americans in California, which had previously been inhabited by less than three thousand. By the end of the year there were one hundred and twenty thousand, and some thirty million dollars worth of gold had been mined. Over the overland trails swarmed a steady stream of covered wagons, incidentally building up the Mormon Empire, which asked to be admitted to the Union as the State of Deseret, the land of the honey-bee, with over eleven thousand people.

The year 1848, then, marked for the West the end of the era as a wilderness little known except to trappers and explorers. The United States had added to it 851,590 square miles—seventeen times the size of New York state. The first gold discovery of consequence had been made and the precious metal was thenceforth to color national thought. Three great overland trails were made known and marked by skeletons, burned and broken wagons—broad beaten paths of empire. Over them, for the rest of the century, poured the greatest wave of emigration the world has ever known—to explore, conquer, populate and forever change the wilderness of half a continent and within the span of one man's life. In all history the world was to see no transformation so swift, so complete. Nor will it ever again.

It was a time when like the sun all men's eyes turned westward, a time of great unrest. From the Missouri to the mountains, those great Western plains were a stage upon which countless thousands of men swarmed to play parts more swiftly than could ever be recorded. It is wholly unremarkable that a boy born in such a time and on the edge of such a stage was to assume a role—a part classically adhered to but nevertheless tinctured by his own subtle individuality—more significant than can be recorded fully.

4

In such an atmosphere of unrest and change the boy grew up. It was as if he lived beside an ever moving army. Roads and river were full of people drifting westward.

The statement of a townsman that "Winfield Scott was a blear-eyed sot in this city, and his haunts were the barrel houses and his friends the seedy-garbed wrecks on the whiskey reefs" is only partially true. The first assertion was always indignantly denied by one of his chums, his neighbor James Parker. The last part hits closer home.

Young Stratton had another comrade, Byron Logan, the son of his father's partner in the Logan and Stratton firm. Inseparable companions from the age of three months to eighteen years, they were much alike, these two sons of their partner-fathers. They had been born in the same month of the same year, in the same block of the same street, and were of the same height and disposition. Winfield often clapped him on the shoulder, exclaiming, "Byron, I have a number of friends but you're the only brother I ever had!"

The three youths went nightly down along the river and

sat in the saloons. All of them could hoist a drink and play at being men. But they imbibed more steadily of a more fiery stimulant: the tall tales of the river and the men who had made the trip overland by the way of the three great trails west.

One in particular held Winfield and his two companions rapt and open mouthed. In thousands of saloons along the river and the frontier, men listened to the same tale with even more credulous astonishment.

Deep in the wilderness of the West a new and glistening silver peak had reared aloft like a beacon to them all. Gold had been discovered at the foot of Pike's Peak. Six quills of gold from the Pike's Peak Diggings had been emptied out on a bar in Omaha. A man named D. C. Oakes, using a journal of W. Green Russell, published in Mills County, Iowa, a *Pike's Peak Guide and Journal*, which reported the region to be fabulously rich in gold, and gave directions for crossing the plains. The Peak itself was reported as being almost solid gold. One had only to slide down it on a heavy wooden drag with a knife edge attached to its bottom to scrape off the gold. A simpler method was to start a boulder rolling down the mountain. When it burst apart at the bottom one simply gathered up the nuggets and chunks of gold it had contained, and was rich for life.

To substantiate these tall tales, loafers drew out from their pockets tattered newspapers in which were printed official statements of Horace Greeley and other Eastern journalists. They had gone West expressly to report the truth of conditions and gold findings.

And look! a stubby finger pointed out project after project. Four men from South Bend, Indiana, had sluiced $3,000 in three weeks. Another group from DeKalb County, Indiana, had washed $260 in a day and a half, despite having to carry their dirt half a mile. Four men from Farmington, Indiana, had sluiced $607 in four days. Another group from South Bend had made $305 a day and sold half their claim for $2,500. All good Hoosiers, every one of them. And some of them neighbors!

Winfield and his two chums left the bars drunker than on drink. They puffed out their youthful chests and swore great oaths at the winking stars. Along all the Missouri men were setting forth for Pike's Peak and Colorado. The youth shook hands calloused by hard labor. They were forced to bide their time, but resolved all three to go too.

Young Fuss and Feathers trudged home in a fine mood and flung open the door. Myron, staid and conservative, was sitting with his four daughters. The past few years of trouble had not left the family welded too harmoniously together. He raised his head.

"Some more of this cock-and-bull talk you been listening to, boy?"

The four daughters ruffled up their skirts and bent heads like chickens before a storm. For by now young Stratton had begun to show another side. He had given up his study of the Bible, was moody and irritable at times, and had begun to quarrel with his father. Winfield now snapped back, and another quarrel was on. In a few minutes it was over: sturdy Myron had the squarer chin. He was only amazed that his frail and mild-mannered son should show so much granite beneath his pleasant shell.

Winfield Scott had finished school. For awhile he worked in the Logan and Stratton boat-building yards. He was a good workman and had his father's knack of handling tools and joining timbers. Deciding upon the trade, he was apprenticed to his father's old German friend, Christian Heine, for three years to learn carpentry, mechanics and drafting.

His aptitude for drawing now appeared to advantage. He was considered an unusually fine draftsman, and was always to show how thoroughly he had mastered his trade as a carpenter.

Throughout his apprenticeship he was known as a young man of thoughtful mien, habitually neat appearance (always going to work in a white shirt and collar) and generally mild of manner. But now he had begun to lose his qualifications for the Horatio Alger hero of Jeffersonville. He developed a devil of a temper.

Byron Logan began to cast uneasy eyes when his chum increased his quarreling with his father; he himself, learning the blacksmith trade, was settling down to an easy stolid life. But on the slightest remark young Stratton was likely to explode into an outburst of rage. On the occasion of a rebuke from his master, he grabbed up a hammer and leaped upon old Heine. The intervention of some nearby workmen luckily saved the old German from serious harm.

And Winfield still hung on to his dream of Pike's Peak gold. The long delay was proving more and more troublesome between father and son; they quarreled often.

Near the end of Winfield's apprenticeship, Myron married again. His second wife, Helen T. Cline, was a beautiful young woman much younger than he and "seemed to rise like a specter between father and son." It is quite probable she added at least a little to the dissension between them. Winfield never let her beauty overbalance his sense of propriety. He was still a Young Fuss and Feathers.

One of their quarrels was caused because she insisted on hanging out the family washing on a line in front of the house. Winfield maintained there was plenty of space in the back yard. Myron now came home. He took up for his wife and began to remonstrate with his son. Winfield was obstinate. After a heated quarrel Myron flung out of the house. Winfield grabbed up a rifle; running to the front porch, he sent a bullet whizzing above his father's head.

The incident gave rise in after years to the pious statements regarding Winfield that he "sought to expiate a reckless crime of his youth by erecting a memorial to his father," and that "it was a mercy he died an honored philanthropist instead of a murderer."

Winfield probably thought little of the occurrence; he was too eager to get away. And he heeded little the vague reports from the now almost abandoned Pike's Peak region.

5

Long before young Stratton could set out, even before he had finished his apprenticeship, the region lying at the base of Pike's Peak had made its bid for immigrants and failed. He did not know that except for a few remaining settlers the Great Plains along the front wall of the Rockies between the Platte River valley to the north and the Santa Fe Trail far southward were left to the Indians.

Pike's Peak was still the snowy beacon, visible for fifty leagues, which it had been long before Pike had seen it, only to declare that nothing but a bird could scale its lofty summit. For a half century, after his futile attempt to ascend it, late in November, 1806, it marked for traders, trappers and explorers that region named Colorado by the Spaniards from its fantastic red cliffs and cañon walls, its slow red rivers and red adobe earth. In them all it provoked the wonder, allure and mystery of the mountains blocking their path. One after another they were drawn by its fatal fascination: James Purcell, whom Pike had met and reported as the first American trapper in the region; Ruxton, a wealthy young Englishman who after spending years in the mountains returned to London, could not stay, and came back to die; Dick Wootton, christened Richens Lacey Wootton, son of a rich Virginia tobacco planter who, once drawn into the mountains, settled in a cabin near the group of mineral springs at the base of the Peak. Long's expedition in 1820 came down the Pass to this same cluster of iron and soda, to springs from which streamed the *Fontaine-qui-Bouille* ("the fountain which boils"). Even then the trail had been worn deep into the rocks by the Utes filing down to their sacred tribal springs. Fremont, the Pathfinder, reached the base of the Peak in 1843; Bent, St. Vrain, Gunnison and Gilpin passed leaving their names, like Pike, inscribed upon the map. For all these men Pike's Peak and the deep cañons at its foot held a rare fascination.

It remained for a group of Cherokees from Georgia to swing northward on their trek to the California gold camps of '49. The customary route for the wagon trains lay to the north: up the Platte River valley, taking the north fork and then crossing the mountains—a route safer from Indian attacks than that up the Arkansas Valley. But taking by chance the latter trail and prospecting on their way north along the base of the mountains, they discovered gold in the Cache la Poudre River.

In 1858, after straggling back from California, a new party of whites and Cherokees was organized in Georgia to resume the search for gold near Pike's Peak. Led by William Green Russell they panned some gold from Cherry Creek, south of the Platte. News of their discovery spread like fire across the plains. Wagon-makers and merchants, clerks, farmers and gamblers flung down their pens and tools of trade. All along the west bank of the Missouri they gathered to make their start. The Pike's Peak Rush got under way.

That high snowy Peak seen for days out upon the plains became a beacon for thousands of huge Conestoga wagons hastily chucked full of household goods—"Pike's Peak or Bust" emblazoned upon their canvas—long straggling lines that snaked over the trails. Even carts and wheelbarrows were utilized for transportation, and one man attempted to cross the prairies in a light wagon with a sail, depending on the wind for power. Within a year 150,000 people were swarming across the plains.

By midsummer of '59 more than a third of them were on their way back, disconsolate, broke, hungry, their clothes in rags, leaving their goods strewn beside the trail rather than to compel their gaunt oxen to drag them the hundreds of miles back to the Missouri. Many of the wagons carried the new terse legend painted over the old: "Busted, by Gosh!" Their opinion of D. C. Oakes who had published the *Pike's Peak Guide and Journal* was appropriately left engraved on dozens of fake gravestones scattered along the route:

> Here lies the body of D. C. Oakes,
> Killed for aiding the Pike's Peak hoax.

This backward flow of immigration was partially arrested by the news of a rich gold strike up Clear Creek by Tom Golden, Jackson and an Indian named Black Hawk. The scene of the discovery became the site for the towns of Golden and Idaho Springs, and the camps of Jackson Bar and Black Hawk. This was followed by the strike of a Georgia cracker named Gregory, establishing the Gregory Diggings and Central City. Down at the junction of Cherry Creek and the Platte the heartened gold-seekers began establishing themselves in Placer Camp, Montana City, St. Charles and Auraria, preparatory to radiating still farther into the mountains. Within a year these camps merged into one, Denver, named after James W. Denver, Federal Governor of Kansas.

Among the many groups crossing the plains was that of the Lawrence Party. This party was inspired by an Indian named Fall Leaf who said he had found gold "two sleeps from Pike's Peak" while on the warpath against Arapahoes and Cheyennes. But Fall Leaf went on a drunken spree as the party was about to start and was left behind. There were about fifty people in the eleven wagons drawn by oxen which left Lawrence, Kansas, on May 19, 1858. They followed the Santa Fe Trail up the Arkansas River, turned north and proceeded up the Fontaine-qui-Bouille along the base of the mountains to the foot of Pike's Peak. Here they camped in the Garden of the Gods among the fantastic red sandstone cliffs, and prospected for gold in the nearby streams. By the end of summer they were disgusted and quit. Most of the party moved north to the camps along Cherry Creek. Some returned to Lawrence, evidently after the hide of Fall Leaf. A few remained to plan a town-site named El Paso from its location at the mouth of the pass leading through the mountains. A few lots were actually sold through representatives in Lawrence but no settlement was made.

The settlers remaining, supplemented by a few newcomers the following year, laid out another town-site farther west along the Fontaine-qui-Bouille. It was optimistically named El Dorado, for from its nucleus of log cabins men began to swarm up Ute Pass to the new Park, Blue and Snowy Range Diggings. Discoveries had been made in South Park and camps were springing up overnight: Buckskin Joe, the Pound Diggings to which the inviting name of Tarryall was given, and then Fair Play. By '60 the new town at the entrance to Ute Pass was the principal supply depot for thousands of excited prospectors. El Dorado became Colorado City. There were more than three hundred cabins in town. Choice lots on Broadway were selling for five hundred dollars. The most optimistic, eying the red rock cliffs, the beautiful white sandstone ridges and the red clay underfoot "which when mixed with water makes a mortar durable as iron ore," saw in them the finest buildings this side of Fifth Avenue, New York City. And the most pessimistic conceded that it was destined to be the first and finest city in the Great Territory of Jefferson "before two more years, if no earlier."

Already the settlers were demanding the establishment of a new government of their own for the western half of the immense Kansas Territory. The new frontier portion was to be known as the Jefferson Territory. By 1861 their efforts were successful; the new territory was created just before Abraham Lincoln's inauguration, but the old Spanish name of the region, Colorado, was retained. William Gilpin who had accompanied the Pathfinder, Fremont, was appointed the first Federal Governor of the Territory of Colorado. At the first meeting of the legislature in Denver, Colorado City was selected as the capital. Soon after, they met again in a log cabin along the Fountain. No business was transacted: the news had just come that Fort Sumter had been fired upon. Gilpin and his legislators returned hurriedly to Denver, to establish a new capital. Some twelve years later a man who had preëmpted a homestead east of the Garden of the Gods bought the log Capitol Building for ten dollars and an old overcoat and moved it to the ranch. A notorious roadhouse was run in it later for many years.

With the Civil War, all travel was diverted from the Arkansas Valley route to the Platte, and Denver instead of Colorado City absorbed the growth of the new Territory. Teamsters and freighters found a way over the mountains from Denver into the South Park mining camps, and Ute Pass became again only a trail for Indians. Colorado City cabins went begging for ten dollars. In June a great flood swept down Fountain valley, the course of the Fontaine-qui-Bouille, drowning people and livestock, and washing out crops. In August it was followed by a plague of grasshoppers devouring everything left and stripping the trees of leaves. Colorado City with its deserted log cabins seemed destined now to become like so many others rotting in the cañons, one of the fabulous ghost-towns of the Rockies.

The pitifully few settlers still clinging to the first capital were now confronted with a new menace—swift marauding bands of Indians. The region had always been a disputed and bloody hunting ground despite an intertribal treaty which had allocated the territory. The plains along the base of the mountains between the north fork of the Platte and the Arkansas River to the south were given to the Arapahoes, Cheyennes and Sioux. The plains south of the Arkansas were allotted as hunting grounds to the Kiowas, Commanches and Apaches. The front range of the Rockies and mountains west were given over to the three tribes of Utes: Uintah, White River and Uncomphagre.

Again the plains tribes, pitching their smoke-gray tepees at the mouth of the cañons, filed into the mountains to hunt and to fight their hereditary enemies the mountain Utes. And—as from time immemorial they had made for the medicinal soda and iron springs to dance and drop votive offerings in the sacred waters of the great Manitou—the Utes kept filing down the Pass over the trail that had been a game trail centuries before their moccasined feet had worn it deeper into the rock. The Pike's Peak settlers were safe from neither. To the east, the Indians were massing at Smoky Hill, closing all communication across the plains, as they had to the south. On the north, Denver had been wiped out by fire and was engrossed in rebuilding. Huddled in the town and fleeing periodically from their ranches to a stockade, they settled down to a reign of terror.

A family in the hills near Colorado City was murdered; up along the Monument men were killed and their stock run off; two small boys herding sheep near Mt. Washington were scalped. The whites in Colorado retaliated with the infamous Sand Creek Massacre when the Colorado Cavalry under Colonel Chivington, a Methodist preacher, rode down upon 138 lodges of Cheyennes and Arapahoes under Black Kettle and White Antelope, exterminating almost eight hundred Indians. In August, 1868, the outrages culminated when Little Raven with a band of several hundred Cheyennes passed through Colorado City into the mountains, killing and running off stock on their way.

Pike's Peak and the region at its foot, after a decade of excitement, was again almost abandoned and forgotten.

6

If Young Stratton had heard that his objective was by now less than a deserted village, he gave no sign of it to his father. His apprenticeship was finished. He was twenty years old, master of a trade, and eager to be away.

There were thousands just like him. The Civil War and the renewed vigor of Indian uprisings could no longer check the flow of westward expansion. Men mustered out of service hurried back to homes and villages despoiled or impoverished by the struggle. Prices were high and jobs scarce. And the frontier that they had left, Missouri, Iowa, Indiana and Illinois, had moved westward across the Missouri. It mattered little that the Pike's Peak rush had been for most a factual bust. Wagon-makers and teamsters, carpenters, merchants and housewives, gamblers, farmers, adventurers young and old—all felt the pull of the thousands of unmapped miles spread out from their feet at the edge of America's frontier. Each saw in them the promise of his calling. The trails were known and marked by skeletons, burned and broken wagons, piles of discarded goods; they were broad and beaten paths that any man might follow.

Winfield, now ready for the break, confided in his two chums. Those Shining Mountains of the Spaniards which "would be found to contain more riches than those of Indostan and Malabar, or the golden coast of Guinea, or the mines of Peru," were still enticing to Parker and Logan. They wanted to go—but not just yet.

Winfield was more impatient. He resolved to be the first, or even the only one, to go. Myron was adamant. There were many quarrels. His partner Logan had died, and he had taken old Heine in the firm. And now there came out news of the miserable state of affairs in Colorado; the Shining Mountains had lost their glitter. Young Stratton was too restless and stubborn to relent: anything to get away.

Luckily there came welcome news from Iowa to ease the squabble. Winfield's favorite sister, Anna, had married and moved to Eddyville. Her husband, George W. Chamberlin who ran a drug store there, had offered Winfield work. Myron Stratton relented and forgave his son—and gave him five hundred dollars with which to start.

To this prosaic objective Winfield started out. Sheepishly he wrung hands with Parker and Byron Logan. They all maintained the seeming lie: they were all going to Pike's Peak and meet there to search for gold.

Strange, the secret ambitions of youth! Byron Logan, pounding out his dreams on an anvil, got no farther than Indianapolis and remained a blacksmith there. James Parker went. It took him five years to reach the mountains. But there among the snowy peaks higher than their dreams he met Winfield and together they set out to find their share of riches. Byron Logan was not forgotten. There came the day (if only a day) when they three stood again united, this time on the snowy peak they had dreamed of, with its gold in their hands. . . .

Eddyville, Wapello County, in southern Iowa still retained a wild dash of the frontier, which had moved westward. Transportation had long been carried on up and down the Des Moines River, supplemented by old trails running parallel with it. Every fifteen or twenty miles there was a crossing, and here sprang up a trading-post. Eddyville, on the north bank of the river, was one of the most important of such crossings.

It had grown swiftly, being on the Oregon Trail and a wintering place for the long wagon trains west. Ezra Meeker, the Oregon pioneer, had stopped here for almost a year en route. When Stratton arrived in 1868 it was still an important if not large town. And here, settled with his sister, he took up his work as a clerk in Chamberlin's drug store.

The work was soft; it was a long way west of home. But the steady stream of emigrants filing past (with or without benefit of his liver pills) aroused his unrest immediately.

A mortar and a pestle seemed trivial tools for one who still faintly hankered to crush out gold nuggets. He lived frugally on his pay, ate heartily of his sister's cooking, and kept his $500 tucked down his pants pocket. Within six months his brother-in-law, Chamberlin, suggested partnership; he needed steady help. It was the excuse Stratton needed. He wrote a letter home to James Parker's brother, R. G. Parker, suggesting that he come to Eddyville as Chamberlin's partner instead, and making the necessary arrangements.

Then he set out farther west with a cousin named Hornaday, a jeweler, the brother of the W. T. Hornaday who later became famous as superintendent of the New York City zoo. They got as far as Sioux City on the Missouri River. It was the edge of the frontier. Standing on the bank he could look across the river to an unbroken thousand-mile expanse.

Abrupty he left Hornaday and went down the river to the old Mormon crossing. Here the Winter Quarters on both sides of the Missouri had grown into towns. The camp on the east bank, called Miller's Hill in honor of a Mormon elder, had become the permanent settlement of Kanesville, and then changed its name to Council Bluffs. Across the river lay Omaha, the key to the opened West.

For twenty years it had been the starting point for two of the three long overland trails. In the winter, when the river between the two towns was frozen, men crossed by throwing straw on the ice so the wagon wheels could take hold. In the summer, steamboats puffed upstream and emptied cargoes of freight, horses and mules, and hordes of men eager to get outfitted and set forth. There were as many saloons as stores. In front of them men swapped news and supplies, quarreled, fought—and went on west.

Young Stratton did not know it, but he entered Omaha as time struck its second great hour. If he could have heard it he would have known it was also striking his own. . . .

He had been born in the year that the three great wagon trails were firmly established across the continent. Now, by another odd coincidence, he had set forth in the very year that saw the establishment of the first of the transcontinental railroads following these old trails. For now a new class of men was crossing that tawny sea of plains with rod and transit. Mile by mile shiny lines of steel crept through the lush prairie grass, through mud and sand. The Union Pacific, started from Omaha, was building on past North Platte and Julesburg, Colorado.

Stratton crossed the river to the liveliest town in the country. As it had been the outfitting post for wagons, it was now the supply depot for the railroad pushing west. Car and engine-houses, machine-shops, were built; huge mercantile establishments sprang up; the railroad was spending a quarter of a million dollars a month in town. Among the thronging crowds of business men and pioneers, railroad gangs and men of every trade and profession, the young carpenter with his still new carpet-bag looked what he was, a country boy away from home for the first time. And like a frightened rabbit he dived for a hole from which he could cautiously peer out at a world gone suddenly mad.

It was May 10, 1869, just twenty-one years after Brigham Young had led his people over the Mormon Trail to the Promised Land; and the last golden spike was being driven with a silver sledge to connect the Union Pacific with the Central Pacific near Promontory, Utah. Every city got the telegraphic message: "Hats off." In Omaha a hundred guns were fired in salute; bells rang, whistles tooted and the town went on a spree.

Stratton, not yet twenty-one, mild, aloof and frightened half out of his wits, slipped through the streets like a ghost. He was less than an individual: he swung with the tide. It was running west, and it caught him up and bore him with it.

His first friend was a hearty, gruff teamster named Joe Donovan who had been discharged from the federal army. He took the boy in hand and together they went to Lincoln. Here Donovan got a job teaming and hauling lumber for the erection of the insane asylum and other buildings.

Stratton came out of his trance with a hearty will. Lincoln was on the boom and he was a full-fledged carpenter just turned twenty-one. He dug in to work. Donovan and Stratton picked up two friends. One was a blunt old carpenter from Nova Scotia named James D. Raymond. The other was a slim young fellow named Edwin J. Eaton who was assistant postmaster in town. The friendship of the four was to carry through many years. But for the two years they were in Lincoln, it seemed based on the avid interest they maintained in the news drifting from the rails farther west.

Connecting with the Union Pacific at Cheyenne, Wyoming, a new branch, the Denver Pacific, was building down to Denver. When it got there, the four reassured themselves, there would be a bigger boom than ever.

Stratton, however, was taking no chances. He was working steadily, and from his savings he was buying two pieces of real estate. For all his seeming interest in the Colorado which had captured his boyish fancy, there was enough of thrifty, shrewd Myron in him to peg down to solid ground.

7

About the same time that Stratton left home for Pike's Peak, another man to the southwest set forth to the same snowy beacon. There was little comparison, and nothing in common, between the young carpenter and this capitalist engineer. But at the foot of Pike's Peak they were to meet; and in a town yet unbuilt and even undreamed of, theirs were to be the only statues erected on the streets. And Stratton, working in Lincoln, seemed to be waiting only for him to lay the way.

The man was General William J. Palmer who had served during the war with the Fifteenth Pennsylvania cavalry. At the present time he was superintendent of construction of the Kansas Pacific railway reaching out across the prairies.

For a year he and his engineers had been surveying possible routes through the territories of Colorado, New Mexico and Arizona to the Pacific Coast. Meanwhile, like a slow snake, the railroad crawled behind him. At the rail-ends the lurid cow-camps of Abilene, Wichita and Dodge City broke out, as the cattle kings and trail-drivers turned their herds of longhorns north to strike the advancing railroad. Here gathered thousands of buffalo-hunters, traders, trappers and surveyors branching out across the plains. And here began again the long lines of covered wagons and the faster stage-coaches of the Leavenworth and Pike's Peak Express, and the Wells, Fargo and Company. General Palmer was in a hurry. Already the Kansas Pacific had reached Sheridan, Kansas, and was crawling to the next rail-end, Kit Carson in eastern Colorado. In July, 1869, he set out for Denver by way of the Arkansas valley. In his wagon-coach near Antelope, Colorado he wrote:

We rode all night across the Smoky Hill fork and have been all day until now, 10 P.M., coming up the Arkansas valley. In a few moments we go on to Colorado City and should reach there about this time tomorrow night. Just before sunset, we came in sight of the mountains, Pike's Peak, the Spanish Peaks and the Green Horn range. A thunderstorm came on and the clouds threw themselves into grand and fantastic shapes, blending with the mountain peaks so as scarcely to be distinguishable. We have just crossed a pretty river called the Fontaine-qui-Bouille up which we shall travel all night, reaching the foot of Pike's Peak about breakfast time.

Two days later he wrote again.

For 120 miles along the Arkansas we drove along not far from the base and generally within full view of the Rocky Mountains. The long ride was by moonlight. I spread out my blanket on the top of the coach back of the sociable driver and slept soundly in the fresh, keen air until awakened, perhaps by the round moon looking steadily in my face, when I found the magnificent Pike's Peak towering immediately above at an elevation of fourteen thousand feet and topped with a little snow. I could not sleep any more with all the panorama of the mountains gradually unrolling as the moon faded and the sun began to rise; but sleepy as I was, sat up and drank in, along with the drafts of pure air, the full exhilaration of that early morning ride.

At Colorado City, General Palmer was even more impressed by something heretofore ignored by the crazed gold seekers—scenery. He bathed in the ancient medicinal waters of the Utes from which flowed the "Fountain that Boils" up which he had traveled. He drank from the soda and iron springs, and rode through the Garden of the Gods, looking at the fantastic, eroded cliffs and pillars of red sandstone that had given Colorado its name. Not only was he sure that there would be a famous summer resort here soon, but, "I fancy that an exploration of the Monument or the Fountain might disclose, somewhere up where they come leaping with delight from the cavernous walls of the Rocky Mountains, where one perhaps might make his future home."

General Palmer was an enthusiastic tourist with an eye for a homesite of his own. He was also a potential railroad-builder, and he had not forgotten to wonder where to lead the Kansas Pacific. His first visit became the stone that was to kill all three birds. He left with the significant observation that "this section is near the line of a railroad that in a few years must be built from Denver southward to the Arkansas, and so on by the San Luis Park to Mexico. This was the first distinct conception on my part of the Denver and Rio Grande railway." . . .

That September, with his engineers, he made the first move, riding "from Sheridan across the plains directly to this spot . . . our object being to ascertain whether an advantageous route could not be found for the Kansas Pacific railway, enabling it to reach shore and striking the mountain base somewhere hereabouts to follow northward through an inhabitable country to Denver. We were some ten days on this reconnaissance, during which we met considerable buffalo, three bands of wild horses, and antelope in such numbers that we were scarcely out of sight of them in the daytime from the Kansas border up to the present townsite. . . ."

The next year, on June 24, 1870, the first train of the Denver Pacific and the first train in Colorado arrived in Denver from Cheyenne. And on August 15th the first train over the Kansas Pacific followed it into Denver. General Palmer was in a hurry; the last ten miles of track were laid in ten hours. It was the farthest west the railroad ever got toward the Pacific Coast. Palmer was more interested in building down to Mexico City, and he immediately began work to start a new line southward.

The Denver and Rio Grande Railway Company was organized. General Palmer was determined to build as far south as the Soda Springs as soon as the money could be raised. This was a clear-cut problem: there was no national subsidy in land or money, no state or county aid; there were less than ten thousand white people in Colorado south of Denver, less than a thousand in El Paso County, and only eighty-one people in Colorado City; there were no mining booms requiring machinery, no crops or herds requiring transportation, no passengers and freight to haul.

But there was a natural site for an important town at the junction of the Monument and Fountain valleys, at the mouth of Ute Pass—a place that with its magnificent scenery and mineral springs could be expected to become a notable health and pleasure resort. On this General Palmer capitalized. If he could get money to lay the first seventy-six miles of line to the foot of Pike's Peak, he was sure that the rest would come easily.

It was a time when the "colony plan" was popular throughout the country. Horace Greeley, agricultural editor of the *New York Tribune*, was advising young men to go West generally, and specifically to join him in establishing a Colorado colony—the beginning of the colony that founded Greeley. Meeker's colony had already been enlisted in the East. And Carl Wulsten's colony of ninety-one German families from Chicago, fully equipped and every man a soldier, were bound for the Wet Mountain Valley in western Colorado.

General Palmer decided on a colonization plan: forming

a land company with capital to lay out a townsite, plant trees, construct irrigation ditches and aid in building, while selling tracts and lots along the right-of-way to arriving colonists to help finance the railway and provide earnings thereafter.

Governor Hunt, acting as General Palmer's agent, bought up some ten thousand acres along the Monument and Shook's Run about six miles out on the plains from the entrance to Ute Pass. Most of it was vacant government land, and for its purchase Agricultural College scrip was used. This abundant scrip, issued primarily for the purpose of aiding various states to acquire large tracts of land to be used for establishing agricultural colleges, could also be used in locating any unoccupied government land. The current price paid for it by General Palmer was eighty cents an acre. The rest of the land consisted of homesteads bought up from discouraged settlers. It is probable that the whole ten thousand acres were acquired for less than one dollar per acre.

On December 1, 1870, a subscription paper was sent out. Subscribers to the railroad securities for the first section of seventy-six miles to the base of the Peak were to be accorded the privilege of subscribing, pro rata, to a land and townsite investment called the Mountain Base Investment Fund. This embraced large tracts of land selected at advantageous points along the projected route where investors might confidently expect quick returns and good profits from arriving colonists. About one-half the capital of this land company, as also that required for the initial seventy-six miles of railroad, was raised in England among friends of Dr. Bell, who became vice-president of the Denver and Rio Grande.

Construction of this "best known railroad in America"

began on January 1, 1871. It was a narrow-gauge line The rails were bought in Europe, and the first narrow-gauge engine built in America for it was appropriately named the *Montezuma*. After the fashion of ships, all engines were named: *Tabi Wachi*, *Ute*, *Cortez*, *Ouray*, *Mosco* and *Hardscrabble*.

In June the Colorado Springs Company organized and selected this as the name of the new town. The townsite was plotted, lots were appraised, and General Cameron of Greeley was engaged to take charge of the infant colony.

On the morning of July 31, 1871, at eight o'clock, the first stake was driven in Colorado Springs. And on October 26th the Denver and Rio Grande was formally opened as the *Montezuma* puffed into town bearing two passenger cars named the *Denver* and the *El Paso* on its first lap to Mexico City.

News of this "baby railroad" and the new town at the foot of Pike's Peak spread over the country. In Lincoln Stratton and his friends pricked up their ears. James D Raymond, the blunt Nova Scotian, packed up his tools and left for the new town the instant he heard the first stake had been driven. A few months later the teamster Joe Donovan swore at his mules for the last time and straggled west. By the spring of '72 young Eaton was afflicted with the fever. No more licking stamps for him: he was going to be a Colorado cowboy.

Only Stratton remained with a good job and two pieces of property. But by August he too had made up his mind With a roll of blankets, a carpet-bag and three hundred dollars hidden in his clothes, he set out for the peak that had long ago inflamed his fancy—for Pike's Peak and the Shining Mountains.

PART TWO: MOUNTAINS

"In gold mining, as in art, distance not infrequently lends enchantment to the view."

2. MOUNTAINS

IT WAS LATE in August when Stratton reached Pike's Peak—at last! He scrambled hurriedly out of the narrow little coach at the end of the rails and set down his carpetbag and roll of blankets. Gripping the lump in his clothes that was his concealed three hundred dollars, he stopped to stare about him. There it was, looming like a cloud above the foothills to the west, a majestic silver cone in a turquoise sky. Pike's Peak—the most majestic and best known peak in America! And the mountains, an unbroken blue rampart stretching from north to south as far as he could see, so close that the deep cañons stood out above the cottonwoods along the creek—the Shining Mountains of the Spaniards!

He was really Out West at last, but the people on the platform refuted the comforting thought. True enough, there were a few old Indian squaws squatting down with buffalo robes to sell. But his gaze was held by a group of foreigners and Englishmen in tweeds listening to a distinguished looking man in expensive riding boots. It was the regal General Palmer who had built the Rio Grande and laid out the town. Young Stratton remembered those shiny boots. But he humbly gathered up his blankets and bag, and strode up the hill past the new hotel where people dined from English china and English silver. He could never have suspected that the time was to come when he was to refuse to attend a banquet in his honor in the hotel, with General Palmer waiting among the others for him to appear.

The new town was just a year old. As an old lawyer remarked, "Colorado Springs was like unto a community upon the nether shore of a petrified ocean." New streets were being laid out with a team of mules and a plow. The first newspaper was being published in a tent. All mail was still being sent to Colorado City, three miles west, and General Palmer's valet brought it over on horseback. Knock-down, portable houses were shipped in from Chicago and put up until permanent ones could be built. There were only two or three hundred people living in town, but in the register of the new hotel opened on January 1st were the names of 3,647 tourists—largely from abroad. The people lived on hope and scenery.

It was easy for Stratton to find his old friend Joe Donovan. Nor did he waste time getting a job; on seeing the booming town his hands itched for saw and hammer. Late that afternoon he went with Donovan to find Raymond. This was the James Raymond they had known in Lincoln, who had preceded them to Colorado Springs. Raymond had a carpenter shop in Pike's Peak Avenue.

"You remember Stratton, don't you? He just came in from Lincoln and wants a job. Can you put him to work?"

Raymond looked up from his bench. "Sure! As soon as he wants."

Donovan said nothing about a job for himself. He hadn't quite got around to working yet. Stratton forgot to mention the three hundred dollars stuck down his jeans, and as there were but few rooms in town it was arranged for both of them to sleep in Raymond's shop in the shavings. That night Stratton spread his blankets over a soft pile of fragrant pine shavings and went to sleep with a smile. He was twenty-four years old and had a comforting roll of bills; by raising himself on one arm he could see through

A Colorado mining camp, Silverton.

Ore trains on the Ute Pass.

he open door the snow-crowned Pike's Peak in the clear ummer night, and already he had a job.

James D. Raymond, blunt old Nova Scotian, was a hard vorker taking every advantage of the building boom to nake himself into one of the first contractors in town. One f his best investments was the employment of Stratton, lso a hustler, for their friendship was the only thing that aved him from spending his last years in a poorhouse.

Colorado Springs was located on the plains opposite the nouth of Ute Pass about six miles away. The road leading vest along the creek, through Colorado City, had a coninual stream of tourists going to the old Indian soda and ron springs. Here at the foot of Pike's Peak and in the nouth of Ute Pass was growing up a little resort village amed after the Ute's Great Spirit, Manitou. Raymond late hat summer had secured the contract to build the Manitou Iotel there, and on this job Stratton went to work. He vas the inside man or draftsman. The foreman of the carenter gang in which he later worked was a man named). K. Lee and one of the carpenters was a J. D. Rogers. Vith both of these men Stratton struck up a friendship. Vith Lee especially he spent his spare days roaming the earby mountains. For a prairie man they always held a eculiar fascination. He was never tired of looking at the ueer eroded cliffs and the white and red formations. He ame home with his pockets filled with bright pebbles and pecimens.

After sleeping in Raymond's shop with Donovan for sevral weeks, Stratton moved into a room of his own and took is meals at Mrs. Stevens' Boarding House. It was one of he most popular places in town. The hitching rack outside vas lined with horses and teams from every camp in Coloado, and the long table boasted men who had combed the mountains. Possibly Mrs. Stevens' young daughter Ella was an attraction, added to the platters heaped with the venison and bear which always hung outside the butcher shops. Ella certainly preferred the tall, slim young carpenter with the bright blue eyes who sat quietly listening to his rivals' tales. She allowed him to take her to dances at Foote's Hall.

From his arrival, Stratton seemed a most promising young man. He was three things he never was afterward: he was hungry, sociable and interested in carpentry. But he never at any time let any of them interfere with his private business and ambitions. Less than a month after he had arrived in town Stratton dug out his roll for a worthy purpose. On September 4, 1872, he bought with his employer, Raymond, a lot in town for $300, and the next March he bought out Raymond's half-interest.

This town lot, which made him a landowner at the age of twenty-four, Stratton always held with sentimental regard. On the back of it he built a small shack and moved into it, although he still took his meals at Mrs. Stevens'. He was now a proud member of the community, and being a home-owner he was duly appointed a member of the Babcock Volunteer Fire Company. The members met frequently and discussed uniforms. They were divided into groups to have care of the engine, to man the pump, and to look out for the water supply—Stratton being appointed a pipe man and later detailed to work one of the small machines.

That spring he quit working for Raymond, and on June 21, 1873, an advertisement began to appear in the newspaper:

GRANNIS AND STRATTON
CONTRACTORS, CARPENTERS AND BUILDERS
PIKE'S PEAK AVENUE NEAR NEVADA AVENUE
COLORADO SPRINGS, COLORADO
CONTRACTS TAKEN AND DESIGNS FURNISHED

The new partnership went off with a bang. A news item read, "Mr. Grannis, of the firm of Grannis and Stratton, has purchased the red lot on the northwest corner of Weber and Kiowa, opposite to the Presbyterian church. The condition of the sale was that he should at once put on it a first-class residence, and we understand that he intends to erect a residence that will be superior to any in town." That they did a good job on it is attested by the fact that it was continuously occupied for over sixty years by three generations of one family. For two years later Grannis sold it to a man named W. S. Jackson to live in with his bride, Helen Hunt, who became famous as the author of *Ramona*.

A month later the new firm received another good contract and under Stratton's direction put in the woodwork of the new stone Episcopal church. Then quite abruptly something happened; still impulsive, Stratton forgot for once that a successful young man cannot let his sympathies interfere with business.

R. W. Grannis, his partner, was evidently a fine man, but it was also evident that his wife at times proved troublesome, particularly when he came home drunk and beat her. She finally obtained money from her home in New York, and after being abused by her husband again, confided her troubles and plans to Stratton and some neighbors, Mr. and Mrs. Rouse. The affair was carefully planned and carried out. Mr. and Mrs. Rouse early one evening went over and detained Grannis on the front porch. Stratton had the more chivalrous job. He carried a ladder to the back of the house, helped Mrs. Grannis out of the bedroom window, and rushed her to the railway station where she caught the train back to New York.

By mid-morning Grannis discovered the role his young partner had played in the conspiracy. They met in front of the shop on the main street in town. Grannis was mad as a hornet, and Stratton, always hot-headed, lost his temper. It was a fist fight to the finish with a crowd gathered to cheer the winner. Both men were badly battered. On the next day, August 2nd, a formal notice of dissolution of partnership appeared in the paper. Underneath it was printed the notice:

Winfield Scott Stratton begs to inform the patrons of the late firm of Grannis and Stratton that he will continue the business of contractor and builder at the old shop on Pike's Peak Avenue and solicits a continuance of their favors, assuring them that he will spare no effort to give them satisfaction.

It was soon evident that Grannis had received the worst of the affair, losing both wife and shop. Stratton received all the business. His first customers were his partners in the conspiracy, Mr. and Mrs. Rouse. They were building a stone house on Cascade Avenue and had let the contract for the woodwork to Grannis and Stratton. They now dealt with Stratton exclusively and let him finish the work.

J. D. Raymond, his old employer, was always ready to recommend Stratton as a "Number One mechanic. He makes his own designs when he has contracts of his own and is a first-class finisher; so much so that when there is any fine work to be done, like making the drugstore showcases, Stratton is called to do it." Now, securing a contract to build several villas for wealthy D. Russ Wood, Raymond stepped aside and let Stratton secure a contract for additional villas on the same job. Luck was with Stratton; it was a mild and open winter and he was able to work without interruption.

Now Stratton was perhaps the busiest man in town. He bought another lot and built a house on it, soon began another beside it, and then built his own shop on his downtown lot just across the street from Raymond's carpenter shop. In the midst of these activities Wood offered him the job of building two large two-story buildings.

To secure this contract and to have the necessary help, Stratton took as partner his friend and co-carpenter for Raymond, J. D. Rogers. That he anticipated better luck with the new firm is apparent from the advertisement which appeared on November 29, 1873:

ROGERS AND STRATTON
CONTRACTORS,
CARPENTERS AND BUILDERS
PIKE'S PEAK AVENUE
ESTIMATES MADE AND MATERIALS FURNISHED IN EITHER BRICK, STONE OR WOOD. JOBBING OF ALL KINDS ATTENDED TO.

The editors reported that "both are known to be first class workmen and we hope that they will build up a flourishing business."

It so promised from the start. The trustees of the school board commissioned them to make school desks, and within a month the firm was making money.

For a twenty-five year old carpenter, Stratton used his head as much as his hands. No one put anything over on him. Four days after his quarrel with Grannis he filed a mechanics lien for $516.42 to protect his claim on material and labor furnished on their work, and later filed another against one of his clients. Neither was canceled until paid.

And on December 2nd, Stratton opened his first account in the County Bank for $263.15. It was a personal account, separate from that of the firm's for building purposes; he was taking no chances on another quarrel.

Young Stratton had almost forgotten Pike's Peak save

that it loomed up before him as if at the end of the avenue, a constant reminder of the now hazy desire that had brought him West. He had been in town only a year and a half, and already at twenty-five he was pointed out as one of its enterprising young builders.

2

Stratton was tall, rather slight of build, and generally quiet and mild mannered. His eyes were the most distinctive thing about him, but even his best friend could never quite remember what they were like other than that "they were very light. Some would call them blue and some would call them gray. His eyes were very light." In all ways he was a man who tended to be obscure and preferred to remain aloof. But everyone liked him, and for the time he entered into the life of the town with vigor and enthusiasm.

He was popular among the younger people, Ella being always ready to accompany him to any dance. The older men evidently respected his judgment. In November, 1873, he was empanelled for jury duty in an inquest over the death of Judge Baldwin at the slaughter house.

W. H. Baldwin, or Judge Baldwin as he was familiarly known, was quite a noted character in town. There were few things he had not done in a life so melodramatic that it seemed he must be charmed. As a boy he had been scalped and left for dead by a band of Indians. He recovered and several years later moved to Colorado. While tending sheep he and a companion were again set upon by marauding Indians. His companion was killed, but just as the Indians grabbed Baldwin by the hair and were ready to split his head with a tomahawk and take his scalp, they saw his scalp lock had already been removed. It was a superstition among the tribe that ill luck or death would follow the warrior who stooped to the folly of harming a man already scalped. They dropped him with a whoop and fled. Baldwin sadly gathered up his companion's body, rounded his sheep and walked to town.

For years he kept a small band of sheep out on the Divide. On rare occasions he came to town "and got fuller than a goat and used to make speeches and tell us how to run the town here and he was real nice." One night on his way home, probably again full as the proverbial goat, "he stopped off at the slaughter house right below the water reservoir here, and in trying to find a place to lie down in the slaughter house he got up into a corner and fell through a hole and went into a well and was drowned."

After due and thoughtful deliberation, as shown by the above testimonial facts, Stratton, Donovan and the other jurors solemnly did affirm "that the said W. H. Baldwin came to his death by accidental drowning."

A few weeks later Stratton took part in a more joyful gathering. Elaborate preparations were made to celebrate Christmas with a big entertainment. Tom Wanless owned a two-story building in town and contributed the upper story for the occasion. Men brought pine branches and kinnikinnick from the mountains for decorations, women loaned curtains to make Wanless Hall a fit place for the occasion, and programs were printed. Preparations were so extensive that the party was postponed until December 27th and Tom Wanless had to go to Denver to get enough chairs to go around.

When the big night arrived, Stratton, dressed up in his Sunday-best, was one of the first to arrive, escorting his landlady and her daughter Ella to their chairs, and then standing at the door to act as usher. As the entertainment got under way, his friend J. D. Raymond and his best girl rose and nervously slid up to Stratton. They wanted to go out for a walk around the block. Would Stratton keep his eyes on their chairs? Stratton nodded solemnly and let them out the door. After a time Raymond came back with his best girl clinging to his arm and giggling. Nervously, Raymond whispered to Stratton, and they slunk to their chairs. In the first lull of the evening Stratton strode down the aisle, jumped on the stage in front of the big Christmas tree, and announced that his old friend and employer had just popped the question to his best girl. The party broke up immediately and took time out to rush with congratulations to the happy couple. Order was established only by the announcement that the feature of the entertainment was to be a song by the Santa Claus of the evening entitled, "This Is the Opinion of Billy Macomber."

The people quieted immediately. Knowing Billy Macomber, they all suspected that his musical opinion might concern itself with the town's most touchy subject. When the townsite was first laid out the Colorado Springs Company was determined that it should be one place completely pure and undefiled by that common denominator of the West, the saloon. A clause was inserted in every land deed providing that intoxicating liquors should never be sold upon the premises and that if this condition of sale was broken the property should revert back to the seller. However, Colorado City just three miles away was full of saloons. And that summer a most peculiar place appeared on the main downtown street corner in Colorado Springs. One walked in the door, quietly laid down a quarter on a counter, and stepped back a pace. Miraculously, then, the counter revolved. The quarter vanished and in its place stood a drink of whiskey. It was aptly called the "Spiritual Wheel" and sometimes, the "Wheel of Fortune." The success of this was influencing other establishments in town to operate on a less spiritual basis, and the worthy residents were becoming alarmed.

Billy Macomber was an "outside man" for General Palmer and had care of the irrigation ditches in town, thus being firmly addicted to water. But it was as a composer that Billy loved to be known. He was not exactly modest, and admitted that "I composed songs that would fit the case pretty well. I composed many songs to amuse people here. Most of these songs were able to stand alone but one or two of them, maybe, would fall down once in awhile."

The composer regarded "This is the Opinion of Billy Macomber" or "The Whiskey Ring" as his most inspired work. He says of it, "I had sung the song before I sang it in Wanless Hall but it hadn't been printed and the boys wanted me to get it printed so that they could all sing it if they wanted to. Like the Doxology, you know. They wanted something that could go around. The song was old enough to stand alone—about a month I should say—when I sang it at the party. This noted song was a song of the times. It consisted of vocal and instrumental music."

So now, modestly eager to have it assume its rightful place beside the Doxology, Billy jumped on the stage, tore off his Santa Claus wig, and began his song:

So what I am going to sing—is about the Whiskey Ring,
That was formed by men, no doubt, with good intention.
The first to start was Root, then Cowell followed suit,
With other sharks too numerous to mention.

With that clause in the deed they never can succeed,
And why they try, to me it is a wonder.
There will come a reckoning day when the forfeit they must pay,
And that is the opinion of your friend Billy Macomber.

A prima donna could not have done better. The song was an instant success and the composer was hailed with cheers and shouts. Among the confusing acclaim, Mr. Cowell and his wife got up and slipped away; they had been in the audience.

Said Billy later, "I hit Cowell pretty hard with the song because Cowell owned the place individually up here and under his clause in the deed he lost his property. He kept a saloon and we were fighting him. He was the only fellow who got it in the neck."

For once he failed to take all credit due him. Three weeks later Stratton was called for jury duty on the case of the Town of Colorado Springs against D. W. Root and Joseph Reef, also accused of violating the liquor clause—Root being the other man named in Billy's "Whiskey Ring."

The case aroused the interest of the whole town. The first trial was brief. Stratton and the other eleven jurors were out but a short time and then discharged by the judge. The second trial was warmly contested. Some of the witnesses didn't know "what they drank was whiskey or what it was." The jury disagreed after being out all night and was again discharged. On the third trial the jury agreed, and the defendants were found guilty. Stratton during all three trials was firmly opposed to liquor and supported Billy Macomber's celebrated opinion. One month later Root shot himself to death.

The case brought to a head the liquor question. The election of five town trustees was approaching, and it proved to be a wet and dry contest. For the first time in the history of town separate tickets were in the field. On March 28th Stratton and his partner Rogers enthusiastically endorsed the temperance ticket and campaigned to secure 103 more signatures to save the town.

It was a significant episode, for years later Stratton and liquor were to rouse the town to another hullabaloo that has not yet died down.

During that winter Stratton experienced for the first time the storms that did so much to keep the high Colorado mountains virginal in their cold blue beauty. He did not know it, but these storms were the prelude to a greater one within him that changed him completely.

About midnight on January 2nd he was awakened by the loud clatter of his small shack and the shop in front. He jumped up, dressed and ran outside. Cowell's place was on the corner. Next to it and separated from Stratton's shop by a hundred-foot open prairie lot stood one of the colony's important shanties. A terrific chinook was blowing loose planks off the houses. A sudden draft sucked out from the shanty's chimney a blaze of sparks, whipping it across the vacant lot toward Stratton. He grabbed his coat and ran to Cowell's place. Billy Macomber and some others were loafing inside. Stratton flung open the door and pointed outside.

"Look there! Those sparks are making right for my shop!"

They all flung out into the wind. Filling buckets of water, they awakened the woman inside and put out the fire. As a dutiful member of the Fire Company and expecting more trouble, Stratton did not return home but remained dressed and ready the rest of the night.

About six o'clock in the morning he happened to pass Major McAllister's house. The Major called out to him. He too was frightened by the wind, and was standing in the front door fully dressed with a child in his arms, prepared to rush outside if the wind commenced to blow the house away. He had just contracted for the building of a new house on Cascade Avenue; although Stratton was not his contractor, the Major asked him what to have done to make the house safe against winds. The specifications called for walls one brick and a half thick—about twelve inches. On Stratton's advice they were increased another brick, making twenty inches thickness, and the roof was ironed down to the masonry with two-inch iron rods.

It was good advice; the house with the same iron rods was still safe over sixty years later, and McAllister's child in arms was to repay the favor.

Then on April 18th, after a mild dry winter, snow began to fall. That day and night and the next day and night it fell continuously until the snow was three feet deep on the level prairies and some six feet deep in the mountain cañons. No wind accompanied the storm and there were no drifts. The town was completely cut off from the outside world. Old Washington, the Ute Chief, stated that the snowfall had been exceeded only by one four hundred moons ago, some thirty-four years, when he had been a papoose. Then it snowed for five sleeps, five days and nights, and the snow was high as a man's head. He stated many of the Utes were frozen to death through being lost in the snow.

The storm stopped construction on the D. Russ Wood villas, almost finished, and the two Wood residences. Construction at best was difficult owing to lack of water for mixing mortar. Most of it had to be drawn and carried from the creek or one of the nearby wells. As the snow began to melt and run through the irrigation ditches, Stratton devised an ingenious scheme. He dug a ditch and sunk three barrels beside it, level with the ground. These barrels kept filling with water as fast as the men emptied them with buckets.

Construction was hurried along, and Stratton did not

accept any new contracts. He was at one of the major turnings of his road. Already he was getting ready for a new venture.

3

Back in 1860 a man named John Baker had heard from the Navajos of gold in the San Juan range extension and mysterious regions of the Sierra Madre mountains in southern Colorado, the wildest and most inaccessible region in Colorado, if not in North America. Gathering a horde of men estimated at from one to five thousand, Baker penetrated the mountains by way of New Mexico as far as the headwaters of the Rio de las Animas, the River of Lost Souls. It was appropriately named. But although it was reported that they picked up garnets and rubies off the ground, and a noted geologist staked his reputation on its being the most extensive diamond field in the world, they could find no gold. The men separated into small groups to work their way northward through the wild mountains to avoid the long way home, and almost all of them perished. From this Baker's Rush derived the expression "over the range," alluding to one who has died.

The San Juan region had not been forgotten. A treaty with the Ute Indians in 1868 provided for use of the territory by white men. In 1870 the "Little Giant" gold lode in Arrastra Gulch was opened after samples had assayed from $900 to $4,000 per ton, and by 1871 the Las Animas district was swarming with men. Then, in 1873, the Utes surrendered three million acres to the government and the San Juan region was thrown wide open.

Stratton heard of these happenings with an imagination that grasped at the tremendous possibilities of making a fortune by a single lucky stroke of his pick. Immersed in his carpenter and contracting work, he had almost forgotten why he had started for Colorado. Now it all came back. He was wild for the first chance to make his fortune in gold or silver.

It presented itself almost immediately. A man named John C. Dunn had arrived in Colorado Springs from the San Juan region with just the thing—a wonderful claim just opened and ready to be worked, the Yretaba Silver Lode.

Stratton was not the only one who pricked up his ears and began to figure on getting in on the deal. Judge Colburn's father; his friend James D. Raymond; Matt France, one of the most prominent men in town; Sherman, a mining engineer; Bolton and Wilson were all interested and talking of forming a company to buy and work the Yretaba. Soon Stratton could think of nothing else. The more he talked with these men, the more convinced he became that his future lay in the mysterious blue mountains he had dreamed of as a boy. But the venture would cost him almost $3,000. He began to get the money together.

There were few people who realized just what a smart young carpenter they had in town. During his year and a half in Colorado Springs he had been, on the side, almost as busy buying and selling real estate as contracting and building. In the latter half of '72 he had bought his first lot with Raymond and then bought out his interest—a total investment of $475. During '73 he had bought and sold three other pieces of property. Now, early in '74, he began to buy and sell property with a dispatch and shrewdness that made him appear more a land agent than a carpenter and builder.

On January 31st he bought a lot from the Colorado Springs Company for $288, and on March 21st two more lots for $2,000. On April 2nd he sold the first lot for $800

—a profit of $512 in two months on an investment of $288. And on April 4th he sold one of the latter two lots for $1,500—in fourteen days buying two lots for $2,000 and selling one of them for $1,500. On March 30th he effected two more transfers involving $900.

Stratton was always secretive about his personal affairs, and it is to be wondered if the money to finance these numerous and quick turn-overs of property derived wholly from his profits in building during less than two years. He still retained his two lots in Lincoln, Nebraska, upon leaving there, and it is probable he sold them at this time. His sister, Harriet Newell, had married and was now a widow. It is probable that she advanced him at least $2,000; for under the name of Harriet N. Hamlin, Widow, she had given him the power of attorney; and two of the lots bought by Stratton, at a consideration of $2,000, were obtained from her or at least under her name.

But despite these many sales, some of them for bonds only, Stratton did not have the necessary $3,000. The natural solution was to sell out his contracting business. The ready buyer was one of his workmen, Joseph Dozier, a Virginian from Queen Anne County who had been bound out to learn the carpenter trade in Roanoke when his father had lost his plantation just before the Civil War. Dozier had made the long wagon trip across the plains from St. Joseph, Missouri, and worked deep into the mountains to the camps of Buckskin Joe and Fairplay. From here, going broke early in '73, he had walked down Ute Pass to Colorado Springs, securing work with Stratton as a journeyman carpenter for enough money to bring out his family. Stratton at the time owed him about a hundred dollars in wages and in April made arrangements with him to lease his property, giving him an option to buy.

Stratton joyfully concluded arrangements. The snows had melted; it was spring; and on May 2nd appeared the appropriate advertisement:

> People who want small cages for birds can find an abundant variety at Wilson and Wood's, these gentlemen having just received a large stock. Young men who are in need of cages for birds of larger growth, can be accommodated on application to Messrs. Rogers and Stratton, Mr. Whipple, Mr. Raymond or any other builders. It's surely time for mating and marrying.

All but for Stratton. No cages for him; he was eager to be off to the mountains. He had sold his lots and houses and given up his business, but in return he had received two pieces of paper over which he pored nightly.

One was a Quit Claim Deed to "an undivided 150 feet of the Yretaba Silver Lode located on the easterly side of Cunningham Gulch just below the upper falls" sold him by John C. Dunn for $2,000. The other was also a Quit Claim Deed for another one hundred feet of the same property he had bought from a man named Isaac Calder for $800, "subject to the notes given by John C. Dunn for the total principal sum of $10,125."

Where the other $7,325 was coming from, or whether the other men in Colorado Springs would decide to go in on the venture, Stratton did not know or care. He had wasted no time in getting an interest of his own in the mine. Channing Sweet, father of one of the governors of Colorado, met him on the street and cautioned him against going into any mining deals.

"You had better look out. You will lose your money."

"Well," replied Stratton breezily, "I am a young man and if I do I can go ahead and earn some more."

His cocksure independence and assurance certainly must

have been a sales argument for John Dunn, for within a few weeks four other men cautiously advanced money toward the venture. On May 26th Stratton, Colburn, Wilson and Sherman set out for the San Juan country to see the Yretaba. Four days later the following notice appeared:

> The firm of Rogers and Stratton has been dissolved, Mr. Stratton having left to try his fortune among the San Juan mines. Mr. Stratton has been a resident of the town from its earlier days, and has contributed to its growth by the erection of a large number of its principal buildings. We wish him success in his new field.
>
> Mr. Rogers has associated himself with Mr. Joseph Dozier, formerly of St. Joseph, Missouri, who brought with him first-class recommendations and who is already favorably known to most of our people.

The transfer of this carpenter shop was the turning point in the lives of both Dozier and Stratton. Dozier took up contracting and became one of the town's most prominent builders for a quarter of a century. Then he also succumbed to the irresistible gold fever. For Stratton, too, the sun had risen. He was off to make his fortune at last.

Raymond, also, was more interested than he let be known, for at the last minute he purchased an interest in Stratton's interest in Yretaba. The first news of the party was published in the *Gazette* early in July. It read: "J. M. Colburn and W. B. Sherman returned from the Yretaba mine—apparently not satisfied with conditions."

A week or two later the men returned home and the town read:

> We learn that the committee sent down to inspect the Yretaba Mine reported unfavorably, and that the stockholders have decided to make no further payments, but to take the

mine for the first payment, 'one fourth the purchase price,' this being the provision they were to have if the mine failed to come up to the reports of the sellers. The stockholders believe they will ultimately come out even.

This was mere whistling to keep up their courage. They knew they had all been suckers and that Dunn had foisted on them a worthless mine. And yet so entrancing were the deep gulches dotted with camps and claims that they were all bit by the gold bug. They forgot the Yretaba and within six months were buying into other claims in the San Juan. Sherman bought an interest in the Ouray Lode; Matt France and Sherman went in on the Rocky Mountain Chief Lode; and the Silver Wing Lode was subscribed to by many other men in town including Reef and D. Russ Wood.

Stratton was no exception. He was the hardest hit of them all. That one trip down into the wild San Juan erased from his mind completely every thought of continuing the prosaic task of erecting buildings. He returned broke and dirty, but at a ranch on the way back he stopped to wash his overalls before entering town.

The next day, on July 24th, he sold his shop outright to Joseph Dozier for $1,000. Dozier had been busy. He too had been south, erecting the first buildings on La Veta Pass—storerooms for traders and teamsters—and had sent for his wife and daughters. Stratton moved out of his little shack behind the shop and went to board and room with two old maids named McDonald. He had in his pockets $1,000 cash, and in his head exorbitant plans for the Black Crook and Era Tabar mines which he had seen in the San Juan mountains.

Without work or anything to occupy his time in the little room he shared with Henry Jenkins, Stratton almost went crazy with inactivity. He waited each day for quitting time to talk with his old friend D. K. Lee, Raymond's carpenter foreman. By January he could restrain himself no longer.

In the dead of winter, on January 7, 1875, he and Lee set out for Chalk Creek on the upper Arkansas near Granite on a prospecting trip. They hired an old freighter, High Winslow, to haul their supply of flour, sugar, bacon and dried fruits. Ute Pass was deep in snow and part of the time they were forced to plod along on foot behind the team. On the top of the pass in a beautiful little valley ringed by snowy mountains they were forced to spend a week at the house of Mrs. Sam Hartsel (the name later being given to a railroad junction). Here they heard that some gold was being taken out of the streams emptying into the Arkansas, and they pushed on as quickly as possible to Chalk Creek to build a cabin.

Lee gives an excellent account of their life and hopes in a letter written on February 13th from Gold Valley, six miles below Granite, at the head of the Arkansas:

> Enclosed you will find Three Dollars for which renew my subscription to the *Gazette*. We find it monotonous in the evenings here in the mountains and cannot get along without your excellent paper. Though we are having splendid times batching in a log cabin, we are always anxious to know how our friends are prospering in the little city of Colorado Springs.
>
> Times are expected to be brisk in this section next summer, and a bright future is anticipated. There are three organized companies busy at work here on the River, one from Denver, one from Pueblo, and the third, "The Arkansas River Ditch and Flume Company."
>
> The latter are putting in a dam and early in the spring will take out a ditch draining the river bed for a mile and a half. The old settlers foretell great success. Mr. Ralstin, the head

of the company, tried to organize at the Springs but was not able to find persons with pluck enough to invest in the enterprise, but on going to Denver he succeeded in getting up the company and the work is now being pushed forward.

It is said there is no gain where there is no risk, but the miners who are acquainted here all unite in saying that it is simply a matter of a little investment so as to do the work properly and the risk comes up missing. While prospecting up the river yesterday I came upon two miners who were taking out a dollar an hour each, but they were so much troubled by the water that they could only work about three hours a day—the rest of their time being occupied in drawing off the water. A little investment would save time and the greater part of their labor, and they could work to a better advantage; but they lack the means and are obliged to do the best they can. Such men are full of pluck, however, and expect to come out all right. As one of the miners remarked to me: "The past may have been bad; the present may be still worse; but there is the ilegant future."

Three years later the future was to be most "ilegant" indeed, Granite being just below the site of Leadville.

But the optimism of Stratton and Lee was soon worn away by the icy streams up and down which they waded hunting for a likely show of color. Stratton spent most of his time three miles down the river building a cabin for a "widow-woman" who expected to be married that spring. Late in March they decided to quit the district. Lee wandered northward, returning to Colorado Springs that fall. Stratton headed south toward his first love, the San Juan region.

At Del Norte he waited for the deep snows to melt before he could cross the mountain ranges into Baker's Park. Most of the time he loafed in a branch store run by Alva Adams who also owned a hardware store in Colorado Springs. Both Alva and his brother Billy were to become governors of Colorado, and his son a United States Senator. Here he struck up an acquaintance with Harry B. Adsit. Early in April the two men crossed the mountains into Howardsville, camping together at the head of Cunningham Gulch.

Baker's Park, named after John Baker who had led the first disastrous rush, was the center of the San Juan country. It was still wild and almost inaccessible, traveling being chiefly accomplished on snowshoes. There were only seventy people in the region including thirteen women. Silverton boasted only twenty-two houses, Howardsville and Bullion City but eighteen. The sawmill was idle, and of lumber quoted nominally at fifty dollars a thousand feet none was to be had at any price. But the rich showings of silver ore drew and held men like magnets. One of the mountains was so seamed with mineral veins of great width that they could be seen two miles away. It was appropriately named King Solomon. The Begole had come to be known as the Mineral Farm because the locations on it covered forty acres and the veins twelve acres. Surely in such a place, thought Stratton and Adsit, they would make a rich strike.

From their camp in Cunningham Gulch the two men each morning set forth on their own to find a place to stake out. Adsit on the morning of April 21st climbed up King Solomon and found a place not yet claimed. He drove his discovery stakes, locating the North Star mine. Forty years later he was still chuckling over it from the Hotel Mirabeau on the Rue de la Paix, Paris.

Stratton climbed up the opposite Green Mountain and located the Black Prince. Nothing came of it and he relocated the Yretaba as the Black Crook. Then he looked over the Ouray, Silver Wing and Rocky Mountain Chief Lodes that his Colorado Springs friends had bought. But surprisingly now, after a lapse of only a few months, they looked worse than his own. He fell in with another prospector equally discouraged, named Walter Mitchell. All summer they climbed the peaks, struggled up gulleys and down into matted ravines hunting for something that either of them might recognize for ore. Toward fall they returned to Green Mountain. Now they had it! They were sure of what they saw. They rushed back to town and at twilight on October 25, 1875, claimed "by right of discovery and location 1500 feet linear and horizontal measurement on the Silver Cross Lode along the vein thereof, with all its dips, variations and angles; together with 150 feet in width on each side of the middle of the vein at the surface; and all veins, lodes, ledges, and surface ground within the lines of the said Claim."

It was an optimistically big bite, but there was nothing to chew on. They almost broke their backs before the heavy snows, digging deep enough to assure themselves there was nothing under the grass roots but worthless country rock.

Worn out and discouraged, Stratton returned to Colorado Springs. This time he did not bother to stop to wash his overalls. His first venture in mining had been a complete bust.

4

It was a dull Fall for Stratton. He moved back into the boarding-house of the old maids McDonald, preferring their sedate and uninquiring manner to the exciting hubbub at Mrs. Stevens' and Ella's ingratiating smiles. Occasionally he hired out as a carpenter to Raymond and Dozier, but only for a few days at a time and for an intricate piece of cabinet work. Raymond, however, had succumbed to the same lure that had taken his foreman Lee and Stratton from him. Unable to make the San Juan trip, he had begun prospecting in the nearby cañons. That winter he was caught in the cave-in of a prospecting hole up Bear Creek Cañon, suffering severe injuries. To recuperate he gave up his business and went back to St. Louis.

Late that fall D. K. Lee returned to town after a summer which had been as disappointing as Stratton's. The two men resumed their friendship on the basis of mutual consolation. Lee recovered his spirits more quickly. He admitted that keeping company with two young ladies had done much to help him. As a matter of fact, he stuttered to Stratton one afternoon, he had half-way promised to take them both to a dance at Odle's Hall that very night. Why wouldn't Stratton be a good sport and help him out? Stratton grudgingly consented to go along.

The evening was quiet but auspicious. Of his two obvious admirers, Lee escorted a plainly dressed but pleasant looking girl who lived with her mother and stepfather in a little house on Tejon Street just below where Stratton boarded. She was about seventeen years old and the jutting fact about her was her name, Zeurah V. Stewart. People were always calling her Ora, Oro or Zura. She had been born at Stewart's Mound near Kewanee, Illinois, her father dying when she was a child. Her mother then married another man by the name of Stewart, who was, however, no relation to the first. They had come to Colorado because he was afflicted with asthma. He was now repairing shoes in Colorado Springs.

Stratton escorted Lee's other young lady, but in his somber mood paid little attention to her save to learn that her name was Miss Shields. The four went out together several more times. Stratton, for the time at least, proved an unsatisfactory swain. Then he and Lee swapped girls.

Suddenly Lee married Miss Shields. And on July 26, 1876, Stratton married Zeurah Stewart. The Pastor of the Presbyterian Church, Henry B. Gage, officiated at the ceremony which was duly witnessed by Isaac H. Stewart and Mrs. Orelia Stewart. The date and facts are pertinent in light of what followed.

From the very first there was an air of mystery about the whole affair. The two young couples no longer were companions. Stratton and Zeurah kept to themselves, repelling old friends and making no new ones. What little romance there might have been between them was almost instantly dispelled. Day and night neighbors could hear Zeurah weeping and Stratton storming. And they soon learned to keep their inquisitive noses on the safe side of their own fences.

For Stratton, always secretive about his personal affairs, took particular care in keeping his marital mystery under cover. Very shortly after the wedding—but certainly not in the preceding March as has been asserted, for they witnessed the ceremony—Zeurah's parents returned back East. Mrs. Stewart's mother had died of a heart attack in Illinois. From the estate Zeurah received some money. The amount was later stated to be $3,000 and Stratton was accused of spending it for various prospecting trips. He probably did receive some money, for throughout the summer he followed Raymond's example and was out prospecting the nearby mountain cañons. Grubstakes for his trips and living expenses for Zeurah at home must have required more money than Stratton made working in town occasionally as a carpenter.

Certainly their quarreling increased. Zeurah accused him of violent outbursts of temper and unreasonable jealousy. Stratton periodically flung off into the mountains and came home, it is said, to find evidence that Zeurah had been consoling herself with other men. It was a most unhappy lot for the seventeen-year-old bride, and it changed Stratton completely.

The truth of the matter soon came out. Zeurah had been with child for several months before their marriage. There were only two possible explanations. The child had been conceived by him out of wedlock or, as he stoutly maintained, the child was not his.

At any rate he packed her up and sent or took her to Danville, Illinois, where she was left alone and without funds. In December she went to her stepfather's home in Cobery, Illinois, and here in January the child was born. It was a boy. Zeurah named him Isaac Henry Stratton, after her stepfather who had given her shelter.

She never saw Stratton again.

Two years later, on January 25, 1879, Stratton obtained a divorce on the grounds that she "has wilfully deserted and absented herself" from him. Zeurah was duly served with a summons as provided by law, but did not file an answer or demur, or even appear. The divorce was granted by Judge E. A. Colburn, Stratton's old friend.

This did not close the most unfortunate affair in Stratton's life. Shrouded in conjectures and embittered by partisanship to each side, it was to lie smoldering for many years and then flame up anew.

This immediately following his failure in mining, it is little wonder that Stratton changed completely. For several months he was gone and unheard of. When he did return, it was to slink into an obscure boarding-house where he kept to himself, without friends. Occasionally, later, he was seen in the company of a Mrs. Demasters, a widow in town; but for the most part he lost all confidence in women and had no use for them after his marriage.

He was no longer the rising young contractor in town with a knack for turning vacant prairie lots into money, and popular with all his clients. He was for the time a carpenter without a job and a prospector who had never made a strike.

Adding to his miserable mood came news from Jeffersonville that his young sister, Mary Ann, whom he had tried to bribe into reading the New Testament, had died. Luckily, an opportunity for work and a change was presented to him by his former landladies, the McDonalds, who had moved to Denver and wanted a house built. Stratton jumped at the job.

After finishing the house, he obtained work at the Golden Gate Mill. A dam was being built just above the present site of the Union Station to block the water which was then run off through the Mill into Cherry Creek. Stratton was hired as a carpenter and wood-butcher—putting in posts, filling sandbags and doing miscellaneous work such as helping to hang the driving wheels of the mill. He roomed and boarded at the Baxter House, a dull and dreary existence on four dollars a day. He was content at night to avoid the noisy crowds drifting to Hop Alley for a bit of fun, and stayed in his room caught between a miserable past and a future that looked no better.

And then one day, by one of those numerous coincidences which always filled his life, he ran into James Parker, his old Jeffersonville chum with whom he had planned to seek gold on Pike's Peak. Stratton's dream for the time had faded considerably. For the last six years that white-crowned peak had been so close a neighbor that he had ceased to thrill at its proximity. And he had learned that mining was for most a heart- and back-breaking occupation which rewarded few for their labor. Always aloof and self-centered, he had been driven by his troubles into a shell he was never to break through. He was no longer a lucky and venturesome youth with tantalizing dreams. He was thirty years old and a man.

Parker cheered him up considerably. His wild ambitions to wrest a fortune from the far mountains were still fresh and robust. Finally, leaving Jeffersonville and Byron still pounding away at his anvil, Parker had started west. Working in Cincinnati, Peoria, Des Moines and other towns along the way, it had taken him five years to reach Denver. And there, right before his nose, rose the blue and silver peaks, the long smoky ranges. In them, he was sure, waited a princely fortune for them both.

The time was propitious for such a cheery prophecy. He had arrived on the stroke of one of Colorado's great hours. He thumped Stratton on the back in wild excitement. It was the Spring of '78; silver had been discovered in Leadville.

5

It was the greatest ore discovery since the Pike's Peak Rush twenty years before. Stratton awoke from his lethargy. After listening to the news which rushed down the mountain slopes like torrents, he could stand no more. His hands trembled with eagerness as he counted his savings at night in his room. This was what he had come to Colorado for!

Unable to wait for Parker, he caught the first train to Colorado Springs. Parker, it was agreed, was to follow him to Leadville later when the road up Turkey Creek was opened. In Colorado Springs Stratton outfitted two burros and set forth up Ute Pass again, past Granite where he had prospected with Lee.

The big rush was already under way. Long trains of mule teams and oxen struggled through the snow over the tortuous pass, wound between silver peaks in a silence now broken by the shouts of mule-skinners and the pistol cracks of their long rawhide whips. Over Ute Pass the road led through a great mountain valley, once the hunting ground of the Utes, now known as South Park. Here they could see the high snowy peaks of the Saguache Range glistening silver against the western sky. Silver! Stratton, trudging beside his burros, gritted his teeth and began the steep ascent up Mosquito Pass "that highway of frozen death" to Leadville, the City in the Clouds, and a fabulous strike.

The region, lying at the headwaters of the Arkansas, was first known as California Gulch. It had been christened by Abe Lee, one of the discouraged Forty-niners on his way back from California. Finding gold in his pan he had jumped to his feet shouting, "I found it! I got it—the hull state of Californy in this goddam pan!"

The production of the early placer miners dwindled from some $3,000,000 to only $20,000 in 1876. A black heavy sand cluttered up their sluices until it was almost impossible to separate gold from the gravel, and this trouble was further enhanced by the difficulty of moving out of the way heavy boulders recognized as worthless. Then W. H. Stevens discovered a supposed lead mine on the south side of the Gulch. His partner, Alvinus B. Wood, also an experienced miner, assayed samples. The stuff ran twenty to forty ounces of silver to the ton, and they found that the heavy sand and big boulders were composed of a carbonate of lead rich in silver. Wtihin two years their Iron Mine paid $200,000 and the secret was out. The rush got under way.

In June, 1877, the first building was erected in Leadville and by August there were six. Then suddenly, as if by magic, the town jumped upon the map. And Stratton trudged into the busiest and most famous town in the country. Coming from the lonely San Juan, he was unprepared for what he saw.

In six months a dense spruce forest had been converted into a town. The hacked stumps still stuck up in the streets which ran through a clutter of log cabins, board shacks, shanties and saloons: "a Monaco gambling room emptied into a Colorado spruce clearing." Sawmills hummed while lines of men stood waiting to jerk away the fresh green planks. Everybody was talking and gesticulating, buying and selling, bonding and leasing, even bidding for a chair to sleep in overnight. Spotswood and McClelland stages drawn by six horses careened down the crowded streets as if they were empty. And the long trains up from Ute Pass emptied hundreds more of miners, prospectors, laborers and gamblers. By night when the miners drifted into town, Leadville looked even more like a street carnival by lamplight with its saloons and gambling houses running full blast.

Stratton, driving his burros to the shelter of a gulch outside of town, quivered with hope and excitement. It was his first big boom.

Within a month or two he began to be discouraged. He had not yet made a strike, not even a discovery worth staking out. The work was difficult, a dreary routine that never changed. It was impossible to leave a thing in camp. Claim-jumping was a daily occurrence. Men had to defend their property down to a frying pan from theft and seizure. He sold one of his burros and packed the other to accompany him on his daily rounds from hill to gulch, from sun-up to dark. By night he was worn out, and flung himself down wherever he happened to be.

And yet all about him great discoveries were being made, fabulous veins of silver exposed to sight, new mines springing up on all the hills.

Wood and Stevens had sold their mine, Wood receiving for his share $50,000 from Levi Leiter, partner of Marshall Field, who was busy making millions from it. George Fryer, an obscure newcomer, wandered up Strayhorse Gulch and located his New Discovery on a hill that was promptly named after him. It became the most famous hill in the district. Then, that spring, occurred an incident which left Stratton open-mouthed but dumb, and set the world to talking.

One of the first residents in the district was a good-natured, hearty fellow named Horace Austin Warner Tabor, commonly known as Haw Tabor. He had been postmaster for the little settlement of Oro, now absorbed by Leadville. He was now first mayor of Leadville and ran a general store. Late in April two old German prospectors ambled in and asked him for a grubstake. They had something in mind, they said. Haw Tabor had grubstaked a hundred other seedy prospectors, but as mayor he was all for doing his part to make the City in the Clouds keep on booming. He allowed the two old Germans to select $64.75 worth of groceries from the shelves in return for a third interest in whatever they found.

The two prospectors set off to Fryer Hill. August Rische was a shoemaker from Missouri, and Theodore Hook had been an iron-worker in Pennsylvania. Neither knew much about mining, but on examining Fryer's New Discovery, thought there might be room on the hill for another. There was.

On May 1st, after digging a thirty-foot shaft, they struck silver ore which assayed 225 ounces per ton. The mine, named the Little Pittsburgh, began pouring money into the laps of the astonished prospectors and Haw Tabor. Hook sold out his share making $153,000, and fled to a farm. Rische sold his for a wad of 262 one-thousand-dollar bills and was finally pulled from the gutter to become an old, broken watchman in the Denver State Capitol. David H. Moffat was the buyer—a man who was to become famous for his dream of drilling a tunnel through the Rocky Mountains.

Tabor, on the Little Pittsburgh, soared to wealth and fame—the first of Colorado's three great mining kings. Within a year the mine was capitalized at $20,000,000. With Marshall Field of Chicago supplying $500, Tabor next bought the Chrysolite and sold his share for $500,000, and then the New Discovery. And Stratton, bewildered and discouraged, sat at his campfire watching the beginning of his meteoric flight to become Lieutenant Governor of Colorado that same year, United States Senator in five years, and world famous as a circus horse thereafter.

Tabor was not the only one whom Stratton watched strike pay dirt with almost incredible luck. An obscure prospector discovered and opened the Robert E. Lee, a mine that was to pour forth $118,500 in silver in one day. And the Morning Star which made Governor Routt's fortune when he had been reduced to a pack almost as empty as Stratton's. All from silver, the bright moonlit metal that had usurped the place of gold in the imagination of men and the marts of the world.

Stratton's ill luck was persistent as the burro at his heels. By July, when Parker finally arrived, he was living under a rock ledge with a piece of canvas thrown up for a tent. Although occasionally he still roamed the hills, he was working as a carpenter building shanties for more fortunate silver-seekers. Again he was glum and unresponsive to Parker's suggestion that they outfit and start out anew. He had been over every foot of ground; there wasn't a piece not already staked out that was worth filing on. Parker insisted, and Parker had the money. The men finally compromised. Silver was selling for $1.29 an ounce but gold was worth $20.00 and Stratton still held some gold claims down in the San Juan. He believed that they might yet produce if only he could keep title on them by doing his year's assessment work. If Parker would go with him and lend a hand, he would then return to Leadville.

Parker agreed. He bought a new outfit and the two men worked their way down the Continental Divide through San Luis Valley to Baker's Park. There in Cunningham Gulch they camped for six weeks doing the assessment work on Stratton's old claims. More men had trailed into the region making new strikes, but Stratton and Parker discovered nothing. Late in August they worked back over the high mountains to Leadville. The shine of Parker's new tools had worn away; their burros were thin and footsore, their clothes ragged and torn by two hundred miles of steep and dangerous trails; and they were broke again.

That night they stood miserably huddled in the glow of a big gambling-house on State Street watching the crowd swarming into McDaniels Theater across the street. From within came the clicks of the little ivory ball playing merry tunes on the roulette, the clink of glass on marble, the chime of bright and newly coined silver. Past them filed a steady stream of avid miners in big boots and with heavy pokes. Then suddenly an incident occurred which Stratton always remembered. The swing doors flew back almost in their faces and a man stepped out. He wore a diamond horseshoe in his cravat; a huge solitaire gleamed on his finger as he struck a match—not to light his cigar, but a greenback in his hand. Seeing the horrified look on their faces, he grinned derisively, touched off his cigar with the burning bill and strode off.

Stratton and Parker slunk away to an obscure saloon.

Pike's Peak (Photo by H. L. Stanley).

There Stratton borrowed ten dollars from another carpenter.

The next morning Stratton got a job building a vault in the bank—a vault in which other more lucky miners could store the silver bullion that he himself had sought so vainly. In a day or two Parker went to work at Grant's Smelter. In it he got his first glimpse of the thousands of tons of rich ore which he had been so sure he was to uncover with his own pick.

The two men lived together until the deep snows, in a small shanty which Stratton built. Then Stratton returned down Ute Pass to Colorado Springs to get his divorce. Parker remained till spring and left Leadville a sadder and wiser man.

Reinforced with a new grubstake he had earned by a winter's work, Stratton went back to Leadville in June. The district had hit its stride and was producing nearly eight million ounces of silver, drawing men from all over the world —even Ulysses S. Grant coming for a look at the "silver city in a sea of silver."

Charles Boettcher, running a hardware store, gave a prospector a $20 cook stove in return for mining shares that later netted him $150,000. John F. Campion had bought the Little Jonny mine to discover in it one of the richest deposits of gold in the world. And Sam Newhouse was laying the foundation of silver on which he built the Flatiron Building in New York. Dozens of other men had made fortunes, hundreds more were growing rich.

Surely, thought Stratton, all these men had done nothing he might not do also. He struck off to the newer camps of Kokomo and Robinson on the headwaters of the Blue River, eighteen miles north. Here at last he was on the top of the world—the high and perpetually snow-bound peaks from which radiate rivers that flow into three seas. But only topographically. His luck was as low as ever.

With the early snows freezing his feet through boot soles worn thin by months of trudging over bare, sharp granite, the backbone of the continent, Stratton once more returned to Leadville. He felt the lowest of the thousands there. And Haw Tabor was, and felt, the highest. He was Mayor of Leadville and Lieutenant Governor of Colorado. He had built a town hall, outfitted a fire department whose members wore red flannel shirts with the name of Tabor in white, moved into a princely suite in the Clarendon Hotel, built next door to the Tabor Opera House, bought half interest in the First National Bank of Denver. His good luck was phenomenal as Stratton's poor luck. He could not stem the wealth pouring into his already overflowing coffers. Even the Matchless Mine he had purchased for $117,000 was paying him an astounding return.

Stratton, hunting about for a job of sorts, happened into the bank for which he had built the vault. This Bank of Leadville was Tabor's converted store. Tabor was immensely proud of it. Remembering the down-at-the-heels carpenter who had done such good work for him previously, Tabor hired him again. He was to erect on top of the building a huge metal disc carved and painted to represent a silver dollar—a symbol under which Stratton labored most humbly indeed.

On the evening it was finished Tabor strolled out, thumbs in flowered vest, and stood looking up at it with a smile of satisfaction. "Silver Dollar—Silver Dollar Tabor!" he chuckled.

A passing Irishman stopped for a look at it with him and exchanged cigars. His name was Tom Walsh, already well known in the Cloud City. He had come to the district from the Black Hills, Dakota, where he had cleaned up a hundred thousand dollars by selling his gold claims during the excitement. Here he had bought the City Hotel, renaming it the Grand, and had just married a beautiful young lady whom he had heard singing in the church choir and who "clapped the name of St. Keven's upon well known Sowbelly Gulch when her husband happened to make a small strike there." He was soon to leave Leadville for Imogen Gulch, far south, and locate the Camp Bird, one of the greatest gold mines in the country which he sold for $3,100,000 after taking from it a profit of $2,500,000. On this "Monsieur Tom" went to Paris to astound the French with his lavish entertainments, to visit King Leopold of Belgium in a special train filled with servants, and to buy his daughter the Hope Diamond—as lusty a playboy as Tabor beside him.

While they were talking, Stratton ambled out of his lodging-house and slowed for a look at his resplendent and famous contemporaries. The passing throng of miners could never have guessed that in those three men—Tabor, the hotel-keeper Tom Walsh and the obscure carpenter Stratton—they were seeing together the three greatest mining men that Colorado was to produce in all its years of fabulous strikes.

Stratton shuffled off. The next day he took the long trail down Ute Pass to Colorado Springs.

He was done with Leadville.

6

Things had been happening down there in the "Saratoga of the West" while Stratton and his burro were plodding hopefully among the wild San Juans and the frosty peaks of the Mosquito and Saguache Ranges.

The boom at Leadville had made it the supply depot for thousands of teamsters setting up Ute Pass with wagon loads of supplies. The narrow Indian trail had given way to a road; the pack mules and patient little burros, usually known as Pike's Peak Canaries, to huge box wagons drawn by three spans of mules. The "skinner" rode the left-wheel mule, driving with a jerkline running to the bridle of the left leader, and using a whip with such dexterity that he could pick out either eye of a fly behind the ear of the farthest mule while turning his own head to spit.

All other roads to Leadville were an endless line of such wagon trains—from Cañon City up the Arkansas, from Denver by way of Turkey Creek, or from the end of the South Park railroad on the Platte. This heavy traffic was a prize that gave impetus to the "baby railroad" of General Palmer and two others. It was also the cause of one of the most dramatic battles in rail history.

Palmer had already extended the narrow-gauge Denver and Rio Grande to Pueblo and toward the mountains west. The tentative route was through the Big Cañon of the Arkansas, over Poncha Pass and through San Luis Valley to the Rio Grande, and thence to Mexico City by way of Chihuahua. The boom at Leadville almost caught him napping; and it awoke his rival, the Atchinson, Topeka and Santa Fe, which had built up the valley of the Arkansas to Pueblo.

The most feasible route to Leadville was up the Arkansas. Its key was the Royal Gorge, a stupendous chasm of red rock walls through which roared the river white as milk (now spanned by the world's highest suspension bridge). Both railroads had claims to the cañon and rushed construction crews to locate and lay their lines. Cipher telegrams between officials were intercepted and decoded, construction gangs were met by armed guards of their rival companies, and the battle began. When hired gun fighters led by Bat Masterson, the fighting sheriff of Dodge City and Tombstone, were imported, injunctions were brought against both companies and the battle was transferred to the courts. The case was finally carried to the Supreme Court of the United States which decided in favor of the Denver and Rio Grande. Under a working agreement the railroad promised not to build south to the Rio Grande, and the Santa Fe agreed not to build to Leadville. On April 1, 1880, the first Denver and Rio Grande train entered the Royal Gorge. The engine which drew it was gaily decorated and appropriately named *Fort De Reemer* after the man who had directed the building of the forts along the right-of-way. Crews working day and night laid the rails to Leadville by July.

General Palmer's success opened the Colorado Rockies to the Denver and Rio Grande. The narrow-gauge line, only three feet wide, began to run wild through the mountains: from Leadville over Tennessee Pass to Utah, from Pueblo over La Veta and Cumbres Pass into the San Juan country, for three years averaging three hundred miles of track each year. As a Denver poet put it:

In the Rocky Mountains, engineers say,
Wherever the water dares to come down,
A railway dares to go up, and they
Coil around the loftiest Titan's Crown
The loops of the lasso of winding track.

Palmer became rich and famous. He built his house in a beautiful box cañon called Glen Eyrie, patterning it after a Tudor castle and importing the stones for the fireplace from England. His little colony, Colorado Springs, came in for its share of glory. It was no longer a village, nor even a

Western town. Scorning the profits of teaming up Ute Pass to Leadville, it proclaimed itself a fashionable resort rivaling any European Spa—the "Saratoga of the West." Visitors from the "Continent" arrived daily. The town began sipping afternoon tea. A meal was no longer "good enough fer a dorg"—the people abhorring "r's."

It was no longer Colorado Springs or even the "Saratoga of the West." It was now "Little London."

Stratton jogging into town, limply astride a shaggy jackass, was most certainly an offensive sight to Little Londoners. If there had to be such depressing occupations as prospecting and mining, why didn't such men keep out of sight among the hills? Though, thank Heaven, the Pike's Peak region's scenic beauty had never been despoiled by the appearance of a mine dump!

Stratton, for his part, felt a stranger in his old town. Five years of chasing to the ends of the rainbow arched between Leadville and the San Juan had impressed on him their indelible mark. Reticent and aloof by nature, the silence of deep cañons and snowlit peaks had made him more taciturn and somber. He rode into town like a lone wolf forever detached from his pack.

Popular and successful as he had been, Stratton was never one of the élite group of Little London's founders. After all, he was only a carpenter who had found success in his trade. And now even this he had forsaken. An ornate carved stairway was nothing compared to the beauty of a piece of gold-bearing quartz—which he still meant to find.

He moved into an obscure lodging-house and got work as a carpenter. Few people knew him. Those who did, remembered his unfortunate affair with Zeurah Stewart. Stratton was left alone as he wished. And now he began a program that never altered: in the winter he worked as a carpenter, and in the summer he set out on another prospecting tour. Slim, mild-mannered, silent, he was persistent and patient as a burro—and just as likely to snap out or kick up his heels at the slightest provocation.

There were many during the fat 80's. Colorado had been admitted as a State in 1876, one hundred years after the signing of the Declaration of Independence. But instead of the "Centennial State" it was more popularly known as the "Silver State" of the Union, producing over $14,000,000 of the white metal each year. And Stratton was always ready to fling down his tools and join the newest stampede.

He had hardly been settled when, that spring, he was off again. Years before, three men, Robinson, Irwin and Pringle, had discovered silver in the Sangre de Cristo range thus named by early Spaniards for the Blood of Christ. Their little settlement they named Rosita. Now came news of Batzelle's big strike. The discovery of carbonate ore in the beautiful Wet Mountain Valley drew a rush of men who created near Rosita the town of Silver Cliff. For a time it became the third city in Colorado, next in size after Denver and Leadville.

By June Stratton was broke and had found nothing. For a month he worked on the new hotel being built, the Powell House. With his savings he crossed to the old settlement of Rosita and established headquarters in Miller Brothers rooming-house. Each day he set out to explore the old dumps and mine workings hoping to pick up a crumb from the earlier strikes. And each night he returned empty-handed. The Sangre de Cristo mountains, like the San Juan and Saguaches, had made him out a complete failure.

But next year there was something better in sight. Mining claims that looked good had been staked along the Eagle River. At Leadville, George Stevens loaded a burro with supplies and established along the river cliffs a store that soon developed into the town of Red Cliff. So Stratton hurried to Red Cliff. Eagle County was formed with Red Cliff as the county seat, but for Stratton the hills were again barren and unproductive.

He rushed from there to the Roaring Fork, not daring to wait till spring. The little camp of Aspen was beginning to mushroom through the snows from new silver discoveries nearby. The ore was so rich that it could be profitably transported to the smelters at Leadville by pack train at a cost of four cents a pound. From Frying Pan Gulch to the Taylor Range, mines began to open. The great Mollie Gibson averaged six hundred ounces of silver a ton, one twenty-four-ton carload yielding $76,500. Schools, churches, hotels, an opera house and three banks sprang up. The town became "the handsomest, most substantial and attractive mining town in the Rocky Mountains." Within a few years its silver production exceeded that of Leadville.

Stratton was a busy man, but not on his own. He was mining, prospecting and putting in tunnels for other men for four dollars a day and board at the St. Nicholas Hotel. He had gone broke again and had been forced to return to his trade.

A year or two later found him closer home. Mines had been opened at Tin Cup. Branching off the road to Leadville at Buena Vista, Stratton followed the new trail up the mountain cañon that today remains one of the wildest and most inaccessible trails to one of the weirdest ghost-towns of the Rockies. One could throw a stone across the deep cañon from either stupendous wall. The town at the bottom was St. Elmo, fantastically named by a woman in camp who boasted of having read a book—the old story, *St. Elmo.*

Thus Stratton's life for seventeen years.

The frail-looking Jeffersonville carpenter shrank into a rospector—strange, unknown breed. The prairie man was ow confirmed to the mountains. All Colorado was his home. ptly it has been called the Mountain State. Here the ockies reach their greatest height and most sublime pro- ortions. Fifty-one named peaks reach higher than fourteen housand feet; over a thousand exceed ten thousand feet. olorado, too, is the Mother of Rivers. For here on the ontinental Divide, the backbone of America, gather the nows and glaciers which feed the streams and rivers radi- ting like the spokes of a wheel. Rivers that flow west to he Pacific, east to the Mississippi basin, and south to the ulf.

But Pike's Peak, the greatest of them all, Stratton hardly oticed. It was always there, white, majestic and aloof, to nark with its melting snowcap the time for him to leave. And eturning, he saw it first—the only welcoming reminder that e was home again and that another fruitless year had assed.

Stratton's life through these seventeen years of manhood ould be most simply told by two pictures: The first to show im in winter, astraddle the roof beam of a new building, ounding away as an unnoticed carpenter with tools which ne may still see in the State Museum. The second to show im in summer—the barest glimpse of a strange, gaunt man assing into the shadow of a dark mountain cañon with a urro patient, plodding, and silent as he.

7

Not to Stratton, nor to Tabor or Walsh, but to the tens f thousands like them but forgotten, grant the time of a ingle mute paragraph—the most inadequate toast. To the sunburned, leather-necked and tobacco-splashed prospectors whose unsung labors in the waste places of America have made us what we are. In icy mountain streams, on barren windswept peaks, in brassy burning deserts and frozen Arctic tundras, they have borne hunger and pain, the cold of night and the heat of day. They have been battered by the elements and reduced by immense solitudes into an unvarying drabness. Plodding, taciturn men, they all wear the same battered felt hats, the same dirty wool shirts and heavy boots. They speak—when they do speak—in the same guarded voice, they know the same hidden haunts of deer and grouse, are skilled alike in the long-forgotten wilderness arts. They have led explorer and trapper, the first advance of civilization. Their lonely campfires have grown to cities of luxury and refinement; their wandering trails mark the route of the thundering Express Limited; and of these insignificant fruits of their heroic labors they are blissfully unaware. They have long turned their backs and sought the farther places. No region is too barren, parched or windswept, too far away. They have gone blithely but slowly, keeping one wary eye open for a piece of likely float, the smallest speck of color. Few, so very few, have found it. But the countless others have never lost their grizzled smiles. No! The prospector, for all his age and misfortune, remains the eternally youthful fellow long after his white beard turns yellow and his rheumy blue eyes grow dim to all but the distant horizon. And when in a forgotten gulch, a lonely hillside, one comes upon his bleached bones, his upturned skull seems still fixed in a derisive grin. Of a strange and incomprehensible breed of men to whom nothing, neither success, failure, riches nor fame, means anything compared to his never ending search—the prospector remains of them all America's wayward child.

In prospecting as in everything else Stratton was a paradox. With new discoveries, camps and towns springing up around him each spring like anemones through the snow, he might reasonably have flung his hat into the air and dug where it landed, as did a friend of his. The odds were with him that eventually he also would make a strike. But after years of chasing through the Rockies after the fickle skirts of Lady Luck, he made up his mind that he ought to know something about ore. At least to make its speaking acquaintance in case he met it on a lonely foray.

The nearest mines were up Ute Pass and in South Park at the foot of Hoosier Pass, old strikes that had boomed Colorado City in the sixties: Tarryall, Buckskin Joe and Fair Play. They were all producers of placer gold, Breckenridge on the Blue River becoming the biggest camp of all.

Stratton had been there once before, having had to pawn his tools to a storekeeper for supplies to get him out of town. He now returned with a different purpose: to learn everything possible about gold ore. After hanging around the dredges for a week, he obtained a job in the Nashold Mill. Here he worked for months learning the amalgamation process of treating ores.

Returning to Little London, he obtained the job of building a house for a friend of his, a lumber-dealer named Crissey. With the money he went to the State School of Mines and took a course in metallurgy. Stratton, the carpenter, then the prospector, was now Stratton the student. He had given up trusting to luck and had settled down to prepare for a methodical search.

Again he returned to Little London to work for a new stake—but not for prospecting. He enrolled at the town's new Colorado College, an institution founded by the Congregational church on a site donated by General Palmer for whom the first substantial building was named. Stratton's teacher in mineralogy was Professor Lamb. From him Stratton learned a valuable lesson: how to test the value of ore with a blowpipe instead of squinting at it in the sunlight and hefting it in his hand. With his first money Stratton blew himself to a copy of Cornwall's *Manual of Blowpipe Analysis* and a shiny blowpipe, and became adept in its use. Now at last he was ready to track Lady Luck to her lair. He needed only the whiff of a fresh scent to be off.

It came within a month; he was just in time! From not thirty-five miles away came the news of a discovery whose samples had assayed $2,000 in gold to the ton. Stratton with all the townspeople stood aghast. The region was a high barren cattle range on the south slope of Pike's Peak itself, the very peak which had brought him to Colorado and which had stood there before his nose all the time. Stratton grabbed his blowpipe and joined the rush up Ute Pass.

When he got there it was to find a thousand infuriated men storming about a shallow mine. The thing was a damned hoax. Somebody had carted up a big bottle of chloride of gold and salted the mine, hoping to sell it to a tenderfoot. While they were trying to discover the perpetrator of the hoax that they might hang him to the nearest tree, Stratton jogged wearily back to town. The affair, known as the Mount Pisgah Fiasco, reminded him too much of his first venture in the Yretaba.

In the fall of 1885 Myron Stratton died at Jeffersonville. The small bequest forwarded to his only son that winter gave Stratton a grubstake with which to really try out his newly acquired education. He bought a saddle horse and pack mule, and set out to the little-known western slope of the Rockies.

Things had quieted down in western Colorado. The Utes,

driven from their old hunting grounds in the San Juan region by a treaty they did not understand, had been pressed farther and farther west. All three tribes, always wandering hunters, could not understand the white man's school, plow and barbed-wire fences. And when the Indian Agent, Nathan Meeker who had founded Greeley, summarily ordered them to plow up their sacred dance ground, they revolted. Meeker and his eleven men were massacred, the agency pillaged and burned. Military action against them was refused by Washington, but the White River Utes were rounded up and removed to a Utah Reservation. Old Chief Ouray of the Southern Utes was not forgotten; in Colorado there are a mountain, county and town named after him.

To Ouray then, Stratton went, a setting wild and picturesque as a Ute war-bonnet. He camped in Imogen Gulch. A dozen mines producing silver ore worth one hundred dollars a ton had been established there, but it had cost eighty dollars a ton to pack it to Silverton, so remote was the district. The high gaunt cliffs were always crumbling, and when an avalanche had buried some of the property under tons of rock the Allied Mines gave up. For weeks Stratton prospected the ground, the very gulch that was later to make Tom Walsh internationally known.

Luck was still against him. His new blowpipe, book and head full of knowledge were useless. He might have known there was no persuading a woman, let alone those three old ladies, Clotho, Lachesis and Atropos, who went on serenely spinning, measuring and cutting their threads without a glance at Stratton miserably returning home.

Busy building a new house costing $4,600—at a nice profit to himself—he was for once too discouraged to heed the next siren call from the headwaters of the Rio Grande.

There an old prospector, Nicholas C. Creede, had discovered the Holy Moses and Last Chance mines soon to be producing $180,000 a month. And in Willow Creek Cañon, Creede sprang into existence as the newest and one of the most renowned of Colorado's rip-roaring camps, a place so rich in mineral and lusty of life that only Cy Warman, the "poet of the Rockies," could characterize it:

Here the meek and mild-eyed burros
On mineral mountains feed. . . .
It's day all day in the daytime,
And there's no night in Creede.

It was the last of the big silver strikes of Colorado—the only one in seventeen years that Stratton had not participated in with failure dogging his footsteps.

He did not know it, but luck for the first time had turned his way; she was letting him cool his heels for the coming storm.

It had been brewing for almost twenty years. The "Fat Eighties" had drawn to a close with the production of silver greater than ever before, $20,000,000 per year. This ever increasing flow of silver from the Colorado Rockies was casting a white shadow over the world at large. The currency system since the days of George Washington had been based on bimetallism, the unlimited coinage of both gold and silver. Then in 1873 the government stopped the coinage of silver dollars and established gold as the standard of value.

Five years after this "Crime of 1873" silver was discovered in Leadville. Colorado became the "Silver State." Strike after strike followed. The Colorado Rockies seemed to hold an inexhaustible supply of silver; enough, as Tabor boasted, to build a solid wall of silver forty feet high and four feet thick along its eastern boundary. As the market price began to drop, mining men and loyal Coloradoans clamored for the right to have coined into dollars all the silver shipped to the mints, and demanded that the ratio of sixteen ounces of silver to one of gold be restored and fixed.

A compromise was reached in 1878. The Bland-Allison Act was passed, directing the Secretary of the Treasury to buy from $2,000,000 to $4,000,000 worth of silver and coin it into dollars.

It was not enough; the supply of silver was so great that the price of silver kept declining. With the election of Cleveland, firmly opposed to free silver, as President in 1884, the political pot began to boil. Colorado newspapers agitated free coinage of silver. Speeches were made, pamphlets advocated the cause. A silver convention met in Denver in 1885. Within a short time a Colorado Silver Alliance was formed. A National Silver Convention met at St. Louis in 1889. Silver had become the one great political issue of the time.

By 1890 representatives from the silver-producing states were so aggressive that they threatened to kill the McKinley tariff bill unless Congress granted them free coinage of silver. The outcome was another compromise, the Sherman Act, which provided for the purchase of 4,500,000 ounces of silver per month by the United States Government.

The passage of this act, which sent up the price of silver to over a dollar an ounce, was joyfully acclaimed by members of almost two hundred silver clubs in Colorado.

Their enthusiasm was short-lived. Something was about to happen. As in Pharaoh's dream, the Fat Eighties were to be followed by the Lean Nineties. Tabor, the Silver King—with his Denver estate decorated by peacocks strutting on the lawn; his Tabor Grand Opera House; his great silver mines in Leadville; his vast holdings in Arizona, Texas, even in the Honduras—was toppling on this throne. Leadville,

Aspen, Silver Cliff, every silver camp in Colorado was about to plunge into an abyss, to be buried forever in an avalanche greater than one of tumbling cliffs.

The silver moon was setting; the golden sun was ready to peep above the Rockies. And Stratton, by a stroke of inconceivable luck, was not in Creede when it rose. A mild, thin man now forty-three years old, his hair grown "white and shiny as bleached silk," he was pounding away with his hammer in Little London, oblivious of the fact that the snowy Peak always before him was to sprout at its grass roots a crop that was to astound the world and alter history.

PART THREE: PIKE'S PEAK

"Hell! The tenderfeet are taking out gold where it is, and the miners are looking for it where it ought to be!"

3. PIKE'S PEAK

BY the spring of 1891, Stratton was getting restless again. Day by day the snowcap on the Peak slipped lower toward timberline. To Stratton, the bare granite summit looked like the bald head of an old gentleman cautiously poking out from his winter covers. Silver was slipping downward faster, but Stratton's feet were itching. Something else would turn up.

One April evening after work he happened to meet a friendly plasterer named Leslie Popejoy on the street. Popejoy had a touch of spring fever too. He didn't know a trowel's worth of mining, but he confessed to having a little money with which he was figuring to take a flier in some mines down along the Gunnison.

"Don't you do it," said Stratton. "You can invest it better close to home. Ever hear of cryolite?"

Plasterer and carpenter got down to brass tacks—and cryolite. The mineral was little known but valuable. It was a fluoride used in making aluminum and most of it had to be shipped in from Greenland. But Stratton believed he knew where there was a valuable deposit somewhere near St. Peter's Dome or up Beaver Creek, not over eighteen miles away. He suggested that Popejoy join him in the venture.

The two men made an agreement: Popejoy to supply the grubstake and Stratton to locate and develop the claims, each sharing equally in the profits.

So Popejoy bought two burros, hand tools, supplies and

a general outfit. They then decided to hire another man for Stratton to take along while Popejoy stayed home on the job to make more money. The man was W. G. Fernay, commonly known as Billy. Although from a good family of means, Billy was not too highly regarded in town. He seldom worked and was often carried home drunk on an ironing board which two friends kept handy for the purpose.

A few mornings later they began packing in front of Stratton's boarding-house. Popejoy came by, gave Stratton fifty dollars, and hurried off to work. Stratton and Fernay kept trying to load their packs on the two burros. One of the mouse-colored "canaries" had been cut by barbed wire which had left a large scab. The instant the pack touched it, the animal brayed and lashed out its heels. Billy stood back and began to swear—the best help he could give Stratton. Within a half hour a crowd had collected to laugh at Stratton. He finally lost his temper and grabbed up a pick handle. His first whack at the obstreperous burro opened the scab. Blood began to pour from the wound.

From the doorway an officious woman screamed out, began cussing Stratton and then ran off to bring the secretary of the Humane Society. Stratton and Billy got busy. While Billy flung a blanket over the beast's head, Stratton hastily flung the pack on its back. Then in great haste they fled down the street.

At the Nevada undercrossing before they were out of town, the pack fell off, spilling flour and beans. Stratton, by now in a devil of a temper at Popejoy for selecting such a cranky burro, replenished their supplies at the last store and ordered the bill for $8.45 sent to the plasterer. That night they camped at old man Wade's cabin and bought a new burro to replace the lamed one, charging the $13.50 to Popejoy also.

It was an auspicious start. For some two weeks they hunted around for the valuable cryolite deposits of which Stratton had heard, but without finding the merest trace. Rather than return to town, Stratton abruptly decided to cross over the Divide into the Cripple Creek district, often called the Womack mining district. He had heard of a gold discovery or two up there on the south slope of Pike's Peak, the very scene of the disgraceful Mount Pisgah Fiasco. And on May 11th, they made their first camp in the district.

Only a mile up and twenty west from Little London, the region was a mass of barren hills clustered beneath the Peak, each over eleven thousand feet high, cut by deep gulches and threaded by a crooked stream winding in and out of sparse aspen thickets and flanked with morasses. For the most part the land was treeless, above timberline, with dreary stretches of bare frost-shattered granite. Yet by its general southward slope it afforded fair pasturage to cattle —a forbidding, high, grazing country which no one could reasonably conceive of holding a speck of color.

The Mount Pisgah Fiasco had flatly discredited the district, but it had not been the first time that wandering prospectors had stopped there on their way deeper into the mountains. During the Pike's Peak Rush of '59 it had been visited by gold seekers; in '74 a gold discovery had been reported between Mount Pisgah and Gold Hill. And still each year a few prospectors like Arequa passed through the gulch which still bears his name, washed a pan of sand from the stream and left with a snort of disgust.

William Womack had originally homesteaded the district. In 1881 his nephew, Theodore H. Lowe, discovered gold while surveying the ranch and located a claim which he called the Grand View. The float he exhibited made little impression. He gave up the claim to another nephew, Bob

Womack, who promised to do some development work on it. For a few years Womack kept up the ranch, digging a little on the claim and puttering around the district looking for gold. Hunting gold and cows did not mix. He went broke and in 1885 hired out as a cowhand on the Broken Box ranch.

The ranch had been sold to Philip Ellsworth, a wealthy young glove manufacturer of New York, who liked the hunting and fishing. But finding the high altitude, intense cold, deep snows and scarcity of feed too much to contend with as a business, he sold out to two Denver real-estate men. Bennett and Myers, the new owners, bought it for a trifle: the hundred and sixty acres, cattle, outfit and fences for $7,500.

Bennett found Womack an indifferent and erratic cowboy, and called him "Crazy Bob." Nevertheless, he allowed him to continue digging for gold provided he covered up the holes so the cattle could not fall in. He even visited Crazy Bob's "gopher hole" and picked up a few samples of ore which he took to a pioneer Denver assayer. "There's no use wasting your money for an assay of this stuff, Mr. Bennett," reported the assayer after one look at the float. "There's no gold in it."

Womack was not discouraged, but intermittently kept working a hole in Poverty Gulch without even staking a claim. Periodically he rode into town and showed samples in the Colorado City saloons. Few paid him any attention until a furniture-store owner, E. M. De la Vergne, pricked up his ears, having had charge of the Orient Mine below Georgetown. He and the manager of his store, F. F. Frisbee, packed up to the Broken Box ranch in January 1891 during a blizzard. It took them three days, and when they begged for shelter, the foreman of the ranch, George Carr, took them for peddlers lost in the storm.

A month later they returned and were shown Womack's old workings. He had sunk a shaft and had encountered good ore. Womack had called his claim "Chance" and had relocated it six years in succession without recording the fact. Now, fearful of losing it, he hurried to town and relocated it as the El Paso. De la Vergne and Frisbee also staked claims, recording them as the Alhambra, El Dorado and Old Mortality. In the certificates the district was named Cripple Creek from the crooked little stream in whose morasses straying cattle had been lamed.

It was winter and bitter cold. Cripple Creek lay frozen under snowdrifts that covered stream, trail and the stake-and-rider log fences of the Broken Box. The white bare aspens shook under the piercing wind that swept down the gulches, ten thousand feet high, and whistled around the white bare face of the Peak that rose above, over fourteen thousand feet high. A barren, high, grazing country, a mere cow pasture on the slope of Pike's Peak, said the townspeople down below. Only tenderfeet could be taken in by the stories that it might be a gold country; real miners didn't give a tinker's whistle for the reports. Another Mount Pisgah Fiasco! Little Londoners proclaimed it was their duty to pronounce the fraud and kill the boom before the mining industry of Colorado was blackened with dishonor.

Yet, with the melting snows and clearing trails, men began to drift into the district: tenderfeet, verdant "alfalfa miners" and old prospectors who would have sunk their picks in the sand hills had the rumors blown in from the Great Plains.

So while Stratton and Billy Fernay were leisurely poking into the district from the south, a hundred men were making camp along Cripple Creek. From the Broken Box ranch, Bennett's foreman, George Carr, wired him that "Prospectors are digging up the range everywhere. Shall I make them jump?" The meaning was obvious; Carr was an experienced old cowman who knew how to use his guns.

Bennett immediately set forth for Cripple Creek, stopping only long enough to find out if he held title to more than surface rights on the Broken Box. Assured that he owned everything "from China to the skies," Bennett hired a civil engineer to plat a town on eighty acres of his ranch. The town was named Fremont in honor of the Pathfinder, but was soon changed to the more familiar Cripple Creek. The prospectors were still laughing at an old cow hobbling about which had become crippled when cowboys had pulled it out of a bog along the stream. The first purchasers of lots for cabin sites had to agree to leave all their lumber to be used in patching fences after the camp was gone.

Such was the Cripple Creek cow pasture that Stratton and Fernay looked down upon early in May.

The sun was sinking behind the Saguache range far west above Leadville. To the north they could see the Kenoshee hills at the headwaters of the Platte, and southward the jagged Sangre de Cristos beyond Wet Mountain Valley with Lost Mountain and the Nipple sticking up nearby, an incomparably beautiful setting.

It was as if they stood on the eastern wall of a giant granite cup, a vast bowl of gold in the setting sun. Already the high bare slope of Pike's Peak was flushing a salmon pink. All around them rose a mass of hills from three hundred to one thousand feet above the surface. Tumbled close together as prairie-dog mounds, they were separated only by deep, precipitous gulches scarcely a half mile apart. Below, through a narrow grassy valley, meandered Cripple

Creek. At its headwaters, two miles high in its amphitheater of innumerable hills and cut off by Poverty Gulch, lay the Broken Box. For once it typified the name with a scatter of cabins, lean-to's and tents—the first jumbled array to bear the name of Cripple Creek.

Billy Fernay was not interested in scenery. The faint crash of a felled pine, the thin blue lines of smoke and twinkle of scarlet campfires meant supper and talk. But Stratton was looking at a ledge of reddish granite that stuck up at the foot of Battle Mountain, a rough and broken outcrop, several hundred feet long on the slope above Wilson Creek. Every prospector in camp had passed it by without a second glance.

"Come on!" growled Billy. Stratton gave his burro a whack and they plodded down the trail.

For almost two months they prospected around. Dick Wootton, the old Indian scout, had picked up good float on Gold Hill above Anaconda Gulch. He obligingly moved his stakes and let Stratton with two other men, Goudy and McKinney, stake out the Gold King beside his Lone Star claim. Stratton then located the Legal Tender and gave it up in disgust, letting some strangers relocate it. Apparently his search for gold was turning out like his quest for cryolite and silver. He began to wonder what Popejoy was thinking about his grubstake.

That night, July 3rd, he sat staring into the embers long after Billy had rolled into his blanket and gone to sleep. The papery-leaved aspens around him rustled in the wind; far down the gulch howled a coyote. Stratton did not stir. The sounds, the warmth of the coals at his feet and the chill at his back, the pattern of the stars in the sky above—all these he had known and felt an incalculable number of times and no longer paid them heed. Nor was he thinking of those seventeen years and the innumerable Colorado ranges that had taken the years of his youth and left him now at forty-three, stranded beside another dying campfire.

He was trying to remember the scraps of geology Professor Lamb had taught him about the region. The country rock was granite of a pinkish tint that had earned for it the name of Pike's Peak Granite. The whole granite area whose culminating point was Pike's Peak, the professor had said, had once been a great volcano whose top had been worn away. Ages ago there had been a mighty eruption. A complex of volcanic rock had burst through the granite in a big "blow-out." This volcanic rock was called porphyry, a purplish rock easily distinguished from the granite. The professor, of course, even knew the name's history: it had evolved from the Greek "porphyra" for purple, used to designate rock which the Romans had obtained from the quarries of Gebel Dokhan on the shores of the Red Sea.

Such musings, even for a man who had been to college, put Stratton to sleep. In Cripple Creek there were no indications of quartz, the usual gangue for gold. Nor were there any bold outcroppings of veins so common throughout Colorado and the world, being known in California as ledges and in Australia as reefs. There was only that immense rib of rock forced up through the granite slope of Battle Mountain above Wilson Creek that he and everyone else had passed by. Stratton rolled up in his blankets and went to sleep.

That night something happened which he never afterward denied in the face of many scoffing laughs. As one put it:

> That night as he lay in the open air under cover of a mountain pine, he dreamed. A bright vision came and whispered that the spot over which he had passed and where the granite rock was found was to be a great mine. Now thoroughly awake, the

carpenter looked up into the heavens, counted the stars and waited impatiently for the sunrise. Old Sol, according to custom, was on time, and when the first rays were discovered above the brow of Bull Hill, Stratton was ready to make the initial move in what he confidently believed would be the first stage on the royal road to wealth.

A true believer further explains it thus:

On the night of July 3rd the vision of fabulous wealth came to him with all the convincing power of revelation. There is something in mental impressions, something in telepathy, as unerring as man's intuitions, whose manifestations are felt and recognized with the force of truth or prophecy, and whose operation is mysterious, occult, baffling thus far the investigations of psychologists.

Poor, sleepy Billy was in the same boat when he was yanked from his blanket at the first streak of dawn. Stratton said himself:

I had scarcely opened my eyes when the impression came to me that on the south slope of Battle Mountain where the altered dike ran up among the briars, was a mine. The impression grew on me. I could see nothing else before me or around me than the tangled briar patch on the south slope of Battle Mountain, with the big boulders, many of them weighing tons. I tried to reason with myself, wondering why I had not been impressed by that locality before, but the mysterious something told me it was no time for reasoning but for action.

It is certain he did not see the half-filled coffee pot. In his excitement to wake Billy, he kicked it into his partner's mystified face. Waiting only long enough to shout his destination to Billy, Stratton jumped to his burro and beat the little beast over the hills to Battle Mountain, He was scared to death someone else might have staked a claim on the spot.

He arrived just as the sun rose above the horizon. The place was unclaimed and deserted, but in the early morning he could hear the faint reports of shots from camp to celebrate the day. It was the Fourth of July, 1891. Stratton staked a full lode claim at the ledge and then another beside it. The first he named the Independence, the other the Washington, both in honor of the holiday.

2

The "vision" might have led Stratton to the spot, but there was no guardian angel to protect it from complications. The first forerunner of trouble was another prospector who arrived within a few hours, on the heels of Billy Fernay, demanding what the deuce.

Popejoy down in Little London had been getting worried. He had bought a complete outfit, given Stratton $50, advanced Billy some wages, and had paid the bills of $8.45 and $13.50 sent him. And now, after two months, he had received no news save that his partners were up on the scene of the new gold camp. So he had sent Fred Troutman, headed that way, to ascertain what gold mines Stratton had located and to see that all of their names were on the discovery stakes.

Troutman poked among the briars and located the stakes, insisting that he was a new partner. The trouble was ironed out. The stakes for the Independence were inscribed with Popejoy's and Stratton's names; and those for the Washington included Troutman's. He immediately returned to town carrying samples from each claim. On July 8th the results of the assays made by Professor Lamb were delivered to Popejoy and Troutman.

Stratton's luck had turned. The sample from the Independence showed 18.9 ounces of gold and .7 ounces of silver to the ton. $380 in gold to the ton! When the news got out the rush to the greatest gold camp in America got under way.

The Washington assay showed only 2.1 ounces of gold to the ton and not a trace of silver. Then and there Troutman gave up his share in the Washington with a snort of disgust.

Popejoy could hardly believe his eyes. It was too good to be true, especially since Stratton had requested more money. He hired a horse and sent Troutman riding back for more samples. But Stratton already was getting touchy about the mine revealed to him in a vision. He refused to allow Troutman to touch a pebble of granite. Troutman was in no mood to argue. He returned to town and after reporting to Popejoy wandered off.

Stratton meanwhile had staked out on July 7th another claim which he named the Professor Lamb, after his friend, and a few days later another named the Black Diamond. Within a week he began to get worried. He had spent all his own spare cash, about one hundred dollars, as well as Popejoy's grubstake, and practically no work had been done on any of the claims. On the Gold King he had helped put down the requisite ten-foot shaft without striking pay dirt. The Independence, Washington, Black Diamond and the Professor Lamb were still briar patches.

There seemed to be only one place to get money. So on the 13th he returned to get more money from Popejoy. Particularly he wanted forty dollars in back wages due the grumbling Billy, although he hoped to get six hundred dollars to develop one of the claims. With him he lugged down ninety pounds of rock from the Independence.

After it had been crushed, a sample assayed by Professor Lamb showed only $11.20 to the ton. Popejoy's pessimism seemed confirmed. He had already spent $275 on the venture, and refused any more help.

Stratton now proved himself as wily as during his real-estate deals of almost twenty years before. He cautiously offered to buy Popejoy's interest in the claims for the price of his grubstake, $275 with interest, giving three promissory notes payable in ninety days. When this was done, he obtained from Popejoy a written agreement of dissolution whereby the plasterer released and conveyed to Stratton all his rights to the claims.

Stratton still was without money. What he did now showed the character of the resourceful and secretive carpenter. He produced the deed to a lot in Denver which he had kept hidden for such a rainy day and sold it for $250. Within two weeks he had sold his house and lot in Colorado Springs, obtaining $500 in cash above the mortgage on it. With this money he paid off Popejoy, who left for Denver to continue at his trade as a plasterer.

Stratton now hastened to perfect the location certificates in his name alone of the Independence, Washington, Black Diamond and the Professor Lamb. Papers had never been filed, the discovery stakes alone showing Popejoy's name.

But how had he protected them from claim-jumping during his absence? Very simply. He had promised Billy Fernay one-half interest in the Washington in payment of the forty dollars due him, provided Billy stayed on the property and helped him. He now returned to Cripple Creek and bought back Billy's half interest for ninety dollars.

Now throughout summer and fall, he tried to develop his four claims. He built a fence of logs around his tent ostensibly for protection against bears, but more probably to keep out ridiculing prospectors. None of the claims produced another sample that assayed gold. His money soon gave out, this time for good. He tried to borrow money from everyone he knew. On one occasion he offered Gillis, a lumber-dealer in town, a half interest in all his holdings for five hundred dollars. He was ridiculed and pitied. He sold his interest in the Gold King, then abandoned the Black Diamond because he was unable to do development work on it.

Billy Fernay, little fed and not paid, left him and relocated it on his own account. He then sold out for five hundred dollars to Stratton's old partner on the Gold King, McKinney, and left on a pleasure trip to his old home in Missouri. The Black Diamond struck ore and he was able to make seventy thousand dollars through transactions in stock. He never returned to Cripple Creek and died in Reno, Nevada, a poor man.

Next, Stratton gave up the Professor Lamb, though sentimentally retaining title to the claim, and turned to his original and remaining two claims, the Independence and Washington.

With uncanny foresight and a luck that from now on never failed him to the minutest detail, he kept his vision-mine, the Independence, face down like a stud-poker ace, and played the Washington.

In October he arranged with Sam Altman to develop it for one-half interest. Altman worked with him for three months and then abandoned it as worthless after spending $950. With a flood of prospectors now pouring into the district demanding lumber, Altman started a sawmill and established on top of the slope the camp of Altman which mushroomed into the highest incorporated town in the world.

A month later, in February, 1892, Stratton hit a streak of gold. He sold the Washington to a syndicate which organized as the Washington Mining Company and began selling shares throughout the State. The price was $80,000, Stratton receiving $10,000 cash and a bond for the balance. Within a few months the lead petered out. The company forfeited the bond and the Washington returned to Stratton.

Shortly afterward Stratton struck the lead again, and gave bond on it to a California party for $150,000. The first payment was due in thirty days, and he had the option meanwhile of shipping ore. From the day the agreement was signed, the vein began to widen. The value of the ore increased to ten dollars a ton. In the thirty days Stratton cleaned up $25,000. And then he received news that the California promoters had been unable to raise the money and the deal was off. The mine was still his.

Lady Luck, with whom he had played tag for seventeen years throughout all Colorado, had finally caught up with him—and on the slope of Pike's Peak.

With money beginning to pour in, Stratton settled down at last to prod among the briars of his dream mine, the Independence. Intuitively right, he had saved it till the last.

The property, a full-lode mining-claim 1,500 feet by 300 feet, lay on the steep slope of Battle Mountain. In following the vein in a shallow discovery shaft, Stratton found that it ran out of the side line in place of extending up the hill inside his claim. The laws provided that any miner could follow the vein if it ran out of his property, but there were so many legal ramifications that it was usually a race and a fight between rival claim-owners. So Stratton with a force of men sank a new shaft near the edge of his property and one night drove a drift into the adjoining White House claim then being patented.

Altman, the highest mining camp in Cripple Creek.

Luckily, he consulted a lawyer who had drifted into camp, a J. Maurice Finn who later struck it rich and built "Finn's Folly" in Cripple Creek, boasting a tropical reception hall, steam-heated and decorated by murals of a famous artist. There was just time, said Finn, to file an adverse claim in the United States Land Office at Pueblo. Stratton hired a man named Charles Steele who with two horses rode the eighty miles of mountain road in eight hours before midnight to protect Stratton's "claim-jumping."

More was to come of the White House property, but for the time Stratton lost the vein. For months he dug up the ground on the Independence claim among the great boulders scattered about, some of them weighing over ten tons. At last in desperation he broke open one of the boulders. An assay from the pieces ran over twelve dollars a ton in gold. From the crushed boulders alone he received $60,000. Then on this very spot he sank an ore chute.

It led directly into the main vein—a vein that day by day widened out and led through porphyry and granite alike, tying up the country rock in a snarl of golden threads, acting like a common cementing material, in pockets and layers of such richness that it "looked good enough to eat."

Stratton's dream had assayed. He had made and developed the greatest discovery in Cripple Creek and was the camp's first millionaire. He was no longer a carpenter. Thereafter he was to be alluded to in a hushed voice as "Winfield Scott the Great," Colorado's greatest mining king.

3

But what had been happening in the world below that he could so easily usurp Tabor's place? He had hammered that silver dollar over the Silver King's Leadville bank too securely into place to suppose it could be blown down by any hurricane.

Well, the metal disc was still there but only as a sadly tarnished symbol. Tabor had been toppled from his silver throne. All his vast holdings in Mexico and the Honduras had been swept away. The millions he had invested turned out to be millions reaped from him by every sort of swindler. The Tabor Block, the Tabor Grand Opera House and his opera house in Leadville, then his mansion on Capitol Hill had been sold to meet his debts. The famed Matchless Mine was closed and filling with water. And Tabor, old and penniless, stunned by the shock, was spending his days sitting in a vacant lot in Denver, staring at the mountains.

"Why?" murmured the deposed king.

"Why?" echoed the new one.

Both were caught up in a whirlwind they had been powerless to escape.

With the election of Cleveland as President in 1892 the free silver question came to a head. Capitalists feared that the heavy purchases of silver under the Sherman Act would result in the replacement of the gold dollar by a depreciated silver dollar. Business tightened, commercial houses began to fail. A rush to redeem securities in gold brought down the gold reserve of the United States Treasury to the danger point, $100,000,000. Then it dropped to $70,000,000.

All winter alarm spread throughout the world. Foreign governments stopped buying silver. Then in June the mints of India closed to silver. In four days the price of silver dropped from eighty-three cents an ounce to sixty-two—less than half its set price.

For Colorado, the Silver State, this was a disabling blow.

Mines and smelters closed. Leadville, Aspen, Creede, every silver camp in the Rockies began to look like a deserted village. In three days ten banks closed in Denver alone. An army of ten thousand destitute workers marched into town and were provided a relief camp under military regulations. Governor Waite came out with the statement that, "it is infinitely better that blood should flow to our horses' bridles rather than our national liberties should be destroyed," and he was thereafter called "Bloody Bridles" Waite. He suggested as a remedy "Fandango Dollars," the scheme being for Colorado to buy the output of its silver mines, ship it to Mexico, and then have it coined into dollars to be returned to the State for circulation.

President Cleveland now called a special session of Congress on August 7, 1893, and urged repeal of the Sherman Act of 1890 whereby 4,500,000 ounces of silver per month were to be bought by the Government. The two Colorado Senators did their best to stem the tide, but were defeated. With the repeal Colorado's silver days were over.

But something else had happened concurrent with the disastrous panic and collapse of silver, an ominous cloud that had its lining, but not of silver.

Gold had been discovered on the south slope of Pike's Peak. Cripple Creek was booming and Stratton's name was on every tongue. From all the silver camps in the West, disheartened miners began to flock to the new boom.

A horde of tenderfoot Little Londoners, alfalfa miners, shoe-clerks, butchers and druggists had already scrambled up the cañons. News of Stratton's discovery had struck town like a bolt of summer lightning from Pike's Peak. Gold from the Cripple Creek cow pasture! Why, the district wasn't twenty miles away as a crow would fly; even by the Cheyenne Cañon stage route it was only thirty-five miles away. And Stratton of all men! Incredulous and astonished at a mere carpenter, they pointed out a house, a staircase he had built. Saner heads wagged wisely. "A lucky little ore pocket" . . . "a unique freak in economic geology" . . . "nothing of permanent value" . . . they repeated. Even the prominent business men shied at the news, remembering the Mount Pisgah Fiasco. "You can't change a country by changing its name," they offered, in place of loans and grubstakes. But in the few months of its first year the camp had produced $200,000 worth of gold.

Cripple Creek—"the $200,000 cow pasture!"

Nothing could stop the flow of men into the mountains. Despite the modern age and the camp's proximity, Cripple Creek was difficult of access. Men had to pack up the difficult mile-high grade over the Cheyenne Mountain road; up Ute Pass on the Colorado Midland train to Florissant and ride by horse or stage the eighteen miles south to camp; or leave the Rio Grande at Florence and cover the thirty miles north to Cripple Creek by Concord stages drawn by six horses. At once the Midland began extending its tracks into the district from the north. A new railroad, the Florence and Cripple Creek organized by David H. Moffat, connected with the Denver and Rio Grande at Cañon City and rushed northward. The road paid for its construction and had a surplus at the close of its first year in business.

At Cripple Creek the new town was booming. Bennett and Myers were fighting to make it the leading camp. The names of Bennett and Myers were successively given to the first streets. George Carr, their foreman at the Broken Box ranch, was Cripple Creek's first mayor. Water was selling for a nickel a bucket; any shack with a roof rented for fifteen dollars a month and was jumping higher as newcomers paid a dollar to sleep in a chair. Two hotels, the Palace and the Windsor, were going up. David H. Moffat, one of Tabor's old partners, switched his interests from

Leadville to Cripple Creek, like a fly drawn to a new molasses barrel. While building the Florence and Cripple Creek railroad, he opened the Bi-Metallic Bank of Cripple Creek as president with Bennett as vice president.

A mile away a new settlement sprang up as Cripple Creek's first rival. Here at Hayden Placer, named after the topographer who had surveyed Colorado for the United States Geological Survey, the Clarendon Hotel was built, the first stop for the stage lines. And throughout all the district new little camps were mushrooming in the deep gulches: Grassy, Elkton, Anaconda, Mound City at the junction of Cripple Creek and Squaw Creek, Goldfield, Hull's Camp, Victor, Altman and Arequa.

From them, from Colorado Springs, from the trail-ends of the world, men swarmed up the south slope of that massive snowy Peak which for almost a century had loomed into the sky, a sentinel and a beacon for a dozen restless races.

No one knew anything of mining and no one cared. "Well, how's Cripple Creek?" any Leadville old-timer would ask on arriving.

"Hell! The tenderfeet are taking out gold where it is, and the miners are looking for it where it ought to be!"

And Stratton, perched on his golden throne, began to wonder if his old baker, butcher or candlestick maker might soon be tumbling him down.

His old druggist, A. D. Jones, had come rushing up the hill shouting, "Where'll I dig boys?"

"Any old place; she's all good," they answered him.

Jones without more ado flung his hat into the air and dug where it fell, locating the Pharmacist, the second mine to ship pay ore in quantity.

The locator of the Elkton went broke and gave half interest in it to pay off a grocery bill of $36.50. The two grocers let in a school teacher named Van E. Rouse who spent his vacation prodding in the hole. He struck the vein and the mine began producing over $13,000,000.

A group of Iowa farmers had been induced to lease the abandoned Jack-Pot and sent their county sheriff, Bill Davenport, to manage the mine. After spending $13,000 of their corn money he was summoned back to Iowa. Bill begged for one more chance and on it struck the jack-pot, two and a half feet of sixty-dollar ore. He went back "wearing diamonds big as hazelnuts—one on his black necktie in a frayed black shirt, one on his finger and a gold nugget chain on his vest." The Jack-Pot paid $1,250,000 in gold.

A. G. White, a rich farmer from Missouri, sank a hole through 120 feet of surface rock with no indication of mineral into the heart of a big ore chute that yielded to the Vindicator company $750,000.

McKinney, Stratton's old friend, had leased his Mary McKinney to a New Yorker who walked up the trail in a plug hat, frock coat and spats, carrying a gold-headed cane. Twelve inches from where he quit digging, succeeding leasers, including Dr. Johnson, a medicine practitioner, struck a vein which enabled the mine to produce over $9,000,000.

Lady Luck seemed to be having a brainstorm. She ran around playing tag with her magic wand. The very grass roots seemed stuck in fabulous ore. Cy Warman, the homey poet, spread the news that "on the summit of Globe Hill in the camp of Cripple Creek they prospected with plows, mined with road-scrapers, and actually shipped the scenery." To this he added the sly observation that "there are men mean enough to doubt the statement." No man could deny the fact. On the summit of Globe Hill the surface dirt, specifically designated as that from the grass roots down six feet, was being contracted for by the wagon load.

From the hillsides erupted new mines and new discoveries. Three shifts of men were driving into Mineral Hill. A new mining company was incorporated just four hundred years after Columbus' discovery of the New World and named the Isabella. The Jolly Tar lode was developing into one of the best mines on Wilson Creek. "Professor Kimball" made gold discoveries by walking around with a willow stick; any mine discovered by him immediately jumped the price, he was so greatly venerated. Another wizard, John Barbee, located the vein of the El Paso with a forked stick. The Anaconda, shipping ore with six-mule teams, had been offered for $400. Now the owners were duly considering $2,000,000 for a controlling interest.

The first mine on Bull Hill, above Stratton's Independence, was located and named the Buena Vista. The first assay from the Rose Maud ran $2,800 to the ton. Gold had been found to assay as high as $100 a pound.

And in Poverty Gulch, Crazy Bob Womack had sold his claim, but others had staked claims like the Rosetta and the C.O.D. Frisbee's Gold King had been bought, the first mine to ship pay ore. The gulch alone was on its way to produce over $7,500,000.

Stratton might well have been dizzy. Old, white-bearded prospectors dug silently and alone up remote gulches. Verdant alfalfa miners in new red shirts squatted along the streams. Tenderfeet went around with handfuls of rock asking what gold looked like. Gamblers sat patiently drumming upon their green felts with diamond-clad fingers while awaiting the evening rush. Store- and saloon-keepers were busy stocking up and nailing new shelves. Railroad men and surveyors, engineers and bankers, swarmed along the wooden walks. Capitalists and financiers brought up to float loans stepped gingerly off the stages and lit fresh cigars with an air of importance. Among them were abysmal failures and men whose names by fame or fortune were to carry through the world and through another generation.

But among them one might have glimpsed two men whose names were almost forgotten in the wild excitement. One was the pathetic and bewildered cowboy, Crazy Bob Womack, who never made a rich discovery and who was to die practically penniless and ignored.

The other was a slim mild-mannered man who slid swiftly along the walks and vanished quietly in the gulches. He cared little to pose in front of the bank smoking a big cigar or to strut over the hillsides looking important as he shouted orders to a mining crew.

Stratton was too busy.

4

No one knew how busy; they couldn't see him. He had moved into a little frame house down in town, but was never there. Not for twenty-two years had he had his picture taken; and now besieged by photographers, he positively refused to grant the favor even to a friend of many years. He was as cagey as a prima donna.

The hordes of reporters, friends and curious townspeople next besieged the Independence. Everyone wanted a look at the famous dream mine. Particularly did geologists wish to study the formation. Stratton was stubborn as the first burro he had started out with from Little London. All visitors were barred from the mine.

Stratton had made mine superintendent the man who had ridden horseback to Pueblo, Charles Steele. He next had located his old Jeffersonville chum, Parker, in Oregon and sent for him. He had also hired Troutman and many other trustworthy friends. These and all miners working under them were forbidden to reveal what was being discovered in the workings.

Cripple Creek, Colorado Springs and Colorado had to stand open-mouthed and watch results.

Stratton was developing the mine cautiously but extensively. The original whim shaft was 73 feet deep. He erected a surface plant and sank a main shaft 404 feet deep from the collar. At each hundred feet levels were established running horizontally from 300 to 900 feet, and from these, cross-cuts radiated in all directions. Then he put down to the north another shaft to 550 feet with similar levels, cross-cuts and drifts.

With such a plant he could have hoisted enough ore to beat the record of the Robert E. Lee in Leadville. But Stratton was not interested in records or running races for production with all the other bonanzas in the district. The capacity of the plant was six hundred tons a day; he never allowed it to be reached. For a prospector who had tramped the mountains seventeen years for a likely piece of float, Stratton exhibited a peculiar restraint. As usual he was a confounding paradox. He instituted the queer policy of reserving ore. Of all the vast bodies of ore that he opened up each day, not a pound was taken out. Foot by foot as the shafts were driven downward, the rich layers of gold were left intact until needed. Then, a veritable Midas squatting on a treasure chest, he dipped in for what he needed.

He still wore the same Stetson hat, long grayed from a creamy white; but he dipped in often enough to buy every claim and mine around him that looked promising: the Lowell for $50,000 cash, the Lost Annie for $35,000, the John A. Logan for $25,000, with others making a total of $169,000. His property now began to look like a town, Independence, with over thirty miners' shanties. At the railroad junction where he loaded his ore, a new camp sprang up which he named Winfield.

And now happened something that proved Lady Luck had not only smiled but had shamelessly taken up residence with him.

To cook for his first small group of men, Stratton had hired an Irishman called Johnny Harnan. Johnny had previously grubbed in the Pennsylvania coal mines, thus having some experience in mining. He saved a frugal stake of three hundred dollars, opened his last can of beans for Stratton's miners, and set up the slope behind the Independence to see what he could find.

It was a long tough slope. When he reached the top of Battle Mountain he ran into a pair of Irishmen disconsolately staring into a miserable little prospect hole called the Portland.

Jimmie Doyle, a carpenter from Portland, Maine, had staked it out on January 22, 1892, the only piece of unclaimed land he could find. It was little wonder that it was overlooked by everyone else. On top of the mountain, squeezed between the Doubtful and the Anna Lee, both full-size lode claims of ten acres, the little piece of land was only one-sixth of an acre. Doyle had to measure it out with a clothesline.

Failing to find anything and needing help, Doyle struck up a partnership with James Burns. They were a well matched pair. Burns was another Jimmie, an Irishman, and also hailed from Portland, Maine. A plumber by trade, he had run away to sea as a boy. Coming home again he learned the machinist's trade and traveled through South and Central America working for the Colwell Iron Works. Abruptly he quit his job and took a fling in the gold and silver mines in Peru, made some money and lost it in Cuba. Dead broke, he landed in New Orleans and won $20,000 in a lottery.

With this he opened an office in Mobile, Alabama, as a cotton broker, went short on cotton, and took to the road again selling sugar machinery. After five years he drifted into Colorado and worked at his trade of plumber and steam-fitter until the Cripple Creek boom.

Rushing up into the district, he located the Tidal Wave, Devil's Own, Mary Alice, the Bobtails and Professor Grubbs. None of them were worth a song. But he and Jimmie Doyle traded each other a half interest in the Portland and Professor Grubbs.

The Little Portland claim looked best; it had the finest scenery.

But, as they remarked to Johnny Harnan when he ambled up the slope from the Independence, they had found only traces of gold. "Sometimes traces and a half," said Doyle, "and if we can't get two of them damn traces we might as well get off of this here hill."

"You boys just ain't diggin' in the right spot," said Harnan. "How much will you give me if I hit it?"

"A third interest," they snapped.

So Johnnie dug in with the two Jimmies. The hole was twenty feet deep, sunk alongside the vein. Johnnie put in a cross-cut at six feet and ran square into gold assaying thirty-two ounces to the ton, worth $640.

The three Irishmen stifled their shouts; they knew they were in for a divil of a fight. The big mines surrounding their little triangular claim would certainly jump it should the news leak out, for according to law they were allowed to follow any vein discovered on their property down along all its dips and angles. It would be easy enough for them to claim that the apex of the vein was on their property and that they were merely following it into the insignificant Portland claim.

So the "Three Jims" as they were popularly known, got

busy preparing for the lawsuits that were sure to come. Over the shaft they erected a little shanty, and worked with utmost secrecy. At night they filled ore sacks with high-grade, packing them on their backs down the mountain side to hide in their cabin on Wilson Creek. The stuff was so heavy that when Burns fell in the darkness, he had to lie kicking until a partner came along to release him. For a year they maintained their secret, smuggling small shipments out to the smelters for bacon and bean money.

One dark night they drove a four-horse wagon up the hill, loading it with several tons. On the way down the axle broke. It was too late to get another wagon. At daylight neighboring prospectors, astounded to see wagon-tracks up the hill, followed the tracks to the wagon load of sacked ore. The secret was out.

The three Jimmies rushed to apply for a patent for a full lode claim 1,500 feet along the vein and 150 feet on each side of it, on the grounds that they were the first to discover ore on the top of the mountain.

The surrounding mines immediately took their cases to court. Adverses and injunctions were filed against the Portland. But with carloads of ore worth as much as $50,000 apiece and as high as $100 a pound, the Irishmen had accumulated already $90,000 to fight the cases. For a time things looked doubtful. They were restrained from taking out ore from a space hardly bigger than a hall bedroom. And when they counted up, there were twenty-seven different law-suits.

At this point Stratton stepped in. It was a safe bet he was overlooking nothing, particularly up the slope. Too, he remembered his own claim-jumping on the White House, between the Independence and the Portland. He gave the three Irishmen $75,000 cash to defend their rights in exchange for stock.

With $71,000 cash and some stock, the four men bought up the conflicting claims, Scranton, Hidden Treasure, Vanadium and Baby Ruth. Then they bought the principal producer and most dangerous rival, the Anna Lee. And then they forced the Battle Mountain Company to sell all the rights and titles to their properties on the mountain: the White House, Captain, Queen of the Hills, and National Belle, paying $50,000 cash toward a full settlement of $265,000.

The purchase settled all twenty-seven suits. The Portland Company was free from litigation and with Stratton's help soon to be free of debt. The little fractional claim of one-sixth of an acre had grown to 240 acres embracing almost 37 claims and was on its way to produce over $62,000,000.

Doyle, the discoverer, made less out of it than the others, in accordance with tradition. Harnan was a director of the company for many years and then moved to Nevada. There he went broke. Penniless, at the age of seventy-four, he wrote the new owners of the Portland asking for a job on the great mine whose vein he had first opened. They wrote back promising him a job "if one became available." Burns, a joyful multi-millionaire, became a little Tabor, rushing about in pointed patent-leathers and building a Burns theater for Little London. But Stratton! He was not their fairy god-father for nothing.

He incorporated the Portland Gold Mining Company, was its most important director, its first president and largest share-holder, owning one-third of its entire issued stock. A short time later he originated the plan whereby the Portland Consolidated was put through, consolidating with it a number of other mines. This scheme added $4,000,000 to the market rating of the Portland, and was considered the best piece of mining financiering ever consummated in Colorado. The golden acres of the Portland were called, and became, a veritable "Gold Factory," the second greatest producer in the district.

And Stratton, quiet, busy Stratton, had made out of it another fabulous fortune. The Independence was known as "King of the District," the Portland as "Queen of the District," and Stratton was more surely seated than ever on his golden throne.

To be sure there were rumbles. Cripple Creek with its discovery of gold coming on the very heels of the silver collapse, was the one bright yellow hope of Colorado, and indeed the whole country. But the trouble had gone too far the panic of '93 spread consternation and misery, and even Cripple Creek came in for its share the following year.

From everywhere discouraged men flocked into the camps to recoup their fortunes. Surprised at not stumbling into a bonanza immediately, they were forced to take jobs. Two dollars and a half for nine hours' labor with a pick, they soon found out, was not the royal road to fortune. They began to slip pieces of high-grade ore into their empty dinner buckets on the way out of the mine. Dishonest assayers would pick up the pieces of "picture rock" at a saloon or in the miner's shanty, crush and reduce it, and pay the man half. As such rich ore abounded in quantities—$40 a pound from the C.K.N. mine, and thirty-seven pounds from the Pike's Peak lode valued at $11,840—these "dinner-bucket shipments" increased steadily. Assayers provided miners with canvas-pocketed belts to wear under their clothing. A Cripple Creek judge on one case decided ore-stealing was not larceny, ruling that "you cannot steal real estate."

Mine-owners tried several ways to stop the practice. One day the superintendent of the Mary McKinney called all the boys coming off shift to his office to have a birthday cigar on him. As the last man filed in to congratulate him, he locked the door and drew a brace of revolvers. Every miner was forced to empty his dinner-bucket on the floor, and each one who had concealed ore was fired. Eventually mine owners resorted to the use of the "change room." Each miner on going off duty took off his digging clothes and passed naked through the "change room" to another room containing his street clothes. In this way no man could wear a belt full of high-grade or secrete lumps of rich ore under his arm pits.

The miners were furious at the shameless imposition, regarding Stratton and the other mine-owners as tyrants who begrudged them living wages while paying huge dividends. They were ripe for soapbox denunciations, and when Coxey's Army marched to Washington three hundred men from Cripple Creek commandeered a locomotive and a box car and sped to join it. The rails were blown up to stop them.

Early in '94 strikes broke out. Several miners' unions were consolidated by the Western Federation of Miners which declared the wage scale to be three dollars a day for eight hours' work. The owners of the Pharmacist, Isabella, Victor and Anaconda declared that any miner who wanted three dollars a day from them would have to work ten hours and eat on his own time.

Stratton after some deliberation straddled the fence: he paid $3.25 for nine hours' work, and with a force of armed deputies surrounding the Independence waited to see what would happen.

The other mine-owners offered $2.50 a day for eight hours' work, and imported scabs. Six deputy sheriffs on their way to protect the scabs at the Victor were set upon and clubbed. The County Sheriff called for state troops which were sent and then recalled when the Governor, "Bloody Bridles" Waite, was informed there was no disorder.

Stratton, watching behind his armed deputies, now saw

about ten o'clock on May 10th a large army of strikers coming over the brow of the hill. The main body stopped at the Strong Mine adjacent to the Independence, while a few approached Stratton's guards. The guards were advised to scatter while there was still time, and they did so. Stratton, unprotected, sat watching.

The nearby Strong Mine, finding it impossible to operate with scabs, had imported a small army of deputy sheriffs, all ex-policemen from Denver. Hearing of this the mob had assembled in front of the mine and now ordered the foreman Sam McDonald and two assistants to come out. They refused and retreated down the shaft. The strikers deliberately broke down the doors of the shaft house and with dynamite blew up the mine.

They then set out to attack the deputies, who had withdrawn to the Arkansas Valley waiting for a thousand rifles and a cannon. Stratton's luck had held. Alone and unprotected in the Independence, he knew that but for chance it might have been himself and the Independence that were blown up.

Approaching Florence, near the station of Wilbur on the new Florence and Cripple Creek railroad, the miners and deputies met in the "Battle of Wilbur." The strike leader and one deputy were killed, six strikers were wounded and six taken prisoner. A day later the strikers found that the three men were alive in the Strong Mine. They were taken out and exchanged for the six miners captured by the deputies, but one of the imprisoned men had gone insane.

The strike had now grown into a war. Clinton Brainard the young lawyer who had drawn up the incorporation papers for Cripple Creek, was found making speeches to the miners and was badly beaten up. A proclamation appealing to the citizens showed the intense feeling:

If you have the blood of 1776 in your veins, in the name of your God, in the name of your country, in the name of your homes, your wives and your children, stand by law and order that this government of the people, by the people and for the people, may not perish from the earth!

All concerned were evidently taking themselves seriously. Governor "Bloody Bridles" Waite rushed up to the camp and began dickering for the strikers with W. H. Moffatt and Hagerman representing the mine-owners. Meanwhile five hundred of the State Militia followed him and began marching up Tenderfoot Hill. The Sheriff with a thousand men began to get suspicious. He was afraid the Governor was siding with the strikers. Now began a race up the hill between authorities while the striking miners, the cause of the trouble, chanted:

The sheriff of El Paso had one thousand men,
He marched them up a hill and he marched them
down again!

For the militia won, crossing over Bull Hill to encamp near the Independence Mine. Stratton was always on the best end of any bargain.

Down in Little London the citizens were in an uproar. Cripple Creek had not only shamed the town by sprouting a gold camp within a crow's flight, but was further disgracing the State by strikes. They had heard, too, of the mysterious man of the war, "General Johnson," who was directing the strikers. He was a West Point graduate, a romantic soldier, and later made a good record in the Spanish-American War. And then one night Governor Waite's Adjutant General Tarnsey stopped over in the Alamo Hotel on his way to Cripple Creek. Near midnight he was called to the lobby downstairs to answer a telephone call. There he was grabbed by a crowd of masked men. In vain the spruce little braggart, "both a blatherskite and a demagogue," got down on his knees, moaning and begging for his life. The crowd took him out to the bluffs north of town and applied to him a beautiful coat of tar and feathers. So attired, he stumbled next day into Palmer Lake and was driven back to Denver. During the investigation Tarnsey insulted the judge of the District Court and was fined for contempt.

Little London!

Up in Cripple Creek the deputies, twelve hundred strong entered town, arrested citizens, kicked and clubbed everyone handy until the National Guard finally restored peace. Then on June 9th, strikers and mine-owners agreed on a wage scale of three dollars for eight hours with twenty minutes for lunch, the mine-owner being permitted to hire without discrimination either union or non-union miners. The "war" had cost the State $75,000 and the County $60,000.

Stratton heaved a sigh of relief. Through all the trouble both himself and his Independence had emerged unscathed. He rode down to town on the train carrying a group of soldiers and officials. In the seat with him was a young newspaper reporter named Frank Huston who, nearing the Woodland Park station, turned to Stratton with a low-voiced question, apparently about the recently settled strike.

Stratton's answer was a yell of rage. He jumped to his feet and grabbing a rifle from the rack overhead, swung it toward the young reporter. A physician in the seat behind grabbed and held him until he was disarmed and politely led to another seat.

This was the multi-millionaire Croesus of Cripple Creek who from his first earnings had hunted up all the stockholders of the defunct Washington mining company and repaid them all their losses, saying that he wished no one connected with any of his mines ever to suffer a loss.

Paradoxical Stratton!

5

Thus, "with the future of the camp accepted as certain, the sun of '94 set and that of '95 rose amid clouds of golden promise."

Despite the strike, the production of the "$200,000 Cow Pasture" had already jumped to over $3,000,000 a year and was beginning to exceed the half-million mark each month with the unheard-of average of over three ounces of gold in every ton of rock shipped. And one-third of all the gold thus produced was coming from Stratton's Independence and the Portland.

The stage was set for Stratton to make his triumphal entry into Little London. Not to stop this time to wash his overalls in the creek, nor to trot down Ute Pass astraddle a shaggy jackass, but to stride in regally, as befitted the "Midas of the Rockies" and the "Croesus of Cripple Creek."

Instead, he swung off the train before it stopped and fled in a closed carriage to his home, where he locked the door to callers. The townspeople, a bit perplexed, waited until he should establish himself in a mansion and invite them to a splendor yet unheard of. The precedent had already been set, and not alone by Tabor with his estate on Capitol Hill flaunting a hundred peacocks on its acres of smooth lawns.

J. Maurice Finn, the obscure Cripple Creek lawyer, had struck it rich in the Mountain Beauty, Caledonia and Royal Oak. From his $300 cabin he moved into the gorgeous

"Finn's Folly" on Crystal Hill, and bought a $50,000 residence in Denver on Capitol Hill.

In Little London, W. S. Montgomery, who located the Hull City placer had built himself a fine residence costing $75,000. So, of course, had Jimmie Burns of the Portland, and the three Woods who owned the great Gold Coin underneath the town of Victor.

To one short street in the north end of town most of these erstwhile plumbers, druggists and livery-stable-owners made a beeline after making their fortunes. Wood avenue was justly known as Millionaire Row; not a house along the street but boasted an owner worth a million from Cripple Creek gold. And they were all wriggling minnows compared to the goldfish king of them all. Where would Stratton move? A carpenter himself, he would certainly show up the neighbors who had shunned him by building a mansion equal at least to General Palmer's Tudor Castle, Glen Eyrie.

And Stratton did buy a house that made them all gasp. An old-fashioned, two-story frame house just a block off Pike's Peak Avenue, the main business street downtown. He had worked on it as a carpenter years ago, building it for Beverly Tucker's father, a doctor in town. Stratton knew it was built securely. Old Tucker had specified a twelve-inch baseboard. When it had been planed down and set in place it measured only eleven and a half inches. Stratton hit the roof with a burst of temper. He made the workmen tear it out and put in a new one to meet the specified size, which necessitated cutting down a fourteen-inch plank. The old house was an everlasting delight to Stratton; he had built it with his own hands. It was set back in a nice lawn, too. The only workman he ever fired permanently was a gardener who neglected to trim its edges after mowing. Settled in his new home with his widowed sister, Mrs. Jennie Cobb, as housekeeper, Stratton began to make 115 North Weber Street a famous and suspected address.

Quietly and unobtrusively he bought a few blocks away on Pike's Peak Avenue the old location of his first carpenter shop sold to Joseph Dozier, and established his office. The first piece of furniture moved in was an elaborate case to contain ore specimens from his mines, which had been carved for him by an old wood-carver in town named Fred Ege. To this office as his personal secretary he brought Thomas A. Ramsay, his bookkeeper at the Independence.

Surely, now, settled in a house and with an office force established to look after his affairs, Stratton was going to make a splurge. After seventeen years of tramping the hills he must be tired of Colorado. He was expected to make a tour of the world. It was anticipated he might move to New York, build his palace on Fifth Avenue, and break into a society more exclusive than even Little London's. Fitz Mack, a prominent newspaper writer living across the street, expressed the consensus in the *Denver Post* when he stated that Stratton was "a fool because he didn't come out and buy a fine yacht and set up a stable and have a good time and see life."

For the latter, at least, Stratton had an excellent opportunity. The new Cripple Creek millionaires on Wood Avenue had got together and made plans for a racetrack at Roswell, north of town. For this "sport of kings" what could be more proper than to select as president the "King of Cripple Creek"? So Stratton received his first bow of homage and was duly made president of the Racing Association. He did not buy a stable or even look at a horse, nor did the honor induce him to buy a fancy team and rig. He continued to pay an old cab-driver three hundred dollars a month to sleep in his carriage in front of his office in case Stratton might want to go some place. But Stratton, as president of the Racing Association, awarded the contract for building the track, grandstand and clubhouse to his old employer, James D. Raymond, who had returned to Colorado Springs.

Day by day he continued his irritating, unspectacular existence—a mild, slim man invariably dressed in a white shirt and collar, a sack coat of a cut that was never changed, and a light-colored Denver-shaped hat of Stetson or Columbia make. He allowed himself one luxury, probably remembering General Palmer's shiny riding boots. He began wearing fine handmade boots. These were made for him by an old shoe-cobbler in town named Bob Schwarz. For hours Stratton would sit watching the old Swiss German pounding away on his bench.

Then one day Stratton swung into the little shop and announced abruptly, "Bob, I've got a new job for you!"

Schwarz laid down his awl and smoothed his greasy leathern apron. "Vel, vat iss it?"

"I'm going to make you general manager of all my mining properties."

"Vat do I know about dose tings?"

"You don't have to know anything," replied Stratton mildly. "I'll tell you what to do. But you've got to keep on making my boots. That's part of the job."

Thereafter the shoemaker was the carpenter's general manager and his closest friend. He had a fine office, a princely salary, and little to do besides making Stratton's boots. It is certain he never licked them. On one occasion they were riding together in a carriage to Manitou. A quarrel started which they kept up for almost five miles. Thoroughly exasperated, Stratton exclaimed, "I'll be damned if I'll ride with you another step!"

"Vell, git out den!" answered Schwarz.

Stratton flung out of his carriage and walked the five miles back to town in a rage while the old Swiss German rode on.

The next morning Stratton went to Bob's room in the hotel. "Bob, I made a fool of myself yesterday. Didn't I?"

"Yess. You did!"

"Well, come on. Let's go to Broadmoor."

Stratton's favorite sister, Anna Chamberlin, had died the preceding summer. His other widowed sister, Mrs. Jennie Cobb, who acted as his housekeeper, was away much of the time. Stratton needed someone else. It was a problem. The few girls he had hired were a nuisance, and they in turn had spread the news that the new millionaire was too eccentric and cranky to put up with. Then he happened to meet Bob Schwarz' best girl. Sophronia was an English girl working as a domestic servant for one of the new Cripple Creek smelting millionaires who had just moved into a handsome home in Little London. Secretly she had confided that she "would rather be a hash-slinger than to work for these rich mining dubs." But under Bob's insistence she moved into 115 North Weber as Stratton's housekeeper. Bob Schwarz had now two reasons for calling. He was the only person in town who continued to be admitted as Stratton's guest.

On sunny afternoons Stratton was usually to be found sitting on the horse-trough in front of the First National Bank, hat off, the wind stirring his thin smooth silver hair. He seldom looked up from his shiny new boots, but one day he suddenly jumped up and waved. Patton, the proprietor of a cigar-store, lazily waved back. Stratton paid him no attention; he was hurriedly crossing the street to intercept a man slouching past Patton's door. Stratton caught up with him, slapped him on the back and led him into the shop. There he borrowed a pencil from Patton and wrote out a check for $5,000 for his companion. The man was Bob Womack who had discovered Cripple Creek. Stratton walked back to his seat on the horse-trough and resumed the moody contemplation of his boots. But he always happened to be too busy to attend the many social functions to which he was invited.

With such goings-on, the élite Little Londoners gave him up in disgust. It was quite evident he preferred the society of shoemakers, servant girls, bookkeepers and a few old friends who were laborers and boarding-house keepers.

Today, forty years later, the antipathy still persists. General Palmer's old butler, now a waiter in one of the prominent hotels, when idly questioned if he knew Stratton, will proudly raise his head and haughtily state, "Of course; everyone knew of him. But he was never presented to me. And never, no not once, was he received at Glen Eyrie!"

Stratton's entry into town and his subsequent reception had been a fiasco. Evidently there was a point of difference between him and his neighboring Cripple Creek millionaires that needed proper illumination.

But how the devil, they wondered, was he going to spend his money?

6

He had already started to spend it, and with a gesture that soon grew habitual: right hand outstretched with money, left hand raised with a finger to his lips.

After repaying the defunct Washington's stockholders their losses, he hunted up Sam Altman and repaid him the exact amount of $950 which he had expended to develop the mine. During the end of the panic he went to the Salvation Army, then considered a disreputable organization, and instructed them to issue tickets for meals and rooms to all the homeless, hungry men straggling down Ute Pass from Cripple Creek. Each month the bills were submitted to him, aggregating almost $85,000. Each Christmas he gave a standing order for coal to be delivered to every poor family in Victor. To Father Volpe, the first Catholic priest to arrive in Cripple Creek, he gave money to erect a church. He then contributed toward the erection of Presbyterian, Baptist and Methodist churches throughout the district to combat the many dens of vice springing up along Myers Avenue. All these contributions were made with the admonition to keep them secret.

But with the clergy of Little London, Stratton was always ready to quarrel. Frequently he declaimed against the expensive and elaborate churches as being out of keeping with the humble teachings of Christianity. The sight of a tall church steeple or an expensive stained glass window was enough to throw him in a fine frenzy. Since Little London was inordinately proud of its name as the City of Churches (most of which, with the city officials, were opposed to the Salvation Army), Stratton's gifts to it and to the Cripple Creek churches added greatly to his social ostracism. To the day he died, Stratton, the boy student and lover of the Bible, was never a member of any church.

He now began giving each year $100 to the Institution for the Mute and Blind to be used for prizes to the best pupils, leaving when he died a bequest of $25,000 to carry on the work. In addition to these yearly sums he contributed $400 to establish a physics laboratory in the institution.

For almost any old destitute miner or laborer whom he ran across, Stratton bought a team of horses, a carriage and a ton of hay, starting them on careers as tourist guides driving visitors around Little London and through the Garden of the Gods. The bicycle craze had struck town, and Stratton walking down the street behind five little girls overheard one of them exclaim, "Oh, I wish Daddy could buy me one of them, all painted red!" Stratton took them inside the shop and bought five red bicycles. The purchase gave him an idea. He ordered a new bicycle delivered to every laundry girl in town so that she would not have to walk to work.

As news of his eccentric generosity began to spread, he was besieged by hundreds begging gifts or asking loans for "old time's sake." And remembering his old Jeffersonville chum, Stratton sent for Byron Logan to spend several weeks in Colorado at his expense. Parker, the third one of the boys who had dreamed of finding gold on Pike's Peak, showed the blacksmith through the Independence, and Stratton presented him with a gold watch the case of which had been made of gold taken from the mine. When the visit was over, Stratton sent him back to Indiana in a sleeper, two one-hundred-dollar bills in his pants pocket and a new bicycle in the baggage car.

One afternoon Stratton heard of a charity tea being given by a Mrs. Whipple, wife of the contractor who had built the first residence on General Palmer's Glen Eyrie estate. He drove over and was announced, a buzz of excitement following his name. Mrs. Whipple rose, quite flustered, and put out her hand to greet the distinguished caller. Stratton calmly put a one-hundred-dollar bill in it and turned away.

"Wait!" she cried. "I'll give you a memorandum. I'll . . ."

"What for?" demanded Stratton. "I don't want any memorandums. You just find the poor people. I'll supply the money."

With all these handouts, Stratton was just getting in trim for a real spender according to his own ideas.

Out of respect to Professor Lamb for whom he had named one of his mines, Stratton gave Colorado College $20,000. Then he offered $25,000 to the State School of Mines. This gift, making possible the completion of the "Hall of Metallurgy," was accepted by the Thirteenth General Assembly of the State which in House Joint Resolution No. 10 affirmed: "The Honorable Winfield Scott Stratton has been the first of Colorado's wealthy mining men to recognize the importance of the School to the chief industry of Colorado."

But Stratton was not to forget the other great mining king even if the State had.

One day Ramsay led into his office an old, broken man with a pathetic, whipped look in his eyes. Stratton stared. He could hardly believe it was the same man he had last seen up in Leadville chuckling at the huge metal Silver Dollar his carpenter Stratton had just fixed into place above the bank. Then he jumped up to grab the man's hand and show him to a chair. "Senator Tabor! Sir, I am honored."

Tabor was on his last financial legs. His great fortunes had collapsed. Reduced to poverty and actually hungry, he was making his last stand against a fate that was soon to overwhelm him and all his family. There was just one chance left. His friends had deserted him, but remembering the many men he had grubstaked and passed out rolls of bills to in his own days of affluence, he had come to Stratton, the multi-millionaire who had taken his place.

The chance, he explained nervously with trembling hands, was this: he still had left of all his fantastic purchases throughout the country, in Mexico and the Honduras an old, undeveloped mine near Ward, Colorado. The silver boom days were over, but he believed there might be gold in this mine. If he could only develop it, perhaps the Colorado mountains would bring his luck back. And if they did—why maybe there might be enough money to open up his deserted Matchless Mine at Leadville again.

"You know, Mr. Stratton, there's silver still in the Matchless. As I always say to Mrs. Tabor, 'Hang on to the Matchless'!"

Stratton winced and turned away his gaze. He knew that the boom silver days were likely gone forever.

"Now, Senator. Don't say another word. You know I deeply appreciate this honor."

He drew out a check book and rapidly scribbled a check for $15,000.

"Will this be enough to get started on?" he asked, sliding it across the table.

A slow flush crept into Haw Tabor's drawn face as he stared at the amount.

"No. No . . . no," he stuttered. "We've got to make it legal. It's just a loan. I'll repay you very soon. But the security . . . ," he hesitated. "I've got a mine left in Maricopa County, Arizona. Will that do?" He brought out a tattered deed from his pocket.

Stratton sighed and rang for his secretary, Ramsay. A note was made out, reading: "Ninety days after date we promise to pay to the order of W. S. Stratton $15,000 with interest at 1 per cent per month from date until paid." This Tabor proudly signed, "The Tabor Mines and Mill Company, by H. A. W. Tabor, President."

When Tabor had gone, Stratton carelessly chucked the deed and papers into his desk drawer. The affair seemed to have left him tired out. He gave orders that he was not to be disturbed; and propping his immaculate boots upon the table, he sat staring out the window and gently pulling his white, freshly combed mustaches. Tabor's, he had noticed, were still uncombed and ragged.

Each day a horde of people came to his office, were sorted and interviewed by Ramsay, and sent in to see him. Whoever they were, whatever their excuses, they all wound up by asking for money. And then one day Ramsay entered his office and closed the door. There was another visitor waiting outside.

"Who is it?" asked Stratton wearily. "And how much does he want?"

Ramsay coughed. He stood on one leg and then another.

"Come man! Who is he?"

Ramsay slid a piece of paper across the table. Stratton reached out his hand for the paper and read the name written there. Then he jumped to his feet and stood trembling, his face grown suddenly white.

"Get him out! I never want to lay eyes on him!"

Then he slipped across the room, cautiously parted the curtains and stared at his visitor waiting in the reception room outside. He was a young man about eighteen years old, tall, slim and lightly built as himself, but with large black eyes. Stratton stared as if mesmerized. It was his first glimpse of his son, Isaac Henry Stratton.

He let the curtains fall. For moments he paced up and down the room muttering, "Damnation! How did he ever hear about me? What's he here for? What's he want?"

There was only one way to have his many questions answered. Ramsay was sent to let the boy in. Then Stratton locked the door from the inside.

Father and son remained together for almost fifteen minutes. When the boy had left, Stratton sent for his lawyer. The boy, he said, was being sent back to Illinois where he had come from; he was to be enrolled at the University of Illinois at Champaign to get an education, and he was to be paid one hundred dollars a month on the condition that he kept out of Stratton's sight. He was not to return to Colorado for any purpose whatever.

"Is that clear?" asked Stratton.

Ramsay and his lawyer nodded.

"Well that's all."

Stratton went home and to bed.

He was ill for some time. These last two visitors had upset him completely. He was beginning to discover that fame and riches may often prove as troublesome a burden as poverty.

Now, for the first and only time in his life, he took a pleasure trip. He went to California in a private car. Within less than a month he was back in Cripple Creek again. The Independence with its responsibilities was something he could not escape.

7

Production in the district had reached and then exceeded the average of half a million dollars monthly. Now, with shipment after shipment of rich tellurium ore, it was being doubled. A million dollars a month from a pasture of scarcely six square miles!

Nothing like it had ever been known: an area so small and so confoundingly rich. Geologists from all over the world arrived daily to hazard theories and conjectures. The Cripple Creek Gold Belt, as it was first known, had comprised an area eleven miles square. Gradually the hundreds of men prospecting the remote hills and gulches drew in to a section roughly eight by seven miles in extent, lying between Rhyolite Mountain and the Nipple. Here the mass of granite was penetrated with dikes of phonolite and contained near its center an upthrust mass of volcanic breccia mainly andesite. Then it became evident that the gold deposits lay in this small center area of some six square miles where the main eruption of the ancient volcano had taken place.

It was as if a column of gold ore rose upright through the solid granite to the very grass roots. On top of this pillar, just four miles southwest from the summit of Pike's Peak, perched the Cripple Creek district proper.

Here, eleven thousand feet high, swarmed men digging into hills and gulches that had taken on names consistent with the original Womack cow pasture: Big Bull, Cow, Calf and Bull Mountains, Bull Cliffs and Grassy Gulch. Others had sprouted newer names, as fresh discoveries were made: Battle Mountain, Gold and Globe Hill, Crystal, Mineral, Galena, Carbonate, Iron Clad, and Tenderfoot Hills, Squaw Mountain and Raven Hill.

The population had grown to over thirty thousand. Cripple Creek had become a riotous town of twelve thousand. Victor, in a year and a half had grown from a lone cabin to a town of three thousand. Altman was the highest incorporated town in the world. Gillett, Anaconda and Goldfield were also incorporated. And with these grew the camps of Independence, Elkton, Mound City, Arequa and Lawrence.

Already 1,250 incorporated mining companies were organized, although half of them had not yet made any serious attempt to develop mines. Mills and ore samplers, gallows frames, glory holes and reduction works dotted hills and gulches between the countless mines and prospectors' holes until the district seemed a solid single camp.

To it swarmed gamblers, saloon men, adventurers and miners, celebrities and New York stage artists. Like George Pullman who originated the idea of sleeping-cars from observing the arrangement of bunks in Colorado miners' shanties, many were to gain fame. Jack Dempsey mucked in one of the mines. Lanky Bob Fitzsimmons, Gentleman Jim Corbett and Jim Jeffries arrived to become models for Fireman Jim Flynn from Pueblo, Battling Nelson and Mexican Pete.

Soapy Smith and Parson Bowers, light-fingered and smooth-tongued, arrived to bunco strangers with gold bricks.

Two Presidents, and William Jennings Bryan who hoped to become one, visited the camp.

Everyone was a spender, and there was much to spend it on. Johnny Nolan obliged with poker, roulette, craps and a faro bank, and the young ladies along Myers Avenue were even more hospitable. "The Petrified Man from Creede" was put on display. At Gillette was staged the only bullfight to be held in the United States, and a coursing meet was established with jackrabbits and greyhounds. Little Londoners played cricket in the shadow of Mount Pisgah, the site of the cemetery where graves were blasted out of solid granite.

Such was the rip-roaring domain to which the mild little carpenter from Indiana returned as king in '96. It was certain he was to need at least a rabbit's foot if he were to keep his throne. A new discovery had just been made which seemed likely to rival the Independence and the Portland.

At the foot of Battle Mountain below the Independence had been a small cattle ranch that grew into the camp of Lawrence as miners flocked into the region. Most of the buildings were log cabins. With the discovery of the Independence and the Portland, the heaviest production of the district swung east from Cripple Creek. The loyal miners began to boost Lawrence as the new boom town.

Then McKinney, owner of the Mary McKinney mine, stepped in. Organizing the Mount Rosa Mining, Milling and Land Company, he sought to get the right to a new

Cripple Creek, with Mt. Pasgah in the background (Courtesy The Denver Public Library Western Collection. Photo by C. L. McClure.

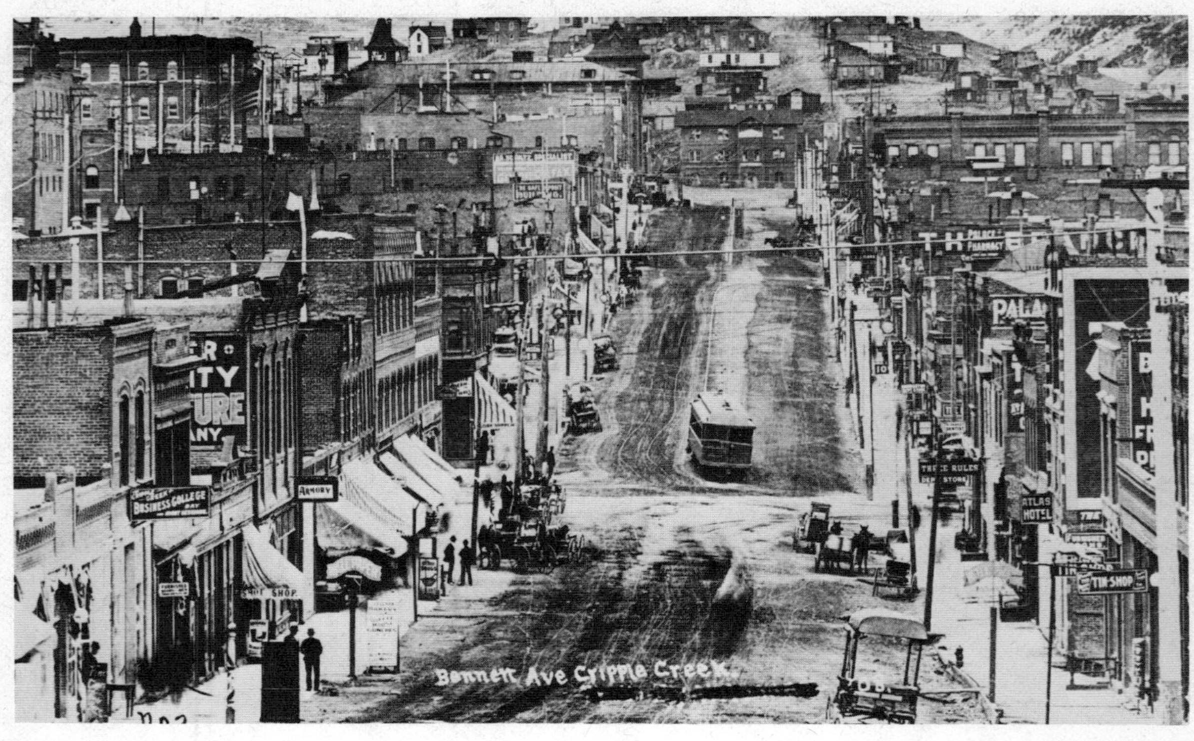

Bennett Avenue in Cripple Creek at the height of the boom days.

townsite, just up the slope from Lawrence, under a placer patent. This was contested on the grounds that the company could not hold the land by a placer claim because the claim did not contain free gold for placering. The company went ahead; to hold the claim the Placer House was erected by Hiram Williams, the Mount Rosa Company receiving title to the location by means of a number of lode claims since they had been unable to obtain the right by a placer claim.

Control of the company was obtained by a new organization known as the Woods Investment Company, which had entered the district. Other buildings were added to the Placer House. Pines on the hillside were cut down for building, and aspens along Wilson Creek for firewood. J. B. Cunningham, later mayor of the new town, was given free lots in return for establishing a sawmill. Streets were plotted and lots placed on sale for twenty-five dollars apiece. If a man did not have the cash he was merely asked to sign a paper as a future citizen of the town. By means of these signatures the three Woods secured the right to a post-office. The new town, firmly established, mushroomed into being as Cripple Creek's only serious rival, becoming the center of the richest producers in the district. The wife of Harry Woods appropriately named it Victor.

The three Woods were shrewd men. Warren Woods, the president, had been engaged in mining throughout Colorado since the Leadville rush. Frank Woods, secretary and treasurer, had been up to Robinson and other silver camps of the Rockies. Harry Woods, the manager, had led the rush from Leadville to the camp of Kokomo in '79 afterward joining his brother in the Robinson Consolidated Mining Company. The company paid large dividends and had never had a failure.

Near Victor they began to acquire sixty different properties including the Panther, Big Theater, May B, Blue Stocking. To their controlling interest in the San Fernando copper mines of Old Mexico they now added the control of some of the best stock companies in the Cripple Creek district: the Victor Mines and Land Company with $45,000 dividends paid out already, the Battle Mountain Consolidated and the Columbine Gold Mining Company.

They opened a brokerage office in Denver, then moved it to Colorado Springs to become the first and largest dealing in Cripple Creek mining stocks. For them Little London named her Millionaire Row, Wood Avenue.

With all their many holdings, the three Woods concentrated on making Victor into the real "City of Mines." A Hotel Victor was their first step forward. Elaborate plans were drawn, contracts let, and excavation started on the choicest location in the center of town.

And now happened one of those unbelievable tall tales that had spread the fame of Cripple Creek. A wandering assayer stood watching the excavation being made for the foundation of the new hotel. He got down and scooped up a few samples of loose dirt. They assayed rich in gold. The blueprints for the hotel were jubilantly torn up and a mine sunk on the spot.

Instead of a hotel a large brick and stone shaft house was erected, the gallows frame being 65 feet high on a stone base 24 feet square. In its first year, 1896, the mine produced $91,750. Four years later it exceeded a million and a quarter, paying $210,000 in dividends, and yielded within five years $5,500,000. Ore averaging $46 to the ton from a vein eight feet wide, and dipping under the town itself.

Victor was no longer a town. It was merely a city with a population of 6,000 occupying the surface of two miles of underground workings and a 3,700-foot tunnel driven under Squaw Mountain to connect the Economic Mill with the first level of the third great mine within a stone's throw of Victor—the new Gold Coin.

Everyone wondered why Stratton seemed little worried about his rival. They did not know what the quiet little ex-carpenter was doing as he strolled casually through the district in his always new boots.

He was too busy building up his own empire to take much note of others. He bought lots in Victor, Cripple Creek, old Fremont and Anaconda. He was a large stockholder in the First National Banks of both Cripple Creek and Colorado Springs. He had large interests in the Omaha and Grant Smelting and Reduction Company, at Denver, and in the two Ore Sampling Companies at Victor and Cripple Creek. At all of these plants he had stored large amounts of ore which he had not yet allowed to be reduced.

On top of Bull Hill, looking down on Altman, he developed two new, rich strikes, the American Eagle No. 1 and No. 2 whose portals were the highest in the district. And all the time he was buying mines and claims: Little Harry (significantly named!), Brooklyn, Lottie, Madison, Lowell, Corrigan, Chief, Smuggler, Pianoforte, The Four Per Cent, Four Queens, Sphinx, Marie Antoinette, Ashland, John A. Logan, Caledonia, Maggie—the list seemed unending.

Besides the little town of Independence there was a camp just north which he called Strattonia. A group of office-buildings and shanties near his holdings, the Logan and American Eagles, was becoming known as Winfield. And a new railroad flag-station was named Independence.

The word was magic. Men threw their hats in the air on hearing of new strikes. They sang and shouted praises of the Mary McKinney, Elkton, Blue Bird, C.O.D. and other great producers. Of the Gold Coin and the Portland they spoke with marked respect. But the Independence—it was a word and a mine that stunned them into, at best, an awed whisper.

The thickness of one ore chute alone was eighteen and one-half feet. Chambers had been discovered that held sylvanite assaying in gold from $250 to several thousand dollars a ton. For two months ore shipped without sorting returned over $450 per ton. This chamber they nicknamed the Bull Pen. With stuff rich as $100 a pound, a man could go down there with an ice-pick and ride up with a year's wages in his pockets.

. . . so it was said. For Stratton maintained his policy of secrecy. No visitors were allowed in the mine and none of his employees were allowed to discuss it off the property. To develop the mine he had obtained the best engineers that money could buy, but still he refused to ship ore as fast as it was mined. Nor did he allow half of it to be mined. What he did ship, yielded an average of 4.6 ounces or $92 in gold to the ton. Levels, drifts and cross-cuts were driven carefully and systematically, but the vast ore bodies blocked out he would not allow stoped. His only answer to his engineers became a classic phrase throughout the district.

"Gold," he said, "is worth more in the ground than out of it."

The Independence, the marvel of the mining world, was not a mine; the thing, they said, was a blooming bank. For as a bank or depository Stratton always used it, extracting ore only when he felt disposed to draw upon his vast account. And the immense yield of over $120,000 a month was never compared with the capacity production of all the other bonanzas in the district; it represented merely the amount Stratton checked out of his mineral bank.

Little wonder that green eyes were turned upon the aloof

and quiet little king sitting on such a treasure and that attempts were made to dislodge him. W. S. Montgomery, whose fashionable home in Little London became the Administration Building of Colorado College, made an early try. He was well qualified. He was a lawyer by profession, having practiced at Red Cliff as an attorney in the celebrated Bull Domingo mine case. He had also edited and published the *Daily Prospect* newspaper at Silver Cliff and the *Leadville Daily Journal.*

Coming to Cripple Creek as a specialist in mining law, he obtained many valuable properties and located the Hull City placer comprising fifty-six acres. Stratton's town of Independence had grown upon the site, whereupon the Independence Town and Mining Company found itself a litigant in an astounding case brought against it by the Hull City placer company. The case was conducted in the Department of the Interior, Washington, and in several local courts. More than $150,000 was expended on the legal war, and eight consecutive decisions were rendered in favor of the Hull City placer. But the case was still pending on appeal in the State Supreme Court, and Stratton smiled down on the town of Independence. Not a shack had been dislodged.

Another storm was brewing, one that seemed likely to give Stratton his first tumble. But inconsistent always, it was like him to do his best to further the cause which meant his ruin.

8

The presidential campaign of 1896 was the tornado that now swept the country with all the accumulated bitterness of twenty-three years. Since the "crime of 1873" the question of free silver had been the cause for dissension, and the panic of 1893 had brought it to a head. Now, in the most spectacular election the country had seen, it was to be fought out at last.

Colorado, the Silver State, was not the only one aroused to a pitch of fanatical frenzy. National issues, national parties, the contestants themselves, were ignored in the one great question: gold or silver. Western Republicans were for free silver; eastern Democrats and Republicans were both for the single gold standard; while western and southern Democrats were for both gold and silver.

The choice narrowed down to William McKinley, the Republican candidate, representing the gold men. But who was to lead Colorado and the silver-mining states in the fight for free silver, to reopen the thousands of closed mines and deserted camps, to restore silver to its parity with gold?

At the National Democratic Convention, a Nebraskan named William Jennings Bryan clambered upon the platform. His speech, thereafter known as the "Cross of Gold," not only won him the nomination for President, but it spread like fire across the country and into the high mountain cañons of the Colorado Rockies. He had expressed the belief and hope of every obscure miner who lifted his pick:

> The humblest citizen in the land, when clad in the armor of a righteous cause, is stronger than all the hosts of error. . . .
>
> The miners who go down a thousand feet into the earth, or climb two thousand feet upon the cliffs, and bring forth from their hiding places the precious metals to be poured into the channels of trade, are as much business men as the few financial magnates who, in a back room, corner the money of the world. . . .
>
> We do not come as aggressors. Our war is not a war of conquest; we are fighting in defense of our homes, our families and posterity. We have petitioned, and our petitions have been

scorned. We have entreated, and our entreaties have been disregarded. We have begged, and they have mocked when our calamity came. We beg no longer; we entreat no more, we petition no more. We defy them!

. . . Having behind us the producing masses of this nation and the world, the laboring interests, and the toilers everywhere, we will answer their demand for a gold standard by saying to them: You shall not press down upon the brow of labor this crown of thorns; you shall not crucify mankind upon a cross of gold!

Cripple Creek was the greatest gold camp in the country and the only bright spot in Colorado. And Stratton was the mighty king of the district. Naturally, as a multi-millionaire capitalist who depended entirely on the undisputed sovereignty of gold over silver, he was expected to cringe before Bryan's fiery "Cross of Gold" address and then fling his millions to the support of McKinley.

It has been written and read by thousands that he was a gold Republican and the Republican distributor of federal patronage in Colorado. He is supposed to have chartered a special train for the Colorado delegates to the National Convention in St. Louis and voted them in a body for McKinley. For this favor, he had only to telegraph McKinley and obtain Tabor's appointment as postmaster at Denver.

Such bosh! Stratton, the unpredictable, could be depended upon to do the opposite to the natural thing. With his fame and fortune staked on gold, he came out for Bryan and free silver.

Why?

"Because," he said, "I believe that free silver is the best thing for the working masses of this country—although I realize that the maintenance of the gold standard would be best for me individually."

The train he was supposed to have chartered was a myth. Colorado had only four delegates to the convention and every one of them was a staunch silver advocate. Henry M. Teller, their leader, was a candidate for the Democratic nomination for President, receiving eight votes on each of the first two ballots, then walking out of the convention. And it was Teller, with Senator Wolcott, who had Tabor appointed postmaster of Denver at a salary sufficient "to rescue him from penury."

Throughout the campaign Stratton kept a big American flag hanging out of his office window with a broad band of white pinned to its lower edge bearing the name, "William Jennings Bryan."

Such a paradox was this gold man in the West sponsoring silver, that the news spread to New York magazines, like the *Cosmopolitan*, which carried stories about him. Mr. Wharton Barker of the Philadelphia newspaper, the *American*, which was also supporting Bryan and free silver, came out to see Stratton and to obtain money for his paper.

"Mr. Barker," said Stratton, "I am a rich man. Richer than I ever hoped to be. I have an immense income. Now, before I speak about contributing to your cause, I would like to know your ideas on the income tax."

Barker saw his anticipated contribution go glimmering; he knew well enough how new millionaires hung on to their money. But honest and determined, he answered in a reluctant voice, "Well, Mr. Stratton, for my part I have never seen why a rich man should not pay his taxes as well as a poor man."

Stratton smiled. "That's right, Mr. Barker. Here is my check for $5,000. If you need more, call on me."

Stratton's belief, even forty years later, would have created a mild sensation along Wood Avenue.

Little London's capitalists and new millionaires were astounded at his stand. They were stunned when they heard a rumor that Stratton had posted a bet of $100,000 in Phil Strubel's Barber Shop that Bryan would be elected. It was a challenge none of them wanted to accept. They scoffed it off as jawbone talk.

Then on Thursday, October 29, 1896, the *Gazette* conformed the rumor with an article stating that Stratton had made an offer to bet $100,000 against $300,000 that Bryan would be elected. He had agreed that if he won he would give the money to the Colorado Springs Free Reading Room and Library Association. If the other side won, the winner could keep the money.

Said Stratton:

> I made the offer and I mean it. The money must be in the bank, and there will be no jawbone talk about it. I understand that the men to whom it was made are going to try to raise the money tomorrow. I did not make the offer because of any information that I have on the election, but I have a feeling that Bryan is going to win. I am deeply interested in seeing Bryan elected. I realize that the maintenance of the gold standard would be best for me individually, but I believe that free silver is the best thing for the working masses of this country. It is because I have a great respect for the intelligence and patriotism of the working people and believe that they will see their duty and interest at the polls is for free silver, that I am willing to make such an offer.

Perhaps he was thinking of the lonely, ruined Tabor and his own seventeen fruitless years as a prospector.

On Saturday the *Gazette* came out with the news that "Stratton's bet will be covered in the East. Mr. L. C. Dana to whom the offer was made, sent a message to New York announcing the bet. Yesterday he got a reply that the money would be covered. He then telegraphed that the New York money must be placed in the Chemical National Bank to the credit of the First National Bank of Colorado Springs."

Then Dana received another wire from New York: "Evening paper says that Stratton wants to bet $100,000 against $300,000. Will take it. Have him telegraph some one here to put up the money for him."

Stratton's attorneys said that he would require the money put up here as he would take no chances of being jobbed out of it on account of the New York laws on betting.

Little London, Cripple Creek and most of the country were wildly excited. If taken, it would be the biggest election bet of the year if not the biggest ever made.

The Associated Press sent a newspaper man to cover the story. As Stratton refused to see him, the reporter waylaid him on the way home. Stratton flew into a rage.

"You've made it up out of the whole cloth! It's all one of your newspaper lies!"

Then the reporter lost his temper. "By God! No damned old millionaire can call me a liar!"

Stratton calmed down, apologized and expressed his respect for the daily press. He gave the man a cigar and strolled serenely on to his house, leaving the reporter without a story and still wondering if the bet had ever been covered.

Nor was it ever known. But, as shrewdly suspected by many, the offer had accomplished Stratton's wily aim. Three days later at the polls in the greatest gold camp on earth, Bryan the silver advocate received almost 3,000 votes to McKinley's 700. And he carried all of Colorado by a plurality of 130,000.

But Stratton's own luck had held. McKinley, by an overwhelming majority from the rest of the country, was elected

President. Silver was definitely out forever. Gold—"bright, shining, yellow, solid gold!"—was thenceforth to be the standard precious metal of the world. Cripple Creek was its biggest camp, and Stratton was still its reigning sovereign.

9

Meanwhile, something else was transpiring in Stratton's own backyard that was to worry him more.

Early that summer a bedraggled workman had arrived in town, going to an obscure rooming-house near the railroad station. After cleaning up a bit he began to call on several lawyers in town. Next he went to Cripple Creek and looked about, spending some time with J. Maurice Finn and riding around behind a prize $2,500 mare from Finn's Folly on Crystal Hill. Then he returned to town, spent five minutes with Stratton, and rushed out to consult more lawyers.

A few weeks later the news came out that he had instituted a suit in the District Court, asking to be declared owner of one-half of all Stratton's wealth and mining properties. The man was the old plasterer who had grubstaked Stratton—Leslie Popejoy.

The story on which he based his claims reviewed in detail Stratton's discovery of the Independence and Washington. He had grubstaked Stratton to the amount of $275 including a general prospecting outfit, Billy Fernay's wages, the cranky burro and additional groceries. He had sent Fred Troutman on a hired horse up to ascertain if his name were properly included on the location stakes of any claims Stratton might have discovered. He had seen the results of the assays, had declared that the properties were not worth developing, and had signed away his rights to a half share of all the profits in return for his original grubstake of $275.

With all this Stratton agreed.

But Popejoy had more to add. He claimed that Stratton had known from the instant he set his stakes that the Independence was a bonanza. He had purposely refrained from obtaining papers, returning to town obviously disgusted claiming the property no good, and demanding that Popejoy furnish $950 more or at least $600 to start development or he would dissolve partnership.

Wherefore Popejoy on the strength of Stratton's assertions had signed away his rights for three promissory notes payable with interest in ninety days. He had then moved to Denver. A poor plasterer with a limited education and too tired to read the newspapers at night, he had not heard of the strike until June, 1894, when he read of the labor troubles in the district. Amazed, he saw notice of the Independence and noted that his name was not mentioned as a part-owner of the wonderful mine.

By the following year he had saved enough money to investigate. He found that two days before their agreement had been signed, Stratton had secured assays showing the mine to be of great value. He remembered how quickly Stratton had produced money to pay off the promissory notes without waiting the ninety days. And Troutman, whom Stratton had driven off the claim without assays, had been employed later by Stratton. By thus wilfully misleading him, Stratton had been enabled to take out papers to the claims in his own name alone. He had defrauded his trusted grubstaker, developed the Independence, and now owned thirty mines or more, shares in the Portland, property in Victor, Cripple Creek, Anaconda and Colorado Springs, interests in many smelting and sampling companies, and many other possessions of great but unknown wealth—half of all rightfully belonging to Popejoy.

To these allegations Stratton replied that Popejoy had at first agreed to supply $950, but had refused to do so when it became necessary to develop the mines. Popejoy, he said, had sold his interest before the locations were perfected, and the Independence did not become profitable until after an expenditure of $2,500 in development work. He also stated that Popejoy, just before bringing his suit, had offered him the $275 note for $407.16, including the interest, which he had refused.

The case dragged through the winter, Popejoy obtaining work as a plasterer. His attorneys were three men in town and another Denver firm of three more, but his chief counsel, though not of record, was J. Maurice Finn up in Cripple Creek.

On April 24, 1897, notice was served on Stratton and Popejoy that the case was set for trial May 3rd.

Two days before the trial Finn came down to see Popejoy. Up to this time he had been encouraging the plasterer, saying that he had a just case. He now urged Popejoy to give up the suit; he could not hope to win over the famous and wealthy Stratton. Popejoy was up on a scaffold plastering in the old Court House. He turned around and looked down. Finn passed him up an Order of Dismissal and a roll of bills.

"Stratton will settle out of court for $40,000. All you've got to do is sign this order. It's the best you can do."

Popejoy scribbled his name, pocketed the wad of bills, and finished his day's work. The next day he left town with his $40,000—minus the $2,250 he had paid Finn for getting it for him.

One year later he was broke, in debt, and had taken the Bankruptcy Act.

For years he was not heard of; then after Stratton had

died he appeared in town again, more disreputable looking than before, and with more news of the case which he had been tricked into settling out of court.

He went to one of the best lawyers in town who specialized in mining law, Norman Campbell, and told his story. He said he had found out many things about his previous lawyer, J. Maurice Finn. Finn had been Stratton's first lawyer, the one who had advised him about jumping the White House claim which had become part of the Portland mine. The Charles Steele who had ridden by night to Pueblo to file adverse papers had been made the mining superintendent of the Independence. Finn, for his part, had been promised a share in the Washington for which he later brought suit for $10,000. It was thus evident that Stratton and Finn were close friends.

Therefore, when Popejoy had instituted his previous suit, Stratton had secretly bought out Finn for a sum of money which he believed to have been $8,000, and had given him thereafter as his counsel a good regular salary of $5,000 a year for several years.

He claimed that "Stratton was lavish and reckless with the use of money to accomplish any end he had in view; that by reason of his violent temper and vindictive and revengeful disposition, and the great power he exercised by virtue of his many financial connections, he held in awe witnesses who knew the facts, and kept many silent who otherwise would have spoken."

These witnesses whom Stratton had "suppressed and kept silent, induced and hired to keep out of the jurisdiction of El Paso County" included Billy Fernay, Fred Troutman, Sam Strong whose mine had been blown up, and many others.

Popejoy also believed that by a careful appraisal Stratton's holdings would prove to be worth $16,000,000. He now wished to bring suit again, in light of these findings, for $8,000,000.

Campbell listened carefully. He was a good and an honest lawyer. Such a suit would create a sensation. Eight million dollars was involved. Stratton was dead and could not answer the charges, but he was still regarded with awe and fear as Colorado's greatest mining king. And Popejoy was the most miserable looking, disreputable client that had ever stumbled over the beautiful Navajo Chief rug on his office floor. Nevertheless, if there were any truth in his assertions, Campbell felt he could not refuse the case.

He insisted, before committing himself, that Popejoy round up the witnesses whom Stratton had bribed and who supported the plasterer's contentions. From these men he obtained sworn affidavits. Still wary of a client who was drunk most of the time, dissolute and dishonest, he made Popejoy give him full power of attorney, allowing him to handle the affair without intervention.

These papers he took to a large Denver law firm and told his story. The firm agreed he had a case and went in with him as consulting attorneys. Campbell returned home and drew up his case.

Popejoy was broke and earning a meager living by doing odd jobs around town. So Campbell expended his own money to pay stenographer's fees and incidental expenses. He copied the affidavits and sent the originals, with his agreement to power of attorney, to Denver for safe-keeping. Then, still more proud of his good reputation than of any money he might obtain, he drew up a notice of attorney's lien. This provided that out of the money derived by winning the suit, one-half of the total judgment was to be assigned to him, and one-third to public educational and benevolent institutions. He had already discussed this with the president of one of these institutions.

Then he filed suit.

For months the thing dragged on. It seemed evident from the start that Popejoy's reputation had endangered the suit, although Campbell was too astute a lawyer to audibly admit he believed any court could be swayed from legal impartiality. For one thing, Stratton's lawyers requested the court to ask Popejoy for security for payment of costs of the suit and to file bond, Popejoy being "so unsettled as to endanger the officers of the Court with respect to their legal demands."

Campbell answered this by a motion for an "Order to Prosecute as a Poor Person," Popejoy being unable to earn more than nine dollars to twelve dollars a week. Then the Court demanded from him a "Bill of Particulars" which would include the names of all the men who had given affidavits and were to be used by Campbell as witnesses. This, stated Campbell, was an unjust demand; it would give the opposing side complete access to the men on whom he depended to win his case.

Meanwhile, Popejoy was getting more and more obstreperous. He finally went out and obtained two shyster lawyers, new in town, who assured him they could squeeze out a million or two for him in no time. The three men burst in on Campbell and demanded that he give up his power of attorney, threatening to wreck his office and beat him. Campbell was obdurate. He had the papers safely hid in Denver.

And all the time Campbell was spending his own money to keep the case going.

The men handling Stratton's affairs were in equal turmoil with Stratton dead and his millions in a tangle. At this time a young lawyer, David P. Strickler, arrived to take charge of all legal affairs, not knowing that he was to be retained for over thirty years. After reviewing the case, he suggested that Popejoy be paid off again. The others were furious. It was a damned hold-up, they said. Popejoy had already been paid $40,000.

Nevertheless, Strickler and Campbell got together, and a motion to dismiss the case was filed and passed.

Campbell notified every one of Popejoy's creditors to be waiting outside his office the day the money was paid. Then Strickler with $3,000 cash arrived. Campbell withdrew the money he had expended and the creditors presented their bills to Popejoy.

With the remainder Popejoy went back to Kansas to eke out a miserable existence at his trade—the man who might have been another Haw Tabor from his grubstake.

The case involving $8,000,000 had been finally settled for a total of $43,000, and out of court.

Today, almost a half century later, there are Little Londoners who still believe that the humble plasterer who staked a carpenter to the richest gold mine on the American continent should have received his just due, and in Colorado's hall of fame be included with Stratton, Tabor and Walsh.

But Stratton's luck—his astounding, perhaps mystical luck after seventeen drab years of failure—had held. It was never to fail him thereafter. He was, and was to remain, the greatest of Colorado's great mining kings.

PART FOUR: LONDON

"O Lord! Keep me from being like some of these Cripple Creek millionaires, afraid of being bored by old friends, insolent in feeling toward those who have not had my luck, and scared to death lest a dollar go by and I not get it."

4. LONDON

WHEN Sophronia, Bob Schwarz' best girl, suddenly threw up her job as Stratton's housekeeper, she left 115 North Weber again to its wealthy and eccentric owner.

For a time Stratton's sister, Mrs. Jennie Cobb, managed it for him, and then she left for California. At periodic intervals other women took her place, supplemented by a continual parade of cooks and helpers. Each stayed a week or a month and passed on, spreading the news of Stratton's intolerable eccentricities. He was so peculiar, so violent in his likes and dislikes, that soon no one in town would work in the house.

Then arrived a Swedish girl named Anna Hellmark. She was of pure peasant stock, with a brogue hardly understandable; and in her faithful, self-effacing way, she was to endear herself to Stratton for the rest of his life. Born in Stockholm, Sweden, in 1862, she had worked as a serving-girl since childhood. Through some political imbroglio of which she would never speak, she was forced to leave Sweden with some friends. She came to the United States and found employment in California and then in Denver. From here an old woman took her to Colorado Springs as a cook. The job lasted but a few months. Anna then heard of Stratton and was induced to apply to his housekeeper for the job of cook.

For the first three days of her employment, Anna did not get a glimpse of her employer. Then one morning a man pushed open the back door. Anna was on her knees scrubbing the kitchen floor. She whirled around to glimpse a pair of new shiny boots. Raising her eyes she demanded, "Vat you vant? Dese boots on dat clean floor vass someting!"

"Do I have to take off my boots every time I come in here?" demanded Stratton.

"Ya!"

Stratton backed off the floor and went around to the front door. In the dining-room doorway stood a young English girl who had been hired to serve Stratton's meals.

"Anna! That's Mr. Stratton! Don't talk like that. He gets awful mad!"

Anna threw up her head and went on scrubbing. Never but once in her life was she afraid of Stratton. But she soon found out that both the English girl and the housekeeper quailed before his slightest frown. That night she witnessed a good example.

Stratton was home for an early dinner. The table was set and a bowl of soup was in readiness when Stratton took his seat. The three women, waiting in the kitchen to serve the next course, were suddenly aroused by a shout. The English girl ran in to see what was the matter.

"You go bring the step ladder in here!" demanded Stratton.

Anna helped her carry it into the dining-room and set it up.

"Now you climb up on it," he ordered the girl.

With trembling limbs she went up the steps and perched on top.

For a moment there was silence. Then Stratton looked up. "Well! Can't you see from up there what's missing?"

The girl had forgotten to put the salt on the table.

The housekeeper also came in for her share of trouble:

Stratton one evening accused her of putting the uneaten pickles left over from supper back into the keg. When she denied it, he grew so angry that he left the house swearing never to eat at home again. Two hours later he returned to eat sandwiches in the kitchen.

One Christmas morning after the English girl had left from pure fright and a Scottish girl, Miss Carmichael, had taken her place, Stratton got up for a late breakfast. A big turkey dinner had been prepared, but for breakfast he was served fried oysters. Stratton wanted some small sausages. There were none in the house, and all the shops were closed. Another storm ensued. Stratton refused to eat a bite of anything. He flung out of the house in a rage and did not return until midnight.

A month or two later came Anna's turn, Miss Carmichael having fled the house. Stratton's favorite dish was a Swedish brown bean soup cooked a long time until it was very thick. He licked out the bowl with evident relish and asked Anna for another. She had hardly set it on the table and returned to the kitchen when Stratton flung out behind her. She had added a bit of hot water to the soup to fill up the bowl.

Anna, staunch, honest peasant that she was, was not to be cowed like the others. "Ya! Dat iss vat I done. Vy don't you say how much you vant sometimes?" The next morning she packed her bag and left town.

Over two years later Stratton found her in Denver and persuaded her to come back. For the rest of his life she was his one enduring attendant, for years the only one in the house. Unlettered, her speech hardly understandable, she assumed her duties as housekeeper with a torturing, self-accusing attitude of unworthiness because she lacked education and graces to receive his distinguished callers. She was his most loyal friend and devoted servant. There is no doubt she loved him. Never married, she gave her life to making him comfortable—and keeping out of his way. Thirty-five years after his death, Stratton was still the greatest thing in her life. A few old newspaper clippings about him, a chipped frame that had held his favorite picture, an old chest of drawers—such discarded junk were her only treasures, and the mention of his name was sufficient to bring tears to her eyes.

But now, enraged by her leaving and by his ill luck with white servants, Stratton happened to remember a Negro woman named Eliza who had previously cooked for him.

During the Cripple Creek labor strike when a group had angrily besieged the house, Eliza had blocked the door with her huge frame. Stratton in gratitude had presented her with a Smith and Wesson revolver, asking her to carry it in her apron pocket thereafter.

"Why, man, I ain' goin' to be no murderer fo' you."

"Oh just shoot 'em in the foot—any place," said Stratton. "I'll pay the bills."

He now got hold of Eliza and made her his housekeeper, in charge of two other Negro girls. They got along excellently. Eliza was big, black as ebony, and beneath her affable nature maintained a mind of her own. With Anna, she was one of the few persons who understood him.

The house was big and comfortable, though not a mansion on Wood Avenue. The reception hall and adjoining parlor were finished in mahogany. Stratton never used them; he had heard that the previous owner, old Dr. Tucker, had died in the parlor. He spent most of his time in the library. It was finished in his favorite wood, hand-polished bird's-eye maple. So were his own bedroom upstairs, his dressers and chests of drawers in the linen-room, and of such wood, too, was the huge picture-frame that held the photograph of his father, Myron Stratton.

The cleaning of these rooms was Eliza's personal job. She was required to report to him each day when she had finished.

"All through now, eh?" he would demand. "Sure now?"

And then he would get down on his knees and with his handkerchief rub the back rungs of the chairs. The slightest speck of dust was sufficient to start a row. In each room was placed a white enamel spittoon. To further test Eliza's thoroughness he would often lift the top and drop a speck of cigar ashes inside and out of sight, which he would look for on the following day.

For now that Stratton could afford peculiarities, he developed enough of them to justify his millions.

"Eliza," he told her. "Never let that ice-box be empty of fried chicken. If I don't eat it, throw it out and put more in."

In addition, she was to place a plate of it and a glass of milk on his bedstand each night, in case he got hungry.

Two weeks later he called her. "Eliza. You know I don't eat much."

"Yes, suh!"

"Then what the hell do you mean by trying to ruin my appetite and starve me? Don't I give you enough money to run the house? Aren't you supposed to be a good cook? Now for God's sake get rid of that fried chicken. It's in the ice-box, in the kitchen, in my bedroom night and day. It's all over the damned house! I can't go any place without seeing it. Get rid of it. Never let me see it again!"

Within a few weeks he made a quick trip with a friend down into Texas and over the Mexican Border to look at a mine. He was gone perhaps three weeks. During his absence, Eliza and the two girls carefully pressed all his clothes and arranged them neatly in his clothes-closet.

Stratton returned home. Early that evening he called Eliza up to his room. He was standing sadly looking into the closet at his pressed clothes.

"Eliza," he asked quietly, "will you do something for me? Get me just one pair of pants that's fit to wear. Just one pair is all I ask. When they wear out I'll buy myself another pair. It's not too much to ask. When a man comes home from a long trip he ought to have one pair of pants he can get into."

"Why, Mistah Stratton. Man, look theah. We broke ouah backs fixin' them. They's pants just pilin' up dis closet."

Stratton took out a pair, sadly running his thumb down the crease. "All just like this. None of them fit to wear. You know I never wear creases in my pants."

Nor did he. Creaseless trousers, his high-heeled boots and gray Stetson hat were the invariable items of his attire. And it was necessary for Eliza to send all his trousers to the cleaners to have the creases removed.

Only once was he persuaded to dress up. The occasion was a party at the El Paso Club. Stratton climbed into a full-dress suit and called in Eliza to look him over; she had formerly been a maid in one of the big homes of another Cripple Creek millionaire.

"How do I look?" he demanded irritably.

He was turning around before the mirror in tails, high collar and stuffed shirt, but in his usual high-heeled boots and Stetson hat.

"You looks scrumptious, Mistah Stratton. But you cain't weah them boots astuffin' out them pants. Gem'man don' do that at the Club. You ain't got no business spo'tin' dat hat either."

Stratton stood still a moment. "I can't, huh? By God, I won't go then!" He ran Eliza out of the room, tore off his clothes, and stayed at home.

It was the nearest he ever came to attending a public function in Little London. And there were few people he entertained at home. Not in two years was there a man who stayed overnight with him. But there were several women. One of them was a Denver woman who spent every week-end with him for months. She always arrived at night on Friday and left Sunday night, driving to and from the house in a closed carriage. She was never seen outside the house during the two days.

One morning while Eliza was cleaning up his room she saw a picture of the woman and her husband on the society page of a Denver newspaper lying on his bed-stand.

"Do you know who that woman is?" asked Stratton.

"No, suh! I don't see nothin' an' I don't know nothin'."

"By God, Eliza! You're a smarter woman than any white one I ever saw. None of them are worth a damn. They'll do anything for money. Anything! Like this woman. She's got everything a woman can want. And still she's after more. They're all alike. I have no use for any of them!"

Another prominent Little London woman sent him an expensive cut-glass vase filled with his favorite American Beauty roses, hoping to curry favor. "What the hell!" he stormed, "a woman sending flowers to a man! Don't I have this house filled with roses myself every morning? And as for that damned vase, throw it out. Or keep it yourself. But get it out of my sight!"

For the most part he remained at home, alone. In his library were several immense couches, wide as ordinary beds; and on these Stratton for hours lay curled up like a woman, his dog Dick at his feet.

He had made a new discovery—a discovery greater than the Independence, a mine of inexhaustible wealth which still day by day grows richer, and to which he and every other man has clear title. He had discovered literature.

The library became filled with books. He grew particularly fond of Balzac. Then he began reading theology, religion and metaphysics. The shelves were lined with his favorite works: Pascal, Henry Drummond, Bible commentaries, the writings of the Duke of Argyll, and Fiske's *The Destiny of Man, Through Nature to God*, and *The Idea of God*. But still his favorite book rested on the table: the old worn copy of Cornwall's *Manual of Blowpipe Analysis* with page 241 turned down for reference to graphic tellurium, which he had always included in his burro-pack while roaming the mountains.

And then one day, sitting in his office downtown, Stratton was led to another discovery.

Living in town was a young schoolboy who was studying violin in his every available moment. The family was poor, the father working at the railroad station, and hard put to it to pay for the boy's music lessons. But young Louis Persinger suddenly thought that the rich Mr. Stratton who stayed at home so much might want to hear him play. For several days he hung around Stratton's offices without success; for some reason the secretaries and clerks didn't seem interested in securing an appointment for him. And then that afternoon he happened to enter the office at the moment the door to Stratton's room was open.

Perhaps Stratton's employees had mentioned to him the persistent kid who had been pestering them. Stratton caught sight of the boy.

"Here! Come in here, sonny. What can I do for you?" he called good-humoredly.

Louis strode into the room. "I been thinkin' you might like to have some music at your house sometime."

"Eh?"

Louis explained about his violin. Stratton, slightly bewildered and amused at the idea, chuckled and answered, "Sure. You come around some night."

A few evenings later the boy presented himself at the house. With him he brought his violin and his mother to accompany him. The music evidently was soothing to Stratton's nerves. For several evenings he lay on the couch watching Louis sawing away at his violin.

"What do you intend doing with that violin?" he asked the boy one night.

Louis told him that one of his teachers believed he had talent and should go to Europe to study and make something of himself. Stratton rubbed his chin a moment. Then he got out his check-book and wrote out a check for a thousand dollars. "There! That ought to help you get started. Let me know when you need some more."

It was the beginning of a career. Louis Persinger and his mother went to Leipzig. They wrote regularly to Stratton, who sent other checks. He wanted them to have the best of everything. In one letter he advised the boy not to sit too high up in the gallery at the opera; that "it wasn't very good for one's health"—meaning, of course, they shouldn't try to get the cheapest seats all the time. With one of his checks the boy purchased the first good violin he ever owned.

Louis never saw his benefactor again. When he finally returned from Europe, Stratton had died not knowing that of the many he had helped the boy was to repay him with a career which fully justified his help and encouragement. After studying violin with Hans Becker, piano, theory, and conducting, he was recognized by Arthur Nikisch as "one of the most talented pupils the Leipzig Conservatory has ever had." After studying with Eugene Ysaye in Brussels, and with Jacques Thibaud in Paris, the young virtuoso launched into a career as one of the outstanding musical artists of the world. He was chosen as concertmaster of the Berlin Philharmonic orchestra, became assistant conductor of the San Francisco Symphony, and leader of the most outstanding American quartet. Following the death of the world-famous Leopold Auer, he was engaged to fill the post vacated at the Juilliard Graduate School in New York, discovering and teaching Yehudi Menuhin and Ruggiero Ricci, and becoming the leading violin teacher in the world.

Stratton, meanwhile, was strengthening his slight acquaintance with another inspiration besides literature—whiskey. It too was to have a far-reaching effect, and it was to help change his life.

2

"While Stratton was known to sight by practically everyone who lived in town any length of time," a *Rocky Mountain News* correspondent says of him, "yet so unpretentious was he that thousands of visitors have passed him by on the street without recognizing the multi-millionaire. Attired in a dark sack suit and wearing a broad-brimmed felt hat, he was accustomed to walk down to his office every morning for years. But lately, when his exceeding generosity became known, he was greatly annoyed by persons who waylaid him on the streets, and this led him to hire a man with a light surrey to carry him to and from his place of business."

It had been his habit on sunny afternoons to sit on the curb in front of his office talking to his coachman, the man to whom he had once given $1,000 for averting a runaway. Now one day he jumped abruptly to his feet.

"By God! I'm getting tired of being pointed out on the street like a prize pup!"

With this he strode into his office and discontinued his afternoon chats on the curb; he had seen one of the tourist-drivers riding by with a load of tourists and pointing him out as one of Little London's sights.

Even within he was besieged with requests for money and aid, with explanations of harebrained inventions he was asked to finance, with circulars and petitions to sign. He was now receiving almost five hundred begging letters daily.

His only statement regarding his unparalleled generosity was simply, "I count my money as a gift from the Father of us all, and I am responsible for its administration as a good steward."

It did not keep him from seeing the results with a clear eye. His friend George H. Adams, proprietor of the Adams Hotel in Denver, asked him, "Have you any idea how much money you have been buncoed out of since you struck it rich?"

Said Stratton: "Yes. I keep account of it approximately. I estimate I have wrongfully had to give up, one way or another, $3,000,000. Where I made my mistake was in the very start. My associates were all working people and boarding-house keepers who were having a hard time to get along. If I had just given them money outright, I would have been the gainer, but I thought to help them by giving them good positions—positions they were incapable of filling. I have had to lay them off, shift them about or pension them, and nine-tenths of them trumped up suits against me."

Now he began to be a little more cautious.

One of his callers was a shabbily dressed woman shown into his office. Stratton listened courteously to her. It seemed her name had been Stratton before marriage. When she was through talking, he smoothed out his white mustaches.

"Madam," he said, "I came from a large family and I have a good many relatives. Some of them are not very well off but not one of them has ever asked me for a cent. You have proved you are not one of our family. I bid you good day."

Some time later the Reverend Thomas A. Uzzell came to him for a contribution for his People's Tabernacle. After three hours of talking, he was given a check. When Uzzell saw written on it the amount of $10,000 he laid his head down on his arms and wept.

"By God!" exclaimed Stratton, his own eyes filling with tears, "you don't feel any better about this than I do. I am not doing anything for you, I am helping those poor people of yours. Now I'm not going to give you another damned penny to build your house, but when you get it all built it will take scads of money to run it and I've got scads. Come to me. I'll stand by you. You know I don't give much to churches. They don't suit me. They are too aristocratic. But you know your work and I think it's just the kind of Christian work that should be done among poor people."

By now, excited and upset, he was weeping more copiously than the preacher. It was two hours before Uzzell could get away.

It was impossible for Stratton to refuse help. Eliza was ordered to keep on hand at all times a supply of meal tickets to a restaurant downtown. "When a man comes to the back door and asks for a meal, don't give him anything. I won't have him treated like a dog and a plate set out in front of him. Give him a bunch of tickets. Let him go down and get what he wants like a man."

And yet he gave her strict orders to keep away all the

Stratton's Independence (center foreground) and Portland (upper right) mines (Courtesy The Denver Public Library Western Collection).

many peddlers who called to sell him odds and ends. One afternoon an old woman called with a leather pillow which she asked Eliza to show him when he came home.

Stratton walked back and forth looking at the pillow. It was of good buckskin and on one side was painted a buffalo bull.

"Goddam it!" growled Stratton. "What do I want to look at that bull for all the rest of my life! Isn't this house full of pillows already? Thought I told you I wasn't to be bothered with all these people. . . . How much does she want?"

"Thirteen dollahs. I likes it. And the woman sho do need it."

Stratton gave her fifteen dollars. "Well, you buy it then, if you want it. But be sure it isn't another cock-and-bull story. When is she coming back?"

The woman was due at seven o'clock. Stratton finished supper and at five minutes to seven put on his hat and went out, noisily slamming the front door.

A few moments later the woman knocked and was admitted into the hall.

"Did he buy it?" she asked.

"No. Mistah Stratton didn't want it," said Eliza.

The woman sat down limply and covered up her face. Her distress was beyond question.

"I likes the pillow though," said Eliza. "And I'se got the money. Heah." She passed over the fifteen dollars to the woman. "And you keeps the change."

At this the woman broke into tears. She was a widow, she said, and the money she had to have to buy medicine for her sick boy. She tried to kiss Eliza's hands.

When the woman left, Eliza closed the door and turned around. Stratton was standing before her with tears running down his cheeks. To make sure Eliza was not trying to put something over on him, he had sneaked around the house to come in by the back door and hide behind the hall portières.

Stratton and Eliza understood each other perfectly. He liked her because she would take no back-talk from him beyond a certain point. To that point he was always squabbling. If his tooth paste or medicine bottles ran low he would empty them down the lavatory and fuss at her because she hadn't kept up a full supply of the few things he needed. With his keen gray-blue eyes it was his habit to stare at his new help as if suspecting them of some intrigue against him. This made a new Negro girl so nervous when she first served him that Stratton made Eliza pay her a month's salary and get rid of her. The two others whom he kept he always tipped every month. To Eliza he gave nothing. When she complained, he burst out, "Any woman who carries my purse-strings like you and is too ignorant to tip herself deserves nothing." And yet he was always spying on her.

One morning after cleaning his room with another girl, Eliza plumped down in his big rocker. "Lawd A'mighty! When Ah gets rich I'se sho goin' to have me a big easy chair like dis one!"

Stratton popped in the door. "Carry it out! Get it out of my sight if you like it that much. But get it out now!"

So Eliza carried it out into the woodshed and stored it with her leather pillow.

In order to give the wash-woman plenty of work, Stratton insisted that clean sheets and table linen be used daily.

There was no telling when or to whom Stratton would give money; it kept rolling in faster than he could get rid of it. It became an insupportable weight he could not shake off.

There were many who tried to be of help. The legal tangles

they got him into aroused in him one of his most violent dislikes, a complete abhorrence of lawyers.

Once he was involved in a lawsuit with an inventor who claimed he had devised a new plan of treating complex ores. According to the story he had interested Stratton who had agreed to furnish $300,000 for the erection of a mill to test the invention, and had then backed out of the scheme.

The inventor had then walked into the office of a young attorney and flung Stratton's agreement on his desk.

"I have here a contract for $300,000 entered into with Winfield Scott Stratton. He refused to fulfill his part of the agreement. I would like to see if I have a case." As the young lawyer scanned the agreement, he added, "Half a dozen other attorneys have told me they can't enforce it."

The lawyer looked up. "I'll take the case for one-half."

"It's yours," came the instant reply.

Stratton's attorney was Charles J. Hughes, later Senator rom Colorado, and one of the best lawyers in the State. Despite him, Stratton lost the case in the district court, the ury bringing in a verdict of $150,000 damages.

Stratton immediately left the courtroom, walked to the office of the opposing attorney and left him a check for $150,000. He then went over to his own attorney, Hughes, who stared at his client with amazement, a slow flush creeping into his cheeks.

"You have settled a case involving $150,000 without consulting your attorney?"

"Why, sure. The jury went against us, didn't it?"

"That verdict," thundered Hughes, "did not amount to a ow of pins! I intended to carry this case to the Supreme Court where it certainly would have been reversed. That man has no kind of a case! Now as for you, Sir"—he leaned cross the desk—"I refuse to handle the business of a client who takes his legal affairs in his own hands. You have acted like a damned old fool, Sir. You will take your legal business elsewhere, and don't ever come into my office again!"

The incident was one of many; Stratton was never able to bear the sight of a lawyer.

At one time he allowed a young man to call at his house. After an hour or two the visitor rose to his feet, apologizing for having stayed so late.

"Oh, that's all right," said Stratton. "I have enjoyed your visit. You are not like most folks, for they come to tell me that they have just started a lawsuit against me, or are about to do so, and you haven't said a word along that line."

Nevertheless, he continued giving away money in sums steadily growing larger, arousing more and more the amazement of Little London. His obvious distress elicited a bit of sympathy from the editor of *Facts*, an illustrated weekly review, who wrote:

> Stratton pays the penalty of his great possessions in a thousand annoyances, in threats, blackmailing schemes, in hard work to keep the money doing something. However, if a kind Providence burdens me in that way I hope He will give me the same kindly heart, the same reckless extravagance in doing what I please with my money that he has given Winfield S. Stratton.
>
> This is not a prayer, but O Lord! keep me from being like some of these Cripple Creek millionaires, afraid of being bored by old friends, insolent in feeling toward those who have not had my luck, and scared to death lest a dollar go by and I not get it.

And then one day Stratton was in his office rummaging through the papers in his desk-drawer. He came upon a packet, unsnapped the rubber band. There was the deed to a mine in Maricopa County, Arizona, and a note for $15,000. Tabor! That was Tabor's note, to whom he had given money. He settled back in his chair and stared out of the window, thinking of the pathetic ruined man who had sat across from him three years ago. After a time he roused himself and rang for his secretary Ramsay to write for him the following letter:

OFFICE OF W. S. STRATTON

119 PIKE'S PEAK AVENUE, COLO. SP'GS., COLO.

September 24, 1898

Hon. H. A. W. Tabor
Denver

DEAR SIR: Mr. W. S. Stratton wishes me to say that he never at any time contemplated the retention of your note and papers as an evidence of indebtedness to him on your part, and in going over his affairs he finds them still on hand contrary to his wishes and intentions. If they remain with him he must list them with the assessor of taxes and in case of his demise could not then be returned by his Executors. He therefore directs that they be returned to you at once and asks that you accept them back again as an expression of his best wishes and good will for your future success.

Respectfully and sincerely yours,
Wm. A. Ramsay
Secretary for W. S. Stratton *

That night Stratton went home feeling a bit better: he had never recorded the deed; therefore both the mine and the $15,000 loan belonged to Tabor. He devoutly hoped they would help Tabor recoup his losses.

It was an ironic jest of a fate that had irreparably turned against Tabor.

* On display at the State Historical Society, Denver, Colorado.

Seven months later Tabor died in hopeless poverty, his mine at Ward having been a failure. Years later Stratton's letter, the note and deed, were found among a trunk load of old papers. On the deed and on the envelope Mrs. Tabor had scrawled in pencil the pathetic comment:

"We thought that Mr. Stratton had recorded this deed it would have saved it for us too bad"

The mine had been foreclosed, and the Tabors would not have lost it had Stratton recorded the deed.

3

Every evening Stratton left his office, hurrying down the steps and jumping into his surrey to be driven the few blocks home to avoid recognition. He rang the bell and immediately opened the door. He ate a scanty meal and retired to his library. Here, curled up on a couch, he read and read; or sat, decanter at hand, drinking and staring blankly across the room at the stern face of Myron Stratton looking back from its gilded frame. In his bedroom was a glass of crème de menthe, in case he had drunk too much. Stratton always believed it was the best antidote for whiskey.

Thus his life day after day with monotonous regularity. Occasionally Bob Schwarz came in, rarely another visitor. Stratton was left alone. He had few friends and welcomed no new ones; and Little London had given him up completely. It was written of him during this time:

> In all things he was [so] different from the ordinary mining millionaire as to almost constitute a distinct type, and for this reason the public took a long time to get used to him. He didn't go to New York, build a palace on Fifth Avenue and make an effort to break into society, according to the accepted idea of what a man with ten or fifteen millions should do. On

the contrary, he stayed here and lived and acted as he had always done. He invested his money at home, built up the town, gave freely to charity without advertising the fact, shunned notoriety, and most of all, accomplished things. For these qualities, more than for the mere possession of great wealth, Stratton will be remembered when most of the other bonanza kings are long since forgotten.

But now, itself ignored, the town completely foreswore him. For his part, "Stratton wanted to be alone. He was such a peculiar man and such a worried man that no woman could have lived with him. His moods were such that no man could have put up with them unless he had to in order to get a salary." Little by little, stories about him began to spread. A fabulously rich crank living alone certainly must be enjoying his selfish pleasures to the full. The house at 115 North Weber began to loom in the imagination as a den of iniquity and vice preposterous as his income. And certainly the number of empty whiskey bottles hauled away lent a credibility to all tales.

Stratton was never seen drunk. He never drank in public. But alone, night after night, he lay drinking, modestly at first, then in increasing amounts. The liquor mitigated his troubles, assuaged his worries, lifted for a time the insupportable burden of wealth that was beginning to crush him under its increasing golden flow.

He began to go to Denver and to make his first investments in Colorado property. For his real-estate agent he appointed Thomas Ramsay, the brother of his secretary, William Ramsay.

The first purchase was of the old Toltec Building at Seventeenth and Stout for $265,000.

Then, over a period of time, he bought up others:

The Tabor property at Seventeenth and Broadway for $200,000.

The Cathedral property at Stout and Fifteenth for $175,000.

The lots on the north side of Welton Street opposite the *Rocky Mountain News* plant, costing $285,000.

The Coronado property, costing $125,000, on which he erected the Coronado Building.

These big purchases, together with his frequent trips to Denver and the stories already grown up around him, gave rise to one of the most fantastic of them all. Stratton has hardly been mentioned without it—the one persistent tale told about him that has never been refuted.

One of the most popular Colorado journalists, in his book, puts it thus:

> . . . Winfield Scott Stratton, an ex-carpenter who could hardly read or write—the same dashing fellow who once tried to register with a blond lady at the fashionable Brown Palace Hotel and when refused, went out, bought the hotel for $800,000 cash, returned to the lobby, fired the clerk and moved into the bridal suite.

Another journalist-biographer writing that Stratton "gave his wife $500,000, and she closed up her boarding-house and sailed for Europe to enjoy herself," repeats the story with the added trimming that it was the manager he threw out.

Still another version shows Stratton dropping bottles of champagne upon the floor of the lobby several stories below his room, and buying the hotel for $1,000,000 when he was made to stop.

None of these colorful versions are true. Stratton personally never owned the Brown Palace Hotel. As a matter of fact, Maxey Tabor, the son of old H. A. W. Tabor by his first wife, was leasing the hotel and continued to be the tenant until long after Stratton was dead, so it would have been impossible for Stratton to have fired the clerk and ousted the manager.

As in most tall stories, there is a common basis to these; they apparently derive from a statement given the State Historical Society by Horace Bennett, the Denver real-estate agent (the same Bennett of the Bennett and Myers firm which had bought the Broken Box Ranch on which Cripple Creek grew into a town). His story is no less interesting:

Stratton, according to Bennett, was asked by Maxey Tabor, for some colorful reason, to move out of the presidential suite at the Brown Palace. In a huff, and without waiting for breakfast, Stratton walked up Seventeenth Street looking for a suitable corner on which to build a better hotel. At Welton he saw some corner lots, occupied by a single building, that seemed to suit his purpose.

Stratton entered the building, ascertained that it belonged to a Mrs. Reithman, and requested an interview. She entered the room with a grim visage.

"How much do you want for this corner?" asked Stratton.

"Fifty thousand dollars," Mrs. Reithman replied, placing the ante high so that she would not have to scale it down too low.

Stratton yanked out his check-book, wrote and thrust a check for the amount into the astonished woman's hand. "Take the abstract to my attorney, Tyson Dines. He will make out the necessary papers."

He then walked into the plumbing shop of W. T. Crean who owned the vacant lots. "What do you want for those lots?" he asked, pointing out the window.

"They are not for sale," replied Crean. "I paid $20,000 for them but I have my business here. This place will keep me for the rest of my life and I'm satisfied."

"You'd sell if you got your price, wouldn't you?"

"No. Not even to that damned fool Stratton!"

Stratton smiled for the first time that morning. Upstairs in their living quarters over the plumbing shop Mrs. Crean was cooking breakfast. A tantalizing odor of sausage, buckwheat cakes and coffee floated downstairs. His drawn face lighted; he sank into a chair. At this moment Crean's little girl, about ten years old, skipped down the stairs, pausing as she saw a stranger.

Stratton smiled and beckoned. She advanced shyly, but the millionaire, now melted into a gentler mood through his olfactory nerves, lifted her to his knee, patted her and gave her a ten-dollar bill. Excited, she flew upstairs.

A moment later Crean's little boy came down. The same transaction was repeated; he too scampered upstairs to show his mother a ten-dollar bill. Mrs. Crean could no longer control her curiosity. She descended for a look at the Santa Claus, then invited him up to breakfast with them.

"You bet I will," was Stratton's whole-hearted response.

After eating heartily, he leaned back and said to Crean: "Now, see here. I've taken a fancy to those lots. I'll give you $50,000 for them."

"Well!" snorted Crean. "If you're fool enough to pay that for them I'm not fool enough to turn it down." And for the first time remembering he had not heard the stranger's name, he asked.

"Oh," his guest answered lightly, "I'm just that damned fool Stratton."

Such a hearty breakfast of buckwheat cakes and sausage had mellowed Stratton's vindictive mood. He lost interest in his plan of annihilating the Brown Palace and its staff, but bought it later when the opportunity presented itself.

It is a pretty story, quite worthy of Bennett who so often declared himself the "Father of Cripple Creek"—as have a dozen others.

The unromantic but interesting facts regarding Stratton and the Brown Palace are these:

Henry C. Brown, the owner, was an old man who had come to Colorado in the early days of the gold rush and had taken up land near Denver. For years he tried to get rid of it but couldn't. Then, as the city grew, his land became the beautiful and fashionable Capitol Hill district. Brown became immensely rich; it was said that he built the Brown Palace out of his income alone.

Then, with the panic and hard times, he lost practically everything. Through his son, James H. Brown, he appealed to Stratton for help. Stratton jumped to his aid with his ever ready check-book.

In order to give the Brown family a chance to sell the hotel without losing it on foreclosure, Stratton purchased a mortgage upon the hotel from the Equitable Life Insurance Company for approximately $650,000—principal and accumulated interest. This successfully forestalled the many judgment creditors. It was agreed that thereafter Stratton should foreclose the mortgage and thus wipe out the judgment creditors.

This foreclosure was finally consummated in 1908 after both Stratton and Henry C. Brown had died, at which time the Stratton estate paid the Brown heirs $75,000 for a release from their right to purchase under Stratton's agreement and to have immediate possession of the hotel.

At the time, *Facts* had this to say about the transaction:

I notice the Denver papers are announcing that Winfield Scott Stratton has saved to the Henry C. Brown estate the famous hotel. That is, he steps in and takes the mortgages and says that without Mr. Brown's consent the building shall not pass from him. That is just like Stratton. What a Good Fairy Bountiful he has been to the former rich of Colorado! The best of it is he is not likely to follow their example. I challenge anybody to show me a business mistake that Mr. Stratton has made since he got his fortune. . . . He is no Tabor, I can tell you, although he is a richer man than that bonanza king ever was. In fact he is brainier than any man who has ever made one of those immense fortunes in this State. To my knowledge he gave Tabor large sums of money for mining purposes just before he died. Henry C. Brown is very old. . . . He can die now in the big palace that bears his name, for Stratton will permit it.

The writer, like the ex-carpenter, had hit the nail on the head for both counts. Stratton had again proved the kind philanthropist—and he meant to make it a business proposition.

He purchased the ground across the street, planning to erect on it an auditorium capable of seating approximately seven thousand. Next, he planned an annex to the Brown Palace. The two buildings he anticipated connecting by a tunnel running under Broadway, a plan practically analogous to one now in operation in Chicago.

It was never to be realized.

Something else was in the wind that was to take his time and interest.

4

By the end of 1898 Cripple Creek was conceded its place as "the greatest gold camp on earth." In less than seven years since its discovery the "$200,000 cow pasture" had yielded $90,300,112; in the year just passed it had produced nearly $15,000,000.

Its only rival was the Transvaal of South Africa, and in the opinion of Sir Morton Frewer, the English bimetallist, Cripple Creek was destined to surpass the production of the Witwatersrandt gold field near Johannesburg. He was right; already the Boers were giving trouble; and with the outbreak of the South African war, Cripple Creek was to lead the world in gold production.

It was still an enigma to geologists and mining engineers. The ore was simply mineralized country rock, ore and waste being hardly distinguishable. One of the first carloads of ore which Stratton had sent to a Denver smelter had been held as waste, the officials believing that a load of ballast had been shipped by mistake. And except for the theory of the ancient Pike's Peak volcano, no one could account for the fact that the gold producing area was limited to only six square miles.

Too, there had always been difficulty in reducing ore. The traditional stamp-mill was little good: as soon as the oxidized surface mineral gave way to unoxidized vein-filling, the percentage of gold saved was too low to be profitable. The ore differed from that of other districts, said Dr. Richard Pearce, who was recognized as one of the foremost metallurgists and geologists, being "in general a telluride; and while it is found in Transylvania and in other portions of this State it is in small deposits, but in Cripple Creek it occurs on an enormous scale and in a wide area."

For a time high grade ore was shipped to the lead smelters at Pueblo and Denver, while the medium was treated in the chlorination plants at Gillette and Florence. Ore containing less than one ounce of gold to the ton left no profit to the Cripple Creek miners. But now a new process of ore reduction, using cyanide instead of chlorine as the solvent for gold, was allowing one-half ounce ore to give a margin of profit. New mills were springing up in Colorado City and Florence; a flag-station on the Florence and Cripple Creek railroad was named Cyanide; and Cripple Creek was given a new impetus.

News of the camp had spread round the world; as Little London had drawn English tourists, so now did Cripple Creek draw English capitalists and promoters. Lombard Street, London, was evincing as much interest in this remote camp high in the Rockies as Wall Street, New York. From everywhere came mining men, promoters, capitalists and journalists: a special correspondent from the *London Financial News;* men with millions to invest from Paris and Brussels; Edouard Cumenge, Ingenieur et Chef Honoraire des Mines; Le Baron de Bellescize; John Hays Hammond, director of operations of the South African mines for Cecil Rhodes and one of the greatest mining engineers in the world.

All were avid to sound out properties, to take options, to form new companies.

Cripple Creek alfalfa miners squatted on their dumps and grinned. One of them had visited London, intending to sell his mine. He stayed a week: the prospective buyers wanted 40 percent profit. The rest of them echoed his sentiments, "that to call a London promoter a hog was an insult to the swine family!"

And when a top-hatted promoter requested an option on

the mine of its Hibernian owner, this wary individual spit over his shoulder and answered with the classic phrase, "Jawbone don't go; pull yer wad or git aff the dump!"

The astounding richness of the camp held strangers spellbound as they read reports and listened to the tales of its mines. Why, the Portland alone had paid $2,539,000 in dividends, and the regular dividends now declared were 24 percent on the value of the stock!

Of all these great producers, these mineral bank vaults sunk in the gulches and on the hills, the Independence was the greatest. It now embraced fourteen claims, a compact body covering an area of one hundred and ten acres. Its underground workings aggregated more than six and one-half miles, and less than 25 percent of this territory had been explored. The principal veins were so rich that they had been named like other complete mines: the Independence, the original vein; the Bobtail; and the Emerson. There had been mined 41,694 tons, but less than two-thirds of this had been stoped, that is, actually mined and not merely removed as the drifts were cut. The average ore yield was 4.6 ounces or $92 per ton. And of $4,000,000, $3,000,000 was clear net profit.

Such were the meager details, for Stratton still maintained his policy of secrecy and dipped in his famous Bull Pen Stope only when he needed cash. His men were well rewarded. Steele, his mine superintendent, had accidentally shot himself to death. Stratton found out that he had been supporting aged parents. He immediately bought a home for them in Colorado Springs and gave them twenty-five thousand shares of Portland stock whose dividends allowed them to live in comfort.

But now for some reason, Stratton broke his silence. He allowed a paper on the Independence to be read before a special meeting of the Colorado Scientific Society. It stated in part:

The Independence is today the most noteworthy gold mine of the Western Hemisphere if not of the world. It is a phenomenon, and the plain, hard, unadorned facts told of its resources sound like Munchausen tales. There appear to be no boundaries to the pay ore below 300 feet, as no matter where the drifts are run, whether in eruptive rock or granite, they tell the same story of gold, gold, and still more gold everywhere. The vein is unique and there is nothing known in the way of valuable ore masses with which to compare it. Now in granite, now in porphyry; the best idea is perhaps conveyed by saying that it is in the uncertain area dividing the two formations—porphyry to the north and granite to the south—one mingling with the other, tying the country rock all up in a tangled snarl. . . .

The main shaft is sunk to a depth of 415 feet, and the 400-foot level is the scene of the most extensive exploitation, drifts being run by the aid of power drills on a systematic plan to thoroughly test the ground. In the 300-foot level the first marvelous gold depository was exposed. Here was found a chamber from eight to thirty feet wide, of sylvanite that runs from $250 to thousands a ton. For two months the average ore shipped without sorting returned over $400 a ton. During the first four months of this present year, more than $650,000 was produced, and prior to January first the yield, all told, while the mine was being opened up, exceeded $1,500,000. At present the sole owner, W. S. Stratton, has curtailed the Independence income to $120,000 a month and hopes to be able to still further reduce it, as more wealth is coming from this rockbound safe depository than he has any earthly use for. On a most conservative basis it has been calculated that there are gold reserves blocked out of $2,500,000 and, in addition, exploitation in all directions is daily augmenting this total.

The Original Antlers Hotel.

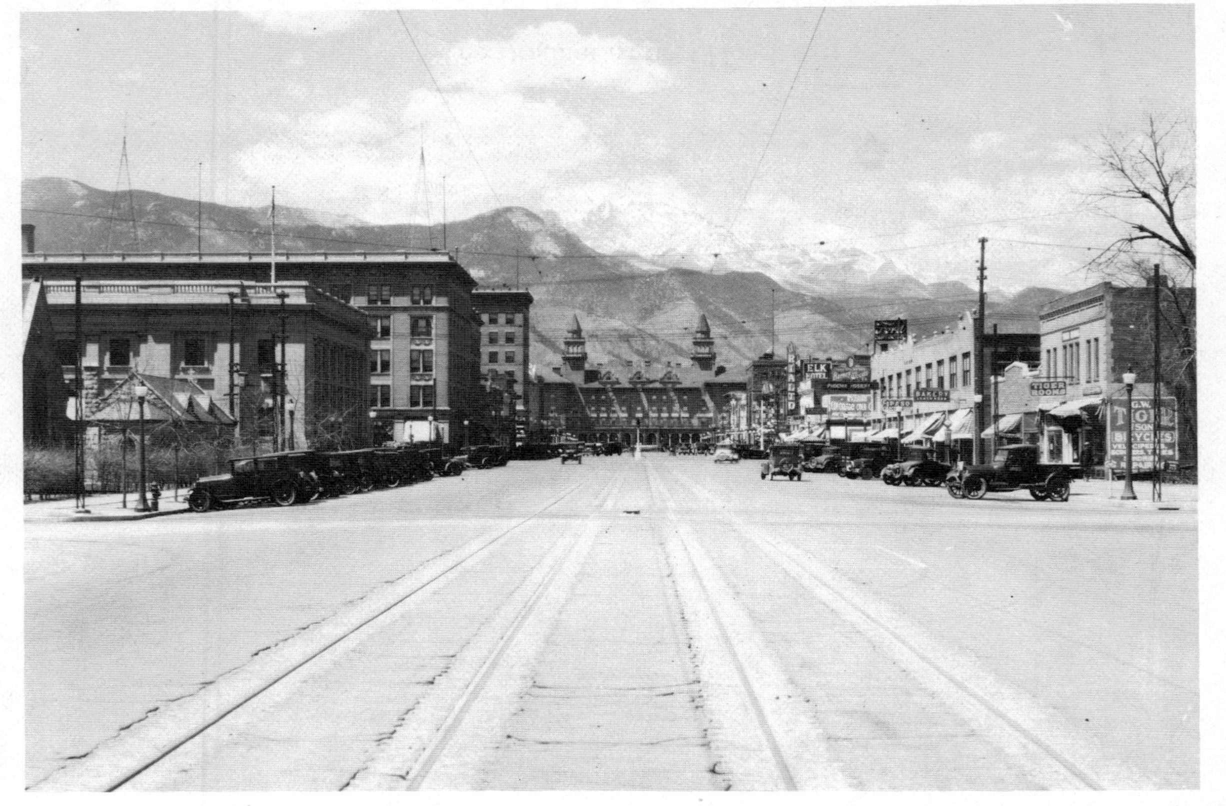

The second Antlers Hotel (Courtesy Stewart's Commercial Photographers, Colorado Springs).

This report coming from a member of the Colorado Scientific Society and American Institute of Mechanical Engineers, a civil and mining engineer, U. S. Department of Mining surveyor, and a consulting engineer, was regarded as most conservative.

But the figures were for 1895. The main shaft was no longer 415 feet deep; it was down 920 feet and the other 625 feet, the two connected at the fifth level (500 feet).

Then Stratton allowed a few visitors in the mine. All were amazed. Hamilton Smith, the eminent English mining expert and agent of the Mining Exploration Company of London, who had been visiting the principal mines of the world, came up the shaft saying, "I never saw a better managed mine than the Independence."

Other reports spread. The Independence was the marvel of the mining world. And Stratton's foresight was as good as his hindsight; he was always different.

Naturally, with all the other mine-owners, he was cautiously approached to find out if he would sell his dream mine. The care and trouble of operating it, they urged, would make him an old man before his time; and indeed he looked ten years older than his age.

Stratton was indignant. "I will not sell my property. I am getting too old to be troubled with a big pile of money. I would have to invest it in real estate and such kind of security. I don't want to be bothered that way. Now, at any time I want, I can take out a few thousand dollars. All I have to do is put a few miners in a stope to break the ore and ship it to a mill."

But meanwhile an energetic young man was busying himself with preparations to make Stratton change his mind.

5

Verner Zevola Reed, author of "Lo-To-Kah the Uncivilized" in the *Great Divide*, issue of 1893, had definitely given up the difficult labor of juggling adjectives for the easier pastime of juggling millions. His transition from author to financier was a gradual one, and his results certainly pointed the moral.

Reed was thirty-five years old. He had been born on a farm in Richland, Ohio, grown up in the farming region of Iowa, and had come to Colorado at the age of twenty-two. For a time he sold lots down along the Fontaine-qui-Bouille for seventy-five dollars at a 10 percent commission. Then he originated the idea of erecting houses in Little London for sale on the installment plan. After selling fifty, he incorporated his holdings as the Reed Building Company.

When Cripple Creek made "its meteoric epiphany into the mining firmament," Reed joined the rush and located the Little Mildred. A short time was enough to convince him there were easier ways to get rich than picking into hard granite; he became a promoter.

His first success came with the Portland Consolidation whereby, during the litigation confronting the "Three Jims," seventeen properties were sold to the Portland Gold Mining Company—the largest transaction till then made in Cripple Creek. Reed got busy with C. C. Hamlin, a member of the law firm of Gunnell and Hamlin which had handled the Portland litigation. The two men formed the Reed and Hamlin Investment Company. Reed's personal secretary was O. H. Shoup, later admitted as a partner, and still later elected as Governor of Colorado.

The firm was immediately successful. They consolidated the Moon Anchor, the Robert Burns and the Champion Consolidated. Little by little they spread out, promoting mines, selling stocks and acting as financial agents for Cripple Creek properties. On the Exchange they made a record sale of one hundred thousand shares of the Portland for two dollars a share. With the sudden interest of Lombard Street, London, in Cripple Creek, Reed suddenly blossomed out; he too established an office at 58 Lombard Street in London. From here he extended operations into England and Scotland, and made frequent trips to Ireland and Germany, finally opening an agency at Arbroath, Scotland—attesting the interest of the world in getting rich from Cripple Creek gold.

"Lo-To-Kah the Uncivilized" and other poor ignorant Indians of the West were forgotten; the top-hatted savages of European stockmarkets were even more ruthless and uncivilized. Reed was now ready for his biggest coup.

Hamlin and the "Three Jims" were not the only men of prominence Reed had met during the Portland deal. He had become acquainted with Stratton himself. He had met Isaac Untermeyer of New York, and had established connections with many London firms including the Venture Corporation. All these he now figuratively took by the scalp-locks and began whetting his tomahawk.

From Stratton, who had always refused to discuss the sale of the Independence, Reed managed to obtain an option on the mine. With this he went to London. Within a few weeks he was back. This time he took Stratton's secretary, William A. Ramsay, with him.

Meanwhile, Stratton was busy at home. One of Eliza's Negro girl helpers got married, and Eliza was also intending to leave his employ for a husband. Stratton abruptly decided to get rid of the third and to employ white help.

It was a propitious time: he had finally located Anna

Hellmark in Denver and persuaded her to return as his housekeeper.

He and the Negro girls parted the best of friends. Eliza had her cherished leather pillow and her easy-chair. To each of them he gave a number of mining shares, and said that he had made provision for them in his will. Eliza had always cast a fond eye at the heavy green and silver window drapes, and Stratton, suspecting as much, ordered her to tear them down and take them for her new house. And now, on a sudden impulse to give the two brides a wedding present, he gruffly demanded that they divide all the table silver between them; he needed new silver anyway. So today, forty years later, one still sees in an old Negro woman's house Stratton's easy-chair, a cut-glass vase, his silver, his brocaded drapes and a heavy leather pillow from which a painted buffalo bull has long faded.

Using this as an excuse, Stratton celebrated Anna's homecoming with new silver. He also began to figure on some slight improvements on the house. They were suddenly interrupted by a cablegram from London.

So early in March, 1899, Stratton and his physician followed Reed and Ramsay to London. Stratton's health had been breaking steadily through strain, worry, work and drinking. A physician was needed at all times, and he had persuaded Dr. D. H. Rice to give up his general practice to attend him. Little London and Colorado generally were dumbfounded to hear that Stratton had at last crawled out of his shell at 115 North Weber. The reason for his leaving was thus ascribed:

> Stratton is tired of being a millionaire. He is leaving Colorado where he gained his wealth. Practically, he is running away from his money and what it brings. It is driving him

from one of his two great interests in life—his mine. In New York or London where millionaires are common enough to excite no remark, he will devote himself to his other hobby—the relief of poverty.

Thus, for the third and last time in his life, Stratton left the mountains of Colorado that had drawn him across the plains almost thirty years before. . . .

He had scarcely been gone a month when Anna Hellmark, his Swedish caretaker left alone in the house, dreamed a peculiar dream: Stratton was lying in bed, white-faced, thin and weak. She rushed to him and sank down on her knees beside the bed. Stratton struggled up, reached out both arms to put round her neck and collapsed upon her shoulder. The weight on her was so great that she was almost borne to the floor. Panting and perspiring, almost exhausted, Anna awoke.

Stratton in England had taken seriously ill.

For days he lay in a hazy coma between life and death. When it appeared he might recover, he was rushed under the care of specialists to the Hotel Metropole, Brighton, on the south coast of England. Then again he was moved to the south of France, at Aix-les-Bains, and again to Carlsbad. Although he gradually improved in health, he was never able to travel about normally while abroad. He had to be carried in and out of his hotel to his carriage for his daily outing, and he never allowed anyone to lift him but Ramsay, who was as much a friend as a business associate. Indeed, Stratton had trusted Ramsay with the entire care of his business and the disbursement of all charitable donations.

Stratton, slowly recovering, lay staring out of the window. The Mediterranean was blue as the Colorado Rockies, the white villas on the hillsides shone bright as snowcaps on the peaks at home. Home! Everything reminded him of home. And then one day something happened as inexplicable as his discovery of the Independence. He had another vision—a vision of what he should do with the vast wealth derived from the inspiration of the former. This time he kept the vision secret; he had long tired of hearing the Independence referred to jocularly as his "dream-mine."

But whatever it was—dream, vision or imaginative fancy—the sudden intuitive revelation was profoundly disturbing. It roused him from the haze of what was almost his death-bed to a clear objective contemplation of himself. In a flash he saw combined in one project his power as the richest mining king of the Rockies and his deep-rooted philanthropical urge to help the unfortunate and needy.

Stratton's wealth at this time was unknown, so secretive was he regarding his dream-mine. It has been estimated that from the Independence alone he had taken about four million dollars. It was probably more, considering his many unknown gifts and investments. But in addition he owned sixteen more mines, his great block of Portland stock worth probably three million dollars, and a vast amount invested in mills and smelters. Whatever the amount, the project revealed in the vision would require more.

He decided to sell the Independence.

John Hays Hammond, the eminent mining engineer who had come from the Transvaal, South Africa, gives in his autobiography the following version of the sale:

> I was asked to make an examination of a mine at Cripple Creek, Colorado, known as Stratton's Independence. This was at the time the greatest gold producer in that famous district.
>
> Its original owner, William S. Stratton, had started out as a carpenter, but he was ambitious and in his spare time took

lessons in assaying. Then he attempted prospecting on his own and discovered the Independence Mine.

The Venture Corporation had been trying to find outlets for its surplus money, and Stratton was now approached and asked how much he would take for his mine. It had not previously occurred to him to sell, but he realized from the eagerness of their representatives that the highly favorable report submitted by T. A. Rickard had made the Venture Corporation exceedingly anxious to buy.

Stratton was invited to come to London at the Company's expense to meet the board of directors. He proved no more tractable in England than in the States. As a last resort, it was decided to give him a banquet. At the appearance of the first course, they offered him five million dollars for his mine. He promptly turned it down.

As the dinner proceeded, the price rose to five and one-half millions. Stratton showed some sign of interest, but was still unwilling. When the figure reached six millions, his eyes opened wider and he began to pinch himself. But his head had started wagging in the negative and he could not seem to stop it.

Except for the price, the contract was ready for his signature. At six and one-half million the pen was placed in his hand. But he said he liked his mine; he couldn't bear to part with it.

In desperation seven and a half million was written in and his fingers were firmly closed around the pen. Still unable to believe his eyes, he affixed his signature.

On such an authority, other writers have embroidered the tale to relate how Stratton was offered $5,000,000 when the soup was served, $5,500,000 with the fish, until, when the liqueurs were served, he was given $7,500,000.

But Stratton, recovering from an almost fatal illness, was in no mood for such a banquet. The price of seven and a half millions is erroneous as his name of "William." And as a matter of fact, he did not sell his mine to the Venture Corporation at all, nor in point of law obtain a nickel for it from anyone.

Stratton's Independence transaction was perhaps the biggest American mining deal ever made. As such, it involved complications more interesting than the wild tale above. It was to give headaches not only to the eminent John Hays Hammond—to whom it was always a sore-spot for reasons to follow—but to some of the greatest minds then known.

While Stratton was lying ill, V. Z. Reed and Ramsay had been busy. Reed was a shrewd man. That he had been able to wheedle an option on the Independence out of Stratton who for years had refused to consider selling his mine attests his salesmanship. He had the financial connections, the option on the mine; he had begun to round up the biggest London capitalists to hear him. There was only one thing needed: the assurance that once a deal was lined up, Stratton would not kick over the traces with the old familiar assertion that he never intended to part with his mine.

And then Stratton had his vision; he wanted to sell his Independence. Jubilantly, Reed hurried back to London. With him went Ramsay carrying full power of attorney for convalescent Stratton.

A tentative plan of sale was arranged. But first the interested London capitalists wanted the opinion of one of the world's most renowned mining engineers.

John Hays Hammond was selected and sent to make an examination of the property. He says:

The manager of the Independence was ill when I arrived at the mine, and the foreman accompanied me on my tour. Although the foreman had known me by reputation and realized I was not easily to be deceived, he suggested that we begin our examination on the upper levels from which the pay ore was being taken. I suspect that he hoped I would devote most of my time to examining that part of the mine. I simply remarked that as the future of the property depended upon the value of the ore found in the deepest workings, I had better start my inspection at the bottom of the shaft.

When we reached the lower levels the character of the development work showed me at once that the grade and amount of ore had fallen off. The foreman admitted that the recent developments in depth had not been encouraging. In order to confirm my conclusion, I sent engineers to sample the mine. Their report convinced me that the estimates made by Rickard and his associate engineers had been altogether too favorable.

In fact, Hammond believed that the rich ore bodies had petered out.

Reed and Ramsay were dumbfounded. Reed particularly; he saw go glimmering the fortune that he himself expected to make by selling his option on the mine. He had insisted that the Independence back in Cripple Creek undergo a thorough probing. For this he had sent T. A. Rickard, State Geologist of Colorado, to appraise the mine.

Rickard and four associates spent six weeks making their report. The Independence, it will be remembered, had six and a half miles of underground workings. They took a sample across the vein every ten feet—a total of 2,016 assays. They divided the mine into twenty-eight blocks and took 1,008 assays along the lodes averaging thirty pounds in weight. The 2,016 assays averaged four and three-quarter ounces of gold per ton. Rickard reported that there were seventy thousand tons of ore in sight with a gross value of $6,712,000 at an estimated net profit of 65 percent. He further stated that he believed $8,000,000 could be extracted.

On the basis of this report the London capitalists accepted—for the present—Rickard's opinion instead of Hammond's. And Reed drew up papers for the largest flotation of a gold mine ever launched on the London market.

Stratton wasn't satisfied. Ill, cranky, stubborn, he read English and American corporation laws, went over the papers with irritating exactness, and sent them back again and again. Ramsay, in fact, crossed the English Channel seven times during the preliminary negotiations. For Stratton, now that he was selling his dream-mine, was taking no chances. He meant to insure the safety of the proceeds for the project revealed to him in the vision.

It was as if he had foreseen the trouble to follow; for so water-tight was the complicated transaction, and with such uncanny shrewdness did he engineer it, that it was to withstand the best efforts of the finest legal minds on both sides of the Atlantic to break it.

The deal, with many ramifications, was briefly this:

Stratton did not sell his mine outright. A new English corporation was formed, Stratton's Independence, Limited, for the purpose of purchasing Stratton's Independence mine, embracing 110 acres and 16 other claims, including the Professor Lamb. As the Independence had exposed and in sight ore bodies worth almost $7,000,000 it was agreed to be reasonably worth $10,000,000.

This contract was entered into with George Butcher of London who was acting in behalf of the company. The company was incorporated with a capital stock of £1,100,000 sterling to buy and work the property. The one hundred thousand shares of one pound each were to be reserved for working capital; the one million shares were to be paid Stratton. Such a transaction was perfectly legal under the laws of both England and America—each permitting the issuance of capital stock in exchange for property conveyed to a corporation.

Stratton was one of the promoters and incorporators. As such, he invested not quite $5 cash, for each of the seven incorporators subscribed to but one share of stock at its par value of £1 to comply with the laws of the Kingdom of Great Britain.

But how was Stratton to get his money?

He was selling his mine. Once rid of it, he didn't intend to be bothered with its working even on the financial end of the transaction. Stratton, in short, arranged most cannily to clear his coat-tails of all entanglements and pocket his money without a chance of a come-back.

He authorized Reed and Ramsay to draw up another agreement with a second company: the Venture Corporation of London. This provided that Stratton was to deliver his one million shares to the Venture Corporation which undertook to sell them on the London market.

On the first 666,666 shares Stratton was to be paid £1.19 per share; for the remaining 333,333 shares he was to receive £2.10 apiece—a total of approximately $10,000,000.

And Reed, who had engineered the deal, was to be paid as a commission by the Venture Corporation $1,000,000 for his option—a fair sized jump from his first $7.50 commission on his first Fountain lots.

This enormous transaction was tentatively approved by both parties.

On April 10, 1899, Stratton's health had recovered sufficiently so that he could leave the baths at the resorts of Southern France and return to England to approve the negotiations.

That same morning, at nine-thirty o'clock, in faraway

London, June 7-1899
This is to certify that I have this day received from C J Hambro & Son of London One Thousand Certificates of One Thousand shares each, being a total of One Million (1,000 000) shares of the Capital Stock of Strattons Independence Limited, the said stock being that certain Lot of shares deposited with the said C J Hambro & Son by the said Stratton's Independence Limited for delivery to me on my fulfilment of instructions given to the said C J Hambro & Son by the said Strattons' Independance Limited

Winfield Scott Stratton
by. William Allan Ramsay.
Attorney

Stratton's receipt for $10,000,000.00 signed by William Allan Ramsey (Courtesy Mrs. Addie A. Ramsay).

Denver, a poverty-stricken old man at last slipped the tether of his troubles. It was H. A. W. Tabor.

Ten days later in Little London, the *Gazette* received a cable from Reed in London and came out with the headlines:

STRATTON INDEPENDENCE SOLD FOR $10,000,000

Cable to Gazette Positively Announces Consummation of the Big Deal

Biggest American Mining Deal Ever Made.

On April 27th, Stratton signed the contract with George Butcher in London, and on April 29th Stratton's Independence, Limited, was created a corporation under the laws of England.

Stratton, despite all the rumors and his illness, had sold his dream-mine and was now the most fabulously rich mining man that the Colorado Rockies had ever produced.

What, sighed everyone at home, would the man do now?

6

He cabled for Schwarz.

The faithful and worried shoemaker vice-president stuffed his carpet bag and caught the first available ship to London. There he presented himself at Stratton's hotel and was shown up to Stratton's room.

"Vell! Vat the hell do you vant now?" he exploded gruffly.

Stratton looked up and smiled. He was pale and so thin his clothes hung on him as though on a cross of sticks.

"Well, Bob, I was just thinking you haven't seen your sister in years and years. Have you?"

Schwarz nodded. Emigrating from Switzerland to America at the age of seventeen, he had kept drifting west and finally settling in Colorado to work at his trade of shoecobbler.

"Well, let's go see her."

First they returned to Carlsbad, the water and baths seeming to help Stratton. Then they went to Vienna and Paris. Stratton was still an invalid: he had sugar diabetes, liver trouble and every stomach disorder, said Bob, that the doctor knew of. And then they went to Schwarz' sister in Constance, Switzerland. They found her living in the basement of the Court House; her husband was a petty, underpaid official. Whereupon Stratton bought her a home and gave her twenty thousand good American dollars. They then returned home, Stratton having been ill three of the six months that he had been abroad.

Back in Colorado, Stratton went directly to the Brown Palace Hotel in Denver for several weeks while his home was being cleaned and slightly remodeled. Every few days he called Anna by telephone to remind her she was not to let anyone in the house—particularly his son, Isaac Henry Stratton, if he happened to show up.

Then, late in August, he made his second triumphal entry into Little London. It was even more quiet and secretive than the first. He arrived at night, fled home in a closed carriage and shut himself in against all callers.

Meanwhile things in London were happening fast. The Venture Corporation and Stratton's Independence, Limited, were making the most of the new deal. There was to be a Greater Britain Exhibit in London under royal patronage. The great mining exhibit of the empire was the chief attraction. It was to be held in the spacious grounds of Earl's Court, London. For five months ore exhibits from English mines all over the world were to be on display. The Venture Corporation was to pay all expenses; the directors agreed it was worth the money as their opening advertising campaign. Already exhibits had been received from Canada, Australia and South Africa. The time was extended so that the famous Cripple Creek display could be shown. Ten tons of ore were sent from the greatest mines of the district, and Claude Sachs, a Colorado Springs man, was made honorary secretary of the Colorado exhibit.

With this under way, the Venture Corporation launched Stratton's Independence, Limited, stock on the Exchange. On May 3, 1899, the *London Daily Financial Times* announced that the capital stock of 1,100,000 shares were offered for sale for twice their par value of one pound and that only 25 percent of the mine's great acreage had been explored by underground workings. And on August 31st, Frederick W. Baker, managing director of the Venture Corporation, 3 Princes Street, London, wrote to V. Z. Reed in Colorado Springs:

> The sale of shares is going on quietly and you will presently be receiving another remittance. The reports continue to be very satisfactory, and from what one can see we shall have opened out this year sufficient new ore to enable us to pay £400,000 in dividends without touching the reserves defined by Mr. Rickard in his original report. . . . The Transvaal affair has rather upset our business but I am hoping this will blow over within the next fortnight. . . . As things look now it seems to me that you will be making as much or more than the Venture Corporation itself. . . .

"Was this fair?" they asked him.

Reed sat back and smiled. So did Stratton. Whatever happened they had the best of the bargain.

And things did happen, with a speed that made them all dizzy.

John Hays Hammond was still growling. The Venture Corporation, optimistic over the Independence, had sent him to appraise Walsh's Camp Bird near Ouray, Colorado. He found that a favorable report had already been made by T. A. Rickard and F. W. Bradley—"who in spite of experience and reputation seem to have lacked the proper qualifications for evaluating mines. Rickard was at the time consulting engineer of the Venture Corporation of London."

Hammond went back to Cripple Creek and the Independence. He now writes:

> When my cabled report was made public in London, there was a crash in the market quotation of the stock. In spite of my unpopularity among those who were gambling in the shares of the Company, the Venture Corporation employed me to replace Rickard as consulting engineer for the Stratton Independent Mine. Under my management the shaft was sunk deeper by several hundred feet, but crosscuts and other exploratory work proved conclusively that the rich ore bodies had petered out.

This was a veritable bomb-shell. Stratton's snubbed and jealous neighbors set up a howl: he had defrauded and hoodwinked the English, had defamed Colorado and made himself more unpopular than ever.

Stratton quietly made one statement. "I was paid $10,000,000 for the mine, but it was more than I ever thought I would get. I thought I would get them to pay me $5,000,000, but they paid $10,000,000. People have said I made them pay me too much, but they paid their own price."

But as yet he had not received all the money. . . .

Then the new owners of the *Denver Post*, Bonfils and

Tammen, eager to boost their circulation by any smelly gos-ip, began to decry the market value of the Independence tock and warn all prospective buyers to beware.

On October 19th, the Venture Corporation wrote Reed rantically:

I daresay you noticed the *Denver Evening Post*, September 5th and the absurd article they had on Stratton. They went o the trouble of sending a copy of this round to all London papers and one or two of them have reproduced it and com-nented on it.

Cannot you manage to stop this sort of thing?

It was only a temporary set-back despite the *Post's* and Hammond's dire predictions; the shares kept selling for the obvious reason that the first buyers were already making money on their investments. And little wonder. The Eng-ishmen, unlike Stratton who had used the Independence as a bank vault, were gutting the mine as fast as they could haul out ore—as high as $500,000 in one month. Little more than a month later, on November 25th, Baker wrote again:

I have written Stratton fully today.

You need have no cause for anxiety whatever about the uccess of the deal. It has caught on thoroughly well now. We have sold between fifty thousand and sixty thousand shares in he last three weeks, but we are considerably hampered over he 60 percent arrangement. . . . Stratton can, over the deal, easily realize £2,000,000 exclusive of his dividends, notwith-tanding his agreement to wave his 60 percent interest over £2.10.0. . . . The reason I have not been able to write Strat-on or Ramsay is that I have been away in Greece. . . . I do not think you need worry about Stratton's getting out of his contract. . . .

Ten days later things were still better. On December 5th, Baker wrote:

> We are selling them [shares] at this moment at the rate of three thousand a day. . . . I have written very fully to Stratton himself, assuring him . . . that the net result of the negotiations will mean him getting at least, with his dividends, £2,500,000. The shares are firm at £3 today and if we could only stop the tape for awhile we could get them higher, but it is no easy thing to lift shares up when there is a constant stream put on the market to satisfy purchasers.

The American issue was launched. On December 9th the Venture Corporation wrote Reed, "We have today received your cable saying that you will take ten thousand shares in the name of Isaac Untermeyer of 30 Broad Street . . . and that Mr. Untermeyer would like one hundred share certificates."

Thus the first year of the deal closed. Stratton's ten to twelve millions were beginning to roll in. And the Independence, despite Hammond's dire predictions, was erupting a steady stream of gold.

One is tempted to guess that for once the great Hammond was put out by a mistake, and that his statement was not the cause for the market crash of the stock. Something else, far greater, was giving trouble: the South African War had started, English troops were being rushed to combat the Boers and the first disheartening reports were turning London heads white.

The Venture Corporation wailed to Reed on January 27, 1900:

> By the end of this month Stratton will have received in dividends and payments from us £970,000, entitling him to receive, after an allowance for difference, up to October 24th, another

£1,030,000, taking the price in sterling. . . . Hambro is negotiating the business with Barings and the Banque de Paris. . . . I think we shall be able to carry the business through, but it will depend to a large extent what the war news is. We began negotiating on fairly favorable news which became better as time went along. Everything now is on the downward track.

. . . One thing is pretty certain: that we have had the worst luck over this deal that ever came to anybody trying to engineer a new scheme, for we have had nothing but Wars, Rumors of Wars, disasters and victories, disasters again, since we took the deal up, but notwithstanding this we find ourselves in a position to give Stratton, with his dividends, £970,000.

He ought to be fairly satisfied with this result having regard to all the circumstances that have affected the matter.

Things did calm down. In 1900, shares of Stratton's Independence, Limited, were selling on the London market again for three pounds and by April 18th more than one half of the stock had been sold—592,000 shares. The Venture Corporation began paying dividends at the rate of £400,000 per year.

Then Stratton reached an agreement whereby he sold the balance of his stock out and out to the Venture Corporation "at such a price as with the cash already received on account of sale of stocks and dividends . . . to make up the total inclusive sum of $10,000,000."

The English company went on gutting the great bonanza. In the first fourteen months ore was mined by them amounting to $3,387,657 with an average value of $71.70 per ton. Their dividends for 1900 amounted to $1,784,000.

By 1908 they had mined $11,049,030 worth of ore.

V. Z. Reed was satisfied. He had put over the deal and made himself a cool million. It was a good start.

For most of the next eight years he lived in France: in

Paris, Nice and an old chateau in the valley of the Loire. He then returned and bought a beautiful seven-hundred-acre ranch near Sheridan, Wyoming. He had a purpose: he had invested in Wyoming oil lands—some of the rich Salt Creek oil fields near Mid West later to be involved in the Teapot Dome trouble. On this he made a real fortune.

And after he died a V. Z. Reed memorial was erected in Mt. Olivet Cemetery, Denver, of Italian Carrara marble 38 feet high, 28 feet long, and 24 feet wide; designed and made in Florence, Italy, by the famous sculptor Raffaello Romanillo. On it was engraved St. Benedict's motto: *Laborare est orare*" ("To labor is to pray")—a last commentary on the author of "Lo-To-Kah the Uncivilized."

But Stratton with a fresh $10,000,000 seemed still restless and unsatisfied. He had a new vision, and developed the two astounding theories that were to make him more famous than ever.

7

But first he had another illness to worry through. He had hardly arrived home before he had to take to bed, doubled up in agony. Nothing would stay on his stomach. All one night Anna rushed back and forth from his bedside with alternate basins into which he vomited continually. She became frightened: it seemed impossible, this violent and prolonged retching.

At last it was over. Stratton sank back exhausted and lay for days in bed. Dr. Rice gave him calomel every fifteen minutes. Stratton was nervous and ice cold all the time. Then gradually he began to drink again, at least three times a day regularly.

He improved in health, but the attack left him more erratic and cranky than ever.

Upon returning home he had given Ramsay $50,000, made arrangements that Anna was to be given $5,000, and made large gifts to all of his employees. As news of these spread around town, following the story of his sale of the Independence for $10,000,000, he was more besieged than ever with countless callers. They flocked in hundreds daily to see him.

Stratton was more stubbornly aloof than before. He positively refused to see anyone. A woman thinking to gain his confidence and a slice of money obtained work in the house with Anna. Stratton became suspicious of her advances. When she entered the room one night, he jumped up, grabbed his revolver and began shooting at the wall above her. The woman left posthaste.

Then he gave Anna strict orders to let no one in to see him. One evening the president of the College rang the bell. He told Anna it was important that he should see Stratton immediately. Anna showed him in and went to tell Stratton. The rumpus and her first scolding from Stratton drove poor Anna to tears. Thereafter she obeyed his orders literally.

Gradually he began to go down to his office for a short time each day. People began to wonder what he was doing. Their suspicions were aroused when they read a notice stating, "Winfield Scott Stratton has purchased the Proper and Accident claims belonging to the Proper Gold Mining Company on Gold Hill. There are about twenty acres and the price was $90,000. Deeds are in the name of Robert Schwarz, a close friend of Stratton's. All of this adjoins a great tract Stratton has secured in that section of camp."

The rumor spread that Stratton was quietly buying up new mines and claims in Cripple Creek at a great rate. And he had just sold out the Independence and his holdings!

A number of prominent men put their heads together and

called at his office. Among them was a well known bank president, a railway magnate, several mining men, minor capitalists and some brokers. They wanted to persuade him to lease out a portion of his new holdings—and to find out what he was doing.

Stratton saw them coming and hastily locked himself in his private office.

At five-thirty, after four hours of sitting in his outer reception room, the committee was still waiting. Stratton was too busy to see them. The committee was not to be put off; as men of affairs they had often found it expedient to be "too busy" themselves to lesser satellites. They posted a man down the hall to keep vigil lest Stratton try to escape by the back door.

Stratton peeked out the window at the fellow patrolling the hall. He was irritable and wanted to go home. At six o'clock he thought of a way out. He quietly opened his window and crawled out upon the tin roof of the one-story building behind the *Evening Telegraph* composing room. Then the bonanza king pounded away at the window, demanding admittance to the editorial rooms. As he crawled in, jumped to the floor and strode to the front door, he shouted jubilantly, "I fooled them that time, didn't I!"

Thus rebuffed at his home and at his office, enraged at a man who had come home from Europe with $10,000,000 and still persisted in minding his own business and living in his ramshackle unpretentious home, Little London wrought herself up into a fine frenzy over Stratton, who hardly seemed to notice the town.

Townspeople began to remember and repeat old stories about him—particularly of his quick temper. They recalled that early in the eighties he had fired a revolver at a man in the obscure lodging-house where he was living. It was repeated that the sheriff had to walk up the stairway of his home in face of a rifle and take it away during one of Stratton's tempers. They recalled his affair with Zeurah Stewart, his attempted attack on the reporter while riding down on the train from Cripple Creek.

The stories gained credence as passers-by at night heard shots being fired in his house; Stratton was practicing revolver shooting upstairs. In one instance at least he did cause concern. He had been drinking more than usual, and when Anna went up to persuade him to go to bed, he grabbed his revolver and waved it at her. It was the only time in her life that she was ever afraid of Stratton. She turned and walked out of the room. The next morning she did not go to his room as usual, but stayed in the kitchen. After almost an hour Stratton came down, said nothing and helped her set the breakfast table.

But still he continued his never ending philanthropy.

He had heard of Tabor's death. And now he heard strange stories of Mrs. Tabor, the broken and penniless widow wandering the Denver alleys with a bread bag under her old-fashioned cape. "Hang on to the Matchless." How often had Tabor repeated that phrase so symbolic of his undying hope!

Mrs. Tabor had made it her life credo, fighting to hang on to that worthless, water-filled old mine against the time when silver should again come into its own. Now she was at the end of her rope: the Matchless had been in litigation and she was about to lose it. It had been sold for $15,000 to satisfy a judgment, and the time for redeeming it had almost expired.

Then something happened. One June afternoon Mrs. Tabor arrived in Leadville. Her mission was a secret, she said, and would make no statement. The old-timers could only watch to see what she did.

She was met at the train by Stratton's former manager of the Independence. They went to the Matchless and spent two hours examining the old mine.

Days later the news got out. Stratton had hired him to make a thorough examination and report on the Matchless, and to manage it for Mrs. Tabor. He had then wiped out all claims against it and secured the title in her name.

It was not long before Stratton received the following letter from the loyal employees of the unfortunate Postmaster Tabor:

Dear Sir: Your generous, timely and financial aid so unselfishly rendered Mrs. H. A. W. Tabor, the noble wife of our late postmaster, the Hon. H. A. W. Tabor, which enables her to retain at least a portion of the vast fortune formerly possessed by her husband, appeals to us as a noble, manly act, which deserves this expression of gratitude and hearty approval of the undersigned letter-carriers and clerks of the Denver postoffice.

The Denver Letter Carriers' Association—Branch 47
The Denver Postoffice Clerks' Association—Branch 46

And to a man the thousands of Cripple Creek miners, erstwhile Aspenites and citizens of Leadville, concurred in similar resolutions published in the *Cripple Creek Morning Times-Citizen.* None of them guessed that within a year they would be passing resolutions against him to a different tune.

The Matchless was never again to produce. It was to lie up Fryer's Hill, its shafthouse crumbling, its workings filling with water—one of the most famous ghost-mines of the Colorado Rockies. But by saving it for Mrs. Tabor, Stratton had maintained her faith in a vanished ideal. For almost thirty-five years she was to cling to it with Tabor's last cry of "Hang on to the Matchless!" ringing in her ears; she was to live there in cold and poverty in its tool shanty; and to die there alone and lonely, forgotten, hungry and frozen to death.

Yes! Stratton was back—with all his foibles, his follies and unbounded generosity. And he had begun to work out the details of his new vision and his two astounding theories at last.

PART FIVE: CRIPPLE CREEK AGAIN

"Gold is worth more in the ground than out of it."

5. CRIPPLE CREEK AGAIN

STRATTON'S first theory was mild enough, but it roused Little London to incredulous amazement.

For years people had been wondering how and when Stratton was going to kick loose and spend the vast amount of gold pouring into his lap. Now with a lump sum of ten million dollars added to his already great fortune, he excited new conjectures and speculations. He had not aped Tabor and the dozens of Cripple Creek millionaires who bought knick-knacks, jewelry and showy estates in town. Nor had he, like Walsh who had just been making his fling, rushed to "do the Continent" in regal style. What in the name of heaven was he going to do!

Stratton quietly stated his belief. He sincerely affirmed that any man like himself who had derived his vast wealth from the natural resources should use it to develop the region from which it had come.

He immediately set about it.

One block from his home Stratton had bought some city lots. These he deeded to the town on condition that it erect a new City Hall on the location. As another corner lot was needed, he loaned the city the necessary money to buy it and to start construction.

He then went to the county officials and arranged to buy the old Court House provided the County built a new one on the beautiful site he designated and helped to obtain—a full-size block.

Next he bought up a large corner property downtown for $70,000 and offered it to the federal government for one-half of its valuation in order to induce it to build a new postoffice, which was later done.

At the mouth of the two scenic Cheyenne Cañons from which had wound the old stage-road to Cripple Creek, Stratton bought up a large tract known as Dixon's Ranch. This was cleared of brush, landscaped with lawns, lakes and playgrounds. In it was built a convention hall and pavilion capable of seating 3,500 people or being used as a free dance hall. Next was added a bandstand. On June 6th, then, Cheyenne Park, more popularly known as Stratton's Park, was dedicated to the use of the city with a picnic held under the auspices of the local Carpenters and Joiners Union. All the planing mills shut down and most of the contractors allowed their men the day off. For years Stratton's money paid the bills: $5,000 a year to maintain the park; $4,000 a season to give band concerts; $4,000 to provide dancing and other amusements.

Here, every Sunday afternoon, he would be glimpsed in his Stetson hat and shiny boots, on the edge of the crowd or skulking behind a tree, but smirking at the increasing crowds.

Now, to induce the people to enjoy the "grand in nature," Stratton conceived the plan of incorporating the Colorado Springs and Interurban Railway Company. He intended to build and operate electric lines in all parts of El Paso, Teller and Pueblo Counties; connecting the County seats, Colorado Springs, Cripple Creek and Pueblo; and running branch scenic lines through the mountains.

His first step was to take over the Colorado Springs

Rapid Transit Company which had accumulated an indebtedness of some $150,000 and had difficulty paying its running expenses.

The move, incidentally, was a boon to one of its owners: Stratton's old chum and assistant postmaster in Lincoln, Nebraska, Edwin J. Eaton, who had preceded him to Colorado Springs to work as a cowboy at the Crow's Roost ranch and later to become president of the Colorado Savings Bank. In little over a year Stratton spent $2,000,000 to modernize the system, building twenty-eight new cars in its own new shops, and extending new lines. Later, the street railway took out $225,000 group life insurance on its employees—the first corporation in Colorado, and the first street railway in the United States to do so. It also financed a home-buying plan for its employees; within ten years 85 percent of its employees owned their homes.

During such an enterprise it was to be expected that Stratton would run into complications. He met them characteristically.

He had bought all the property needed for a loop terminal in Manitou except the key lot. This was held by a Kansas City man who, knowing Stratton's wealth, was asking an exorbitant price. Confused, Stratton went to his secretary for advice.

"All you've got to do," came the reply, "is to run your tracks across it. Let him bring suit, have the property appraised, and buy it at a fair price."

Stratton rubbed his chin. "Well, I could do that. But I'm a rich man and he's a poor man. You pay him what he asks."

Since getting rich, Stratton had made gifts totaling $70,000 to Colorado College. In his will he had another bequest of $250,000. Now, without warning, he suddenly ordered it taken out. Years later it was explained thus:

"A millionaire with philanthropic impulses is naturally expected to found a college. W. S. Stratton had that ambition, but then he reflected that colleges breed lawyers and he refrained."

The real reason is this. Stratton was running his new carline north. The College campus lay in the center of the residential district, and directly in the path of the projected line. Stratton therefore petitioned the school to give his engineers permission to lay their lines across the campus. It was refused. General Palmer donated Palmer Hall to the College and built it directly across the line of the railway. Laying the lines around it in a four block detour necessitated Stratton's spending $25,000. Wherefore, in a huff, he eliminated his $250,000 bequest.

When the line was finished, Stratton made provision for his housekeeper, Anna, to buy a small group of rental buildings across town so that she would always be self-supporting. To ride to and from town, she was given a lifetime pass on the street-car system. Within a few years an anti-pass law was enacted by the State Legislature providing against the issuance of passes and for the infliction of fines and jail sentences for so doing. After Stratton had died, the Public Utilities Commission ordered this last pass discontinued and threatened prosecution if its order was not complied with. Dr. Rice, Stratton's old physician and then president of his estate, told the commission quite flatly just where to go!—and that he was ready to serve sentence.

He neither went to jail, nor did Anna stop riding streetcars on her pass.

Stratton's next gift to the city he had been deliberating for several years, ever since he had bought the expensive

THE DENVER PO

ENTH YEAR. DENVER, COLORADO, SUNDAY MORNING, SEPTEMBER 28, 1902

THE FEAST OF THE BUZZARDS.

PS ARE IN
DIRE STRAITS

Withdraws and Says He Is a Democrat.

BRYAN MAY RUN FOR THE PRESIDENCY

Kansas City, Mo., Sept 27.—The staff correspondent of the World (Democrat) traveling with Mr. Bryan in Kansas says that it is not impossible that Mr. Bryan may not be a Democratic presidential candidate again. The opinion is based on statements by him to close Democratic friends and repeated by them. The article says:

"Personally Mr. Bryan would prefer not to make the race and will probably not permit his name to be used if political conditions remain as they are. But should the Hill-Gor-

REPUBLICAN
DAY IN OHI

Root, Hanna and Foraker O
Campaign.

Cartoonist Steele's view of the struggle over Stratton's bequest to charity, already a major dispute within two weeks of his death (from *The Denver Post*, September 28, 1902).

corner property on Pike's Peak Avenue adjacent to his own offices.

During the early boom days of Cripple Creek, the promoters had stood on that corner in the sunshine trading shares. In 1895 a Board of Trade and Mining Stock Exchange had been organized with one hundred members. The production of the Cripple Creek district had reached almost $8,000,000 a year, and it seemed fitting they should at least have a roof over their heads. Since then, however, they had had little else. And Stratton liked mining stockbrokers as a class as thoroughly as he disliked lawyers.

A few years before, he had authorized some of them to purchase a block of shares in the Plymouth, which he was eager to control. He had set a limit of eight cents a share. Then the brokers came running joyfully to him. They had obtained an option to buy it for six cents a share—a saving to him of $20,000. Stratton shook his head. "I knew those boys in the early days of the district. I believe that ground is worth $80,000 and I want you to pay them that amount instead of $60,000."

With such a feeling, he began to erect on the corner a beautiful new five-story building to house the new Mining Exchange. He spared no expense, time or care to make it the finest building in the city. For the first time since he had laid away his own hammer and saw, Stratton was on the job to see that the thing was built just right: none of these new-fangled shortcuts.

A dozen stories were told of his meddlesome care. When the first brick wall was up three feet, Stratton went up to it in a new pair of Schwarz' boots and kicked out a hole. "If you can't do better than that, you can't work on this building!" he shouted angrily at the bricklayers.

One early winter morning he slipped downtown five minutes after the morning whistle blew. One of the laborers was warming up by threshing his arms against his sides. Stratton was enraged. "If you can't keep warm workin' for me get off the job!"

Periodically he fired whole gangs of men "to teach them a lesson"—only to hire them back the next day with full pay for the day lost.

At last, by December 3, 1901, the building was nearing completion. On that day the Colorado Springs Mining Stock Association published the following letter:

To the Members of the Mining Stock Association,
and Business and Mining Men of Colorado Springs:

The handsome Mining Exchange which has been constructed for our Association by Mr. W. S. Stratton is about completed. Before occupying the Exchange, which is second to none in the United States in point of beauty and finish, it seems fitting that the officers and workers of the Mining Stock Association, in connection with the mining and business men of Colorado Springs, should in some way show their recognition of the generosity and public spirit of Mr. W. S. Stratton who has by his liberality and wisdom given ample evidence of how a broad-minded citizen can best advance the interests of the city in which he lives.

Hence, in order to show our appreciation of Mr. Stratton as a public-spirited citizen, we suggest that a public banquet at the Antlers be tendered him at a date which will be most convenient for him.

Arrangements went forward for six weeks; the date was set for January 16, 1902. And on January 15, the new building was opened, the first call being received in the beautiful new Mining Exchange.

In the *Gazette* of the same day a short article appeared of more than passing interest:

"General Palmer announced to the Chamber of Commerce that he had announced to friends his intention of donating a site of one hundred acres of ground and a cash subsidy of $50,000 to found a sanatorium."

Yes! General William J. Palmer had at last made himself heard. During the year preceding he had sold his share of the Denver and Rio Grande Railroad for $6,000,000 to the Gould interests, and retired to his Tudor Castle, Glen Eyrie, to entertain with majestic splendor. But perhaps he had been a little dumbfounded, with all the Little Londoners, at the astounding generosity of the carpenter who had started Out West with him the same year. Fifty thousand dollars as an offhand cash present to his secretary! The ante was too high for General Palmer. But on the very day Stratton's biggest gift to the city was opened, he did manage to announce to the Chamber of Commerce that he had announced to friends his intention. . . . Indeed, "progress will be keenly watched by the whole community."

On the next evening the huge banquet was held in the Antlers Hotel. There were one hundred and sixty people present, including the General. There were long addresses by six main speakers including ex-Governor Adams and Mayor Robinson, and speeches by ten others. "No eulogium was glowing enough to discourage the next speaker from attempting something in the same vein."

The menu was enough to astound the whole town; it had been published the day before. It included fifteen courses, four kinds of champagnes, cognacs and liqueurs of every description. Even roast quails on toast were served. But the crowning glory of the repast was "Small Tenderloin à L'Independence"!

It was a most successful banquet. Everyone of note was there—except Stratton himself. He, reported the *Gazette*, was "unable to attend, although his absence made the function resemble the play of Hamlet with Hamlet left out."

Stratton made no excuses. His only comment afterward was: "I never dined out but once in my life when I enjoyed it. That was down on a quick trip to Mexico once when my host couldn't speak a word of English, and I couldn't speak a word of Spanish."

2

Such was Stratton's surface life during the two years following his sale of the Independence. Underneath the events ran a swifter, darker stream. . . .

He was living at tremendous speed; his building up of the town was but one of the many things he had in mind. And the millions he was spending hardly dented the surface of his reserves. There was more, more and, with his other anticipated projects, still more money to be coming in. So he lived like a man desperately fighting for breath against the flood of riches slowly choking him.

He was ill, always ill. For days he would refuse to take the spoonful of medicine prescribed by the doctor, then angrily drink up the whole glassful. He ate hardly at all. But day by day his consumption of liquor increased. It was the first thing he demanded on awakening in the morning—a good stiff drink to get him up. There was wine in the house but he never touched it. Whiskey was all he wanted, and he sometimes drank almost a quart a day. One of his old housemaids remembers the pepper and the peppermint always on his cabinet: he used to add one or the other to his drinks to make them stronger still. He was never drunk, but under its influence he began to do queer things. To the townspeople they seemed even queerer. The stories about him kept growing.

Just a year after he had returned from Europe he and his private secretary, Ramsay, severed connections. Ramsay, his trusted friend and business adviser for almost six years, to whom he had given $50,000 as a gift! People pointed it out as an example of Stratton's unreliability. Others maintained that Stratton had discharged him on learning that Ramsay had been "knocking down" on all Stratton's contracts.

Dr. Rice now became his financial agent, and Stratton hired as a secretary a strict orthodox religious man named William A. Lloyd. This was surprising to many in light of Stratton's liberal religious views. Lloyd was methodical, honest and exceedingly cautious. The story is told of Stratton walking into the bank one morning and abruptly requesting a million-dollar loan immediately.

The request was not unwarranted: on one occasion he had as calmly walked into the bank and deposited a million dollars in a single day. And the bank wanted his business.

"Certainly, Mr. Stratton," agreed the president. "You'll give us something for security though—as a matter of record?"

"Sure," said Stratton, "just get in touch with my secretary. He'll give you something."

That afternoon he returned to his office, casually asking Lloyd if he had given the bank anything for security. Lloyd laid the papers on his desk. He had given as security for the million dollars practically everything Stratton owned, worth ten times the amount Stratton had borrowed. Stratton said nothing until that evening when he was ready to go home. Then he called Lloyd.

"Mr. Lloyd," he said quietly, "I am ready to go home to supper. I should like to walk and I think I shall wear my hat. Will you please get the president of the bank on the telephone and ask him if I have his permission to do so?"

Stratton in his early days had never belonged to the Carpenters Union, for under the rules a contractor employing labor could not be a member. Now, on July 16, 1901, he filed application for membership with two other carpenters in Local Union No. 515 of the United Brotherhood of Carpenters and Joiners. He was accepted, probably becoming the country's wealthiest union carpenter, and was in good standing at the time of his death.

He had already become a thirty-second degree Mason at the insistence of Bob Schwarz. Masonry was Schwarz' religion; he had become one of the lodge's most efficient members in instructing candidates for degrees. Now Stratton became an Elk.

As he became more ill and irritable, he took to reading religion of every creed. He became interested in the Order of Emethachavak, and entertained F. P. White, Rabbah of the Order at his house. The Order was a communistic society of vegetarians whose principles were set forth in its book, *The Romance of the Red Star*. White later brought suit on the grounds that Stratton had given him $50 on account toward a contribution of $2,000 which he did not receive. At this time he claimed Stratton believed himself surrounded by good and evil spirits.

And then in July, Stratton became a Christian Scientist. A healer from Denver and two women attendants moved into the house next door in order to attend him.

Now, in full flower, blossomed the worst tales about him. He was regarded as a rake, a libertinous Bluebeard and a Satanic master of super-Bacchanalian ceremonies. And Billy Fitts, a former under-sheriff whom he had appointed as his bodyguard, was considered his procurer and fixer.

In a "Pen Picture of Colorado's Count of Monte Cristo," the omnipresent Polly Pry of the *Denver Post* said of Stratton:

> He seems to have run the gamut of human emotions, and to have fished from the depths of his own distorted mind the black horde of sorrows which infested his pessimistic soul and darkened all the days of his life.
>
> He was moody and misanthropical, given to violent tempers and furious outbursts of rage, suspicious even of his most intimate friends.
>
> He had no morals, no trust, no faith and apparently no hope. His debaucheries are said to have been not alone bad, but positively Satanic. His numerous affairs cost him great sums of money. He was capricious, irascible and absolutely unstable. To be your friend in the morning was no guarantee that he would not be your bitterest enemy in the afternoon. . . .

The stories kept growing. Almost forty years later some of them still persist. Several of his friends were generally known as his mistresses. Another, posing as his niece at one of the prominent hotels, was suddenly ejected and left town without remonstrating. To one of two sisters, he is said to have given $25,000 to marry her off when he tired of her; whereupon both tried to insinuate a third sister into his graces. There is the tale of one who had run a boarding-house in Cripple Creek previously. She was married and had two children. Apparently she was a smart woman. When her husband died, she frightened Stratton out of $100,000 and is now supposed to be one of the respected society women of Little London.

A story is still told by a lawyer of having been visited by a young woman of undeniably good breeding. Her face flushed with real embarrassment as she confided to him that she was with child by Mr. Stratton. Wouldn't the lawyer please ask Mr. Stratton to be friendly enough to give her some money?

The lawyer rose and placed his arm around her shoulders. "Child, I can't do that! You are a child! Why, nobody would believe you. You haven't any proof. They'd laugh us out of court. Haven't you any parents?"

The girl admitted having a mother in Utah.

"Well, you go back home and don't worry. Things like this just happen. And when they do we've got to make the best of them. But don't ruin your whole life by making a laughing-stock out of yourself trying to bring Stratton into court. No good lawyer would dare touch such a case."

Nor did the lawyer apparently condemn Stratton too harshly: he had just happened on a child instead of the usual harpy.

How much or little there is to such stories will probably never be known. There are probably some grains of truth among the wild conjectures. Stratton, always repressed since his unfortunate marriage to Zeurah twenty-five years before, continuously excited by excessive drinking, was living at a nervous tension that demanded some sort of safety valve. And at public opinion he snapped his fingers.

Unlike some other Little Londoners he was unique in never covering up his actions. One of his trusted servants suggested diplomatically that he be more discreet in entertaining women friends at home. His violent rebuke of "Why, by God! Isn't this my house and my life?" expressed his contempt of others' opinion. He bought one of his companions a beautiful satin gown to wear to a ball. When she found that he was not going to accompany her, she tore it into shreds. With another he was sitting up drinking all night, having locked Anna downstairs. They got into a violent quarrel, and then into a fight. During the scuffle Stratton struck her so hard with his fist that he broke her nose. And then at dawn he drove her over to the west side of town to a young doctor to be treated.

Women, women! They were now the bane of his existence. Adventuresses young and old came to Little London for the avowed purpose of snaring him with their charms. They paraded up and down the walk in front of his office and his house. One morning a woman denied admittance by Anna took up her seat on the porch steps. She was still there by nightfall. Anna had to call him by telephone so Stratton could sneak home by the way of the alley. It grew to be a regular route. He was beset by a dozen threats of breach of promise suits. And now he gave orders that no woman was ever to be admitted to his house on any condition, and that no woman was to be admitted to his office unless accompanied by a male companion.

Meanwhile, to offset these, there are stories of his touching kindness to animals:

A great flock of "horn larks" were driven into town by a storm. Stratton could not bear their distress. He bought bushels of grain and employed men to remove the stricken birds from the streets and feed them until they were strong enough to fly.

Learning of this, someone gave him a great eagle. Stratton was delighted. He had a large cage erected for it in his yard. After a time he noted that the majestic prisoner was pining for freedom. He ordered a large beefsteak for the bird and had it driven out on the prairies. There the cage was opened and the eagle released.

For years Stratton had kept his old partner of prospecting days: Dick, a faithful scrubby mongrel. The dog, from high living, was dying of gout and old age. Stratton believed him lonely. So he bought a black spaniel, Jack, for his company. The three were inseparable companions around the house. After Stratton had died, Jack was still faithfully attended by Anna.

But whatever his surface life, Stratton paid it little attention. He had written his will, and in it embodied the guiding principles of the vision that had come to him when he was ill in England. . . .

The will—handwritten, for he would not allow it to be typed—after enumerating certain bequests, directed that all of his wealth be delivered to the trustees of a charitable corporation. This corporation was to be created by Stratton, or by the trustees in case he died, for the purpose of erecting and maintaining a free home "for poor persons who are without means of support, and who are physically unable by reason of old age, youth, sickness or other infirmity to earn a livelihood." One million dollars was to be expended in purchasing a site, building and equipping this home to be known as the Myron Stratton Home in memory of his father. All the balance was to be invested in safe securities, and all the income derived therefrom was to be used in supporting the home. For, as he wrote, "It is my especial desire and command that the inmates of said Home shall not be clothed and fed as paupers usually are at public expense, but that they shall be decently and comfortably clothed and amply provided with good and wholesome food and with the necessary medicines, medical attendance, care and nursing to protect their health and insure their comfort."

In revolt against the common poor-farm of the day he also directed "that no inmate . . . shall be constrained against his or her will to perform any manual service for any inmate of said Home not related to him or her by blood or marriage, nor for any officer or employee of said Home;

nor shall any of such inmates be constrained to perform any manual labor when physically unable to do so."

This was what Stratton, ill in London, had dreamed of doing with the vast wealth from the Independence—itself revealed to him the same way. For months he had brooded over it, drawn up tentative plans, gone over details in his mind. It became the one guiding ambition in his life, for with all his gifts to individuals, to town and county, his wealth had hardly been touched. It became his religion (that nebulous quality described by the *Denver Post:* "His religion was of a practical type, and consisted chiefly in obtaining the approval of his conscience").

After Stratton had drawn up his will, he took it to his secretary, Lloyd, and asked him to read it over that night and tell him what he thought of it. The next morning Lloyd's comment was, "A home for children is fine, Mr. Stratton, but I'm not so sure about old people."

Stratton smoothed back his own white hair. "Well, Lloyd," he said after a time, "old people suffer too."

The will stood as read.

But now for a time, thought Stratton, the Home could wait. He was developing his second theory which was to provide even more money for his cherished dream.

That it concerned itself with Cripple Creek was not surprising. For Stratton, despite his role of benefactor, financier and business man, despite his sale of the Independence for $10,000,000, was still the lonely prospector who had tramped the Colorado Rockies for seventeen years before making a strike. It was in his blood to stay.

A flare-up of the old feeling had disturbed him during the Klondike rush two years before. He had sent out an expedition under the direction of James Casey who had mined in Cripple Creek, Leadville and Creede. Two river boats named the *W. S. Stratton* and the *Florence* were built in Seattle, lashed on the deck of the four-masted, chartered schooner *Bartlett*, and taken up the Yukon to Dawson. Although Casey later located and sold some oil claims to the Standard Oil Company, Stratton's expedition was not a success.

But Cripple Creek! It would always be there for him, the scene of his everlasting luck. In just nine years since he had located the Independence the district had produced a hundred million dollars worth of gold. With its year's production of over eighteen million dollars and the closing of the Transvaal mines during the South African War, it had enabled the United States to procure $118,435,562 of the world's $255,954,654 worth of gold. The country was leading Australia, Canada, Russia, the whole world, in the production of gold. And Cripple Creek's claim was undisputed as the greatest gold camp known.

To it Stratton had turned his eyes again. This time not as a poor prospector, but with millions at his command. And he had a theory—a theory that was to make him more famous than he had ever been, and which was to be remembered as long as the linked names of Stratton and Cripple Creek.

3

On Saturday, June 15, 1901, Stratton's big office was crowded with newspaper representatives, mining engineers and prominent business men. He had a statement to make—the first since he had returned from Europe with $10,000,000 from the sale of the Independence.

The next day the news broke. Sunday papers flashed with glaring headlines the story of what he had been doing for the past two years and his plans for the project ahead:

FROM MULTI-MILLIONAIRE TO BILLIONAIRE
STRATTON'S GREAT CRIPPLE CREEK UNDERTAKING
THE BIGGEST STORY EVER PUBLISHED IN COLORADO

The story printed in the *Colorado Telegraph*, the *Rocky Mountain News* and *Cripple Creek Morning Times-Citizen*, in part, ran thus:

W. S. Stratton, who for years has been famous all over the world as Colorado's most noted multi-millionaire mining king, has conceived, planned and for months has been executing an undertaking which for boldness of conception and magnitude of execution surpasses any mining enterprise ever conceived by the minds of men during all the ages of history.

. . . The Cripple Creek mining district is crossed and seamed by thousands of veins of gold-bearing ore and scores of big ore shoots. There are indications that these ore shoots and veins tend to converge toward a common center. W. S. Stratton has purchased approximately one-fifth of the present productive area of Cripple Creek and all of these veins run into his ground. This would indicate that the great mother vein, the center from which the great veins and ore shoots of the district radiate is directly under the ground owned by Mr. Stratton.

. . . Gold is heavy and it is reasonable to suppose that much larger and richer values of this precious metal will be found as depth is gained in the district. What might be called the surface of Cripple Creek has produced to date $100,000,000 in gold. . . . It is not the dream of a prospector or the unreal vision of an enthusiast, but the sober, clear-headed judgment of a practical mining man, to imagine that in the center of this great volcanic eruption are treasures of gold. . . . He is sinking shafts and running a tunnel to intersect these veins and ore shoots at a great depth. . . . The expenditure runs from $35,000 to $50,000 per month. This great amount is no draft on Mr. Stratton's capital. It does not even represent the entire income from which financiers would call his "gilt-edge securities." It is possible for Mr. Stratton to continue his work on this tremendous scale, and even to increase his operations, for the rest of his life in this undertaking without in any way lessening his fortune or weakening his resources.

. . . The gold found in these mines will be spent for the benefit of the people of this state and this city. . . . It means more to the State of Colorado and especially the people of Colorado Springs and Cripple Creek than any other thing that has happened in the history of the State. . . . If even a small portion of the wealth is uncovered which must be hidden under these hills, Colorado will see the greatest mining boom ever known in the history of the world. . . .

V. Z. Reed, his agent for the Independence deal, made the authorized statement, "If Mr. Stratton succeeds in this project, and I believe he will, he will make the greatest fortune ever made in mining in the history of the world."

John Hays Hammond in London admitted that he believed Stratton had acquired the cream of the undeveloped inside area of the district.

Other opinions held that of all the great mining projects launched in this country, notably the opening of the mother lodes of California, none had been conceived on so tremendous a scale.

Stratton's plans, reiterated others, surpassed the greatest plans ever conceived by Cecil Rhodes.

Few mining men had the courage to oppose this broadside of opinion with the remark that Stratton's scheme was not practical, and that if the veins of the district converged to a common point it would be so deep that it would be impossible to find the ore. They knew he had the nerve; his sale of the Independence had provided him with the means. The general consensus was condensed in the casual remark, "We fellows often thought he was making a fool of himself, but when it came to cash he always had the stack of blues."

The black bold headlines, the frenzied phrases, the appalling news of what he had been doing so quietly for months, the excitement following the release of the story—all this reflected nothing of the quiet manner in which the information had been imparted the day before.

It was a dull Saturday. Outside, the clatter of hoofs and the drone of carriage wheels rose faintly in the still cold air. The room was crowded with nervous reporters, stolid mining men chewing on black cigars and pipe stems, and business men fumbling the watch chains across their vests. Behind the long carved table loaded with papers sat Stratton's legal counselor, his financial agent, Dr. Rice, and two mining engineers. The statement had already been prepared; the voice reading it went on and on, monotonous in tone as the buzzing of the single fly in the room. In the corner sat Stratton himself.

His thin white hair and white Kentucky Colonel mustaches were freshly combed. He wore a stiff collar and black bow tie. Underneath the carven, walnut table his handmade boots rested precisely on the carpet. He looked innocent of the news and was mildly interested in the fly buzzing from one furiously scratching reporter to the next.

There was one interruption. The secretary opened the door to call Mr. Stratton to the telephone. The voice ceased as Stratton stood up; pencils stopped; a reporter hastily pushed back his chair to let the mild apologetic man get by. For a moment there was deathly stillness in the room. Had Stratton already reached that gold-littered floor of the Rockies, they asked each other with tense faces. Then Stratton came back. It had been his old housekeeper, Anna, calling to inquire what he wanted for supper. The voice took up its drone.

When the report had been read, Stratton crossed his legs. Throats cleared with important "hems." No one spoke.

"Maybe there's some questions," said Stratton. "Not that you haven't hit the nail on the head," he amended hastily, "but there's a lot of facts there."

One by one the hearers began to inquire into the details of the astounding project whose significance they were just beginning to comprehend. Stratton was still mild and shy of appearance and manner, yet when he spoke it was with a voice that was firm, definite and sharp-cut as steel.

"It is a wonder that no one has guessed what I was driving at in buying those holdings," he said. "I have invested in all at this time fully $7,000,000 in the Cripple Creek district. I cannot tell you when this plan first occurred to me, for I don't remember. I have followed the development of the district fairly well, and anyone who studies the maps on it cannot but notice that all the great veins of the principal mines apparently meet under Gold or Globe Hill. When they do cross I am of the opinion that they will form some important ore bodies. I am going ahead to find out whether I am right or wrong."

"Will it take you long to find out, Mr. Stratton? Or is it a lifetime job?"

"This is my life mission. I am undertaking a big thing; it will take lots of money and years of hard work, but I believe I am right. To prove this I am spending a small fortune every month. It is averaging me month in and month out from $35,000 to $50,000 and I have been keeping this up for a good many months. You know mining is an expensive thing in Cripple Creek, but it may in the end do some good for the camp."

"Is that the only reason you got back into it again?"

"Why I got into Cripple Creek again I cannot tell," replied Stratton quietly. "It was in my blood to tackle this and the first thing I knew I was at it. I spent $4,000,000 in buying ground and I bought every piece with this one end in view. The veins had to come north and I merely got in their way. From what I have found in the little development so far, I believe I have bought well. Now that I have all I want, it remains for me to develop it."

"How far down you figuring on sinking?" drawled one of the engineers across the table.

"I believe there is ore in Cripple Creek to a depth far beyond the ingenuity of man to mine it out, Sir! I will, of course, go down on any big ore chute I find until human ingenuity and modern machinery fail me. I will not say I am going to sink to three thousand feet or any other depth, but I am going after the ore."

He turned to the other, listened quietly a moment and went on. "At present I am sinking a three-compartment shaft on the Lady Stith claim. I call it the Plymouth Rock shaft because it is upon the property of that company. It is being made 5 x 15 feet in the clear and will be carried down with these dimensions to the point where I strike ore. It is now only 150 feet deep and at that point I am carrying out one of the plans which I intend to follow in all my operations. I am running a drift southwest from the shaft and another northeast for exploration purposes."

"But what about the tunnel?"

Stratton reached out and drew one of the folios on the table to him. He flipped to the page. "We have run the Chicago-Cripple Creek Tunnel in 2,300 feet and will push it ahead for 700 feet more. At that length it will connect with the Plymouth Rock shaft. It is only a prospect tunnel, but will serve us also for air connections and also to carry out a good lot of the prospecting I intend to do."

"What sort of plant will you put on the Plymouth Rock shaft?" was asked.

"Oh, I have not decided yet; it will be a good one. Good for a mile," he added. "We have a good one there now, capable of going 800 feet and we will use this for awhile. When we do change we will put on a steel plant, a permanent one, for we will be going ahead here for years to come."

"Do you think this one, the Plymouth Rock, will be as good as the Independence, Mr. Stratton?"

Stratton smiled.

For hours, all afternoon, he sat there answering questions technical and general on his project, on his philanthropic intentions toward State and community should he succeed, and what he would do next if he failed. He was patient and unexcited. He could afford to be. For months he had been quietly accumulating holdings, drawing up his plans, marshaling his resources. Now the cards were on the table: he let them read the hand for themselves. Quiet, shy, paradoxical Stratton!

4

This then was what Stratton had been doing, so quietly buying claims in Schwarz' name.

Doubters asserted that he would show himself a fool carpenter after being so long favored by mere luck. Others, believing him a modern Midas, waited to hear daily that Stratton had reached the mythical gold-littered floor of the Rockies. But generally the opinion of mining men was expressed by an editorial in the *Pueblo Chieftain:*

Winfield Scott Stratton is credited with harboring and brooding over a mineral theory somewhat like that which caused the sinking of the deep Geyser shaft at Silver Cliff. The man who began and prosecuted that great undertaking figured out that there was a volcano from which had been discharged the mass of rich silver ore found at Silver Cliff, and that he could tap it with a deep shaft at a certain place. Mr. Stratton's idea is that there is a certain point in the Cripple Creek district from which most of the gold veins have radiated or at which they cross and meet. He thinks it is in or about either Gold Hill or Globe Hill, and that it can be found, and will yield a greater amount of rich ore than has yet been brought to light in even the Cripple Creek district. If anybody can arrive at such conclusions, Mr. Stratton is the man to be in a position to do so. . . .

It was really not so new and original as it was startling—this amazing plan that was to make the fortunes taken by Croesus from the sands of the Pactolus, by Solomon from the mines of Ophir, by Cecil Rhodes from the mountains of South Africa, seem a poor man's competence compared to the wealth of Colorado's most successful and most famous miner.

Stratton's "Bowl of Gold" theory as it came to be known was, after all, no more than the old, old dream of men the world over: to tap the great mythical mother lode that men have persisted in believing lay under every continental mountain chain: the Himalayas, Andes, Rockies. It was but a variation derived from the peculiar geological structure of the Cripple Creek district, and its only basic originality lay in Stratton's courageous conception and bold execution of his plan.

The theory went back not only to the first geological conjectures about the region, but to its topography. A high pastoral landscape, without outcrops, its physical appearance alone had retarded the discovery of gold until late. No one until Stratton's first discovery could possibly believe that in such a "cow pasture" lay the greatest gold deposits on the continent.

But gold had been discovered to prove the trite truth that "gold is where you find it." And as strike after strike was made, the theories followed. In ten years its geological structure was determined and accepted. The Cripple Creek region with its many high hills rising on the general south slope of Pike's Peak occupied the ground floor of an extinct volcano whose superstructure had been removed by erosion. Probably it had had an unsymmetrical conical shape, and the present high hills had been covered by a thousand feet of granite whose culminating point was Pike's Peak. This pinkish granite was the basal rock of the region and was assumed to have formed the bed of an ancient sea which received the sediments now composing the sandstones of the Garden of the Gods a mile below.

Most of the mines were situated amid a complex of volcanic rock which occupied the throat of this extinct Cripple Creek volcano.

It was exactly analogous to a high-walled granite cup filled with breccia and erupted rocks like a water-soaked sponge. This explained the reason for its being an extremely wet mining region requiring many drainage tunnels. It also gave rise to the deposition theory of gold ore.

During a great eruption the volcanic breccia had burst through the granite in an aqueo-fused condition. Cooling and solidification took place and contraction followed, resulting in the formation of many fissures. Hot water ascended with great velocity from the depth of the volcano and, nearing the surface, spread more slowly through the complicated fissure system. As it stagnated, deposition and chemical action on the country rock changed the composition of the solution. Precipitation of gold ore took place.

The theory was sound and it fitted the Cripple Creek district neatly. The main producing area was only some six square miles in extent and coincided with the volcanic deposit enclosed by granite walls. It was in fact a Bowl of Gold.

Hundreds of failures proved it true. Almost every mine located outside the granite neck proved worthless; the gold veins lay imbedded in the breccia.

And now followed conjectures and quarrels. How deep was this layer of volcanic breccia? Did it spread out below like an underground lake? Or was it narrow and pinched like a bottle neck? Had the richest deposits been found near the surface or were they yet to be found at depth?

The preponderant belief held that Cripple Creek would have a short life. The shipments of unbelievably rich ore taken from the grass roots had exhausted the richest ore deposits. This was substantiated by U. S. Geological Survey engineers. They held that the ores then seen probably extended to a maximum depth of three thousand feet. According to the deposition theory accepted by all, precipitation of gold ore had taken place abundantly near the surface and sparsely at depth. When the top of the volcano had been removed by erosion, they said, much richer deposits had also been displaced.

Cripple Creek, echoed the many adherents to this belief, was on its last legs and the ore was gradually petering out.

Yet year by year the production of the district kept increasing: $2,010,367 in 1893; $6,879,137 in 1895; $13,507,244 in 1898; and now, for last year, it had climbed to the staggering sum of $18,073,539.

This gave rise to a conflicting theory. The staunchest believers in Cripple Creek held that far richer deposits would be found at depth than had been taken near the surface, and that the district was just now beginning upon an era of mining. They ignored the fact that of 60 of the most important pay chutes 30 were less than 500 feet down, contemptously asserting that the grass roots had barely been disturbed. They based their belief upon the fact that free gold did not occur in the veins except when set free by oxidation. This zone of oxidation did not exceed a depth of 1,000 feet, that being the approximate depth to which oxygen could penetrate through fissures or in water. But in the unoxidized ores gold was still present, in combination with tellurium forming the tellurides, sylvanite and calaverite, and in sulphides forming tetrahedrite, commonly called "gray copper."

Too, all over the gold-bearing area the underlying granite formation showed evidence of disturbance. In many instances it had been penetrated and traversed by vertical sheets of phonolite called dikes—a dike being easily seen where the softer rock had scored away. During the vein deposition the phonolite had been disintegrated and replaced by equivalent volumes of ore in fissure veins varying in width from a few inches to several feet. The resulting conclusion was that the deposition of gold had taken place in fissures after the eruption and solidification of volcanic breccia and was not restricted to its confines. Gold might be found in the granite below.

On this basis Stratton had studied the mines and maps of the district.

There were five general ore zones in the district running from south to north. In these zones he plotted the trend of the veins of their most important mines. On the east, the

Lillie-Vindicator zone system swung to the northwest; the Independence-Portland system he knew had a general northward trend as had the Gold-Coin-Dead-Pine zone; while the two westerly zones, the Elkton-Raven and the Anaconda-Mary-McKinney, swung to the northeast. This disclosed the interesting fact that the ore producing area of Cripple Creek was broad at the southern extremity and narrow at the northern—roughly in the shape of a pear.

He believed that these major veins converged at a central point. And this point he chose as the center of the extinct Cripple Creek volcano: in general, the area occupied by two of the major seven hills of the district, Gold and Globe Hills. The very Globe Hill on whose top men had "prospected with plows, mined with road-scrapers, and shipped the scenery."

Other men who had noted the same trend believed that on the broad southern curve of the pear the veins had risen from deep inside the earth, cooling, then solidifying, as they escaped upward toward the grass roots. Stratton did not. He held that where they converged, deep under Gold and Globe Hills, would be found the primal source of the mineralization of the entire district.

He had then, quietly and without quibbling, begun to buy up all the property in the neighborhood of those two adjacent hills and lying directly transverse to the line of direction of the five great ore zones.

Now, in the summer of 1901, just ten years from the time when as an obscure carpenter he had made his first discovery and put Cripple Creek on the map as the greatest gold camp on earth, he owned six hundred acres of the best patented mining claims in the region, approximately one-fifth of the whole productive area. He had spent $7,000,000 already. He had commenced on Globe Hill to sink the deepest shaft yet driven in the district, the first to go down one thousand feet, and requiring eighteen-foot timbers so large that they would permit of a five thousand foot depth. And with millions behind him he was prepared to begin his gigantic exploitations.

Colorado and the world waited to see what would happen—at Stratton's expense.

5

That June 15th, the Saturday on which Stratton released his "Bowl of Gold" statement, occurred the heaviest June snow recorded in the district. In Cripple Creek fully a foot of snow fell; in Pueblo there were rain, hail and snow, snow-shovels being required to clear the streets; and in Little London the weather was little better.

Stratton trudged home, rang the bell and then opened the door without waiting—a gesture that betrayed the two men within his pleasant shell. Anna came to him in the hall with a glass of liquor; he took it at a gulp and went in to supper. Now she stood in the kitchen doorway watching him pick gingerly at his plate. His white thin face was flushed, his hands trembled slightly, the old familiar signs.

"But Mr. Stratton! You don't eat nothing. What wass it you vant?"

"Don't want anything. Not hungry."

He brushed by her and strode off to the library. "You better lock up," he said turning around. "I won't be in. To nobody, understand?"

"Yes, Mr. Stratton." Anna let out a sigh and began to clear the table.

In his library Stratton closed the door, drew the curtains and snapped on the light. Then he dropped into a big armchair and sat staring at the shelves of books: Fiske's *Destiny of Man, The Idea of God* and *Through Nature to God;* the works of Pascal and Henry Drummond, Bible commentaries. He picked up a volume of the Duke of Argyll and turned a page. And in this deceptive posture Anna found him when she knocked at the door.

"Are you all right, Mr. Stratton? Is there anything what it iss you vant?"

Stratton did not look up from his book. "Just lock up, Anna."

For a moment she stood looking at his neat, studious figure under the glow of the lamp. Then with a worried frown on her face she quietly closed the door.

Stratton listened to her receding footsteps, then with an elated gleam in his big eyes, he went to the cabinet and brought back a crystal tumbler and a bottle almost full of Bourbon whiskey. He sat down in his chair and carefully dusted the bottle in his lap. On the footstool his shiny new boots rested precisely and at ease. In the glow of the light his carefully combed hair gleamed silver. With a steadying hand he stroked his white mustache and poured himself a drink. Setting the bottle on the table close at hand, he sat staring into the brownish liquor in the tumbler. Abruptly, and with a single gulp, he took the long drink neatly and poured himself another. . . .

The night wore on and still he did not stir from his seat.

Across the table in the light of a guttering candle rammed down the throat of a bottle, a bearded old prospector sat watching him: Stratton's favorite painting, "The Miner's Last Dollar," by W. Bancroft, a local artist.

A dog howled at the dawn which as yet only lighted pinkly the high snow-covered peaks. Then suddenly there was a loud slap on the porch outside as the Sunday *Telegraph* slid across the planks and fetched up against the screen, unfolded to show the screaming headlines of Stratton's new project and, underneath, the picture of his mild face with his fastidiously combed hair and mustaches.

Through the drawn curtains inside the library, Stratton gave a jerk; he had been lying face down upon the table, the empty whiskey bottle overturned and sticking to one of the Duke of Argyll's leather volumes.

He crumpled back into his chair, legs and arms outspread, his bow-tie askew and white hair ruffled. His head flew back; and his face seemed to be staring through the hideous mixture of dawn and lamplight at the neatly framed quotation from William Henry Channing, a gift from Thomas Tonge which, he was accustomed to tell his intimate friends, constituted his creed:

> To live content with small means; to seek elegance rather than luxury, and refinement rather than fashion; to be worthy, not respectable; to study hard, think quietly, talk gently, act frankly; to listen to stars and birds, to babes and sages, with open heart; to bear all cheerfully, do all bravely, await occasions, hurry never; in a word, to let the spiritual, unbidden and unconscious, grow up through the common.
>
> This is to be my symphony.

That afternoon he received word from Jeffersonville, Indiana, that his sister, Harriet Newell Hamlin, had just died.

Always superstitious, Stratton was overcome by forebodings. Zeurah, whom he had never seen since leaving her twenty-five years before, had lately died also. So had his favorite sister, Anna Chamberlin, whom he had brought west and buried in Evergreen Cemetery, Colorado Springs. Of Myron Stratton's twelve children there were now left only himself and one sister, Mrs. Jennie Cobb, living in California.

And then his dog Dick died. Stratton buried him under the pansy bed outside his window and resumed his brooding. . . .

It was the year 1902: just over ten years since he had discovered the Independence, just three years since he had sold it for ten million dollars. He was now fifty-four years old.

In less than a decade he had jumped from the obscurity of a journeyman carpenter and penniless prospector to fame as the father of the greatest gold camp in the world, the owner of one of the greatest mines known, and the richest mining king Colorado was ever to produce.

In the last three years he had astounded the country by his gifts to the town, adhering to his theory that vast wealth should be used to build up the region where it had been produced. He had drawn up plans specifying to what use his huge estate should be devoted, according to the vision he had seen. And in Cripple Creek his engineers had bought up over one hundred claims, incorporated into the Stratton Cripple Creek Mining and Development Company, and acquired control of eight other mining companies. They constituted one-fifth of the whole camp, and for them he had expended some seven million dollars. He was sinking the deepest shaft yet to be driven in the district. And all this was for the express purpose of proving one of the most spectacular theories ever originated—his own theory of the "Bowl of Gold."

His wealth still seemed inexhaustible: besides his mining properties he owned vast blocks of real estate property in Denver and Colorado Springs, all the stock of the International Realty Company, the Colorado Springs and Interurban Railway on which he had expended two million dollars, and other bonds, stocks and securities.

And for these short three years he had been living at a speed and under a nervous tension that no one could stand for long; he lived like a man who had long since, in London, received a summons he could not delay in answering.

He had put his two theories to work, his vision on paper. He had provided for his faithful employees, friends and relatives. To Carl Chamberlin, his favorite sister's son, he had written in Brooklyn, promising him the management of the street-car system if he would finish college with creditable grades.

Now something, perhaps another intuition, whispered in his ear. His monthly expenditure on the Bowl of Gold theory had reached $85,000. He wondered if his luck had turned. Afraid that things might go wrong, he drew and signed a check for $250,000 payable to Bob Schwarz. It was to provide for both of them if the scheme fell through, and Bob was instructed to take care of it and not allow him to draw on it.

For weeks Schwarz kept the check. Nothing happened. He finally returned it to Stratton, unwilling to be responsible for so vast a sum.

Then, late in the summer, Stratton was again stricken ill. This time he went to bed with the premonition that he would never get up again.

Anna also intuitively divined the truth. A newspaper reporter thus accorded her action homage:

"A Swede girl who has lived in the house a long time sent for a physician and calmly shut the door in the faces of two Scientists when they arrived to head off the Doctor."

Anna ran back to Stratton's bedside.

And now a peculiar thing happened: he struggled erect, reached out both arms to put around her neck as she sank down on her knees beside the bed, and collapsed upon her shoulder—the same pathetic gesture of final defeat that she had dreamed while he was in London.

Dr. Rice arrived and then brought two more physicians for consultation. Stratton had hypertrophic cirrhosis of the liver with diabetes complications; it was very serious and there seemed little doubt but that it had been hastened by his excessive use of stimulants.

For almost a month he lay there. His sister, Mrs. Jennie Cobb, arrived from San Jose, California, and her daughter hurried on from St. Louis. His nephew, Carl Chamberlin, came from New York. These, with Billy Fitts and Stratton's closest friend, Bob Schwarz, watched by his bedside. A nurse had arrived, but Stratton allowed no one to administer to his wants but Anna who knew his needs better than anyone else.

He now knew death was near. Rousing his mind, he inquired and found that his cash balance in the bank was only $31,000. His secretary was ordered to write a check for $25,000 payable to Schwarz, and Bob was asked to cash it immediately so that there would be no complications.

It was the last check of the thousands Stratton signed.

On Wednesday, September 10, 1902, a wave of excitement swept through the gold camps at Cripple Creek. Men congregated on street corners, in saloons, on mine-dumps discussing the rumor that Stratton had died down in Little London.

"The regret expressed," reported the *Cripple Creek Times*, "was not unmixed with consternation, for it was felt that because of his immense holdings in the district his death would have an unsettling effect upon many mining enterprises." The rumor presaged the storm to follow the collapse of his gigantic Bowl of Gold exploitation.

Two days later Stratton's mind began to wander; it was apparent he could not recover.

Reporters, friends and curious townspeople began to form lines in front of the house. Stratton couldn't die: he had too much money and too many unfinished projects under way. What, argued his business associates and mining engineers, would become of his Bowl of Gold theory? His friends and relatives still held hope; he was only fifty-four years old.

Bob Schwarz told the physicians "they did not know." He had been with Stratton in London when he was so ill, and believed that Stratton's strong constitution would again pull him through. "He is not going to die, I tell you," he repeated. "I know he is not going to die. He will get well."

The Reverend Father Bender came to kneel at his bedside and pray—the only religious man whom Stratton could tolerate. "Mr. Stratton is not a member of any church. He is what we call a humanitarian and is a good and great man. He is a Christian man, and a wonderful student of religion. His library is remarkable for the number of books upon religion which it contains. There are Catholic books and Protestant books and books of nearly every creed on his shelves, and I know he is a great student of religious subjects. I have known him for many years and called upon him as a friend. We were good friends and I felt that I should call upon him in his illness."

On Saturday night Stratton relapsed into unconsciousness, and at three o'clock Sunday morning a change was noticed in his condition. His respiration was not so strong, his pulse had weakened: death was imminent. And yet his tenacity of life was wonderful, his heart action remaining good when it seemed all else was gone. His vitality was amazing.

That evening Stratton roused for a brief instant. He

asked Bob Schwarz to sit down beside him "as you used to do, Bob." The shoemaker did as requested.

"He grasps my hand so tightly," he whispered. "He is not going to die."

And then Stratton relapsed into final unconsciousness.

"He is as wonderful in death as he was in health," said his sister.

And at nine thirty-five o'clock on Sunday evening, September 14, 1902, Stratton slipped effortlessly out of the world in which he had never been really known. . . .

An hour before he died a telegram was received, marked Pasadena, California. It was from Stratton's son, Isaac Henry Stratton. Dr. Rice left the house to telegraph him the simple announcement of death.

As he went out of the house a woman and a man accosted him regarding Stratton's condition. When told he had just died, the man lowered his head and shuffled up the street without a word. The woman murmured "thank you," stood with tears in her eyes, and then slowly moved away in the opposite direction. Unknown and lost in the darkness, they seemed like vanishing symbols of the thousands of unknown people whom Stratton had aided with anonymous contributions.

6

On Monday the newspapers throughout the country carried front-page stories and editorials on the death of the "Midas of the Rockies," "Colorado's Greatest Mining King," and pictures of "The Father of Cripple Creek" and "Colorado's Count of Monte Cristo." The *Denver Post*, *Rocky Mountain News* and *Colorado Springs Gazette* ran sketches of his life.

Stratton's son arrived. He was allowed to view the body, but Carl Chamberlin did not permit him to stay in the house.

On Tuesday, Nellie V. Walker from Chicago, later given a $5,000 contract to execute a design for a Stratton monument, made a death mask of his face.

His body was then taken to the Mining Exchange where it lay in state from one to six o'clock attended by a guard of honor composed of ten employees of the street-car system. Over 8,600 eager and curious onlookers filed past to see what the noted dead man looked like. The line at times reached down to the corner and across the avenue, blocking traffic. There was no call on the Mining Exchange for the day, and at two o'clock every street-car in town stopped for five minutes.

As Stratton's favorite flower was a rose and his favorite color purple, American Beauty roses tied with purple ribbon were hung at his house instead of black crepe. Every business house and organization sent huge wreaths. The demand for roses was so great that the supply in Colorado Springs, Pueblo and Denver was exhausted and it was necessary to send to Chicago for more.

On Wednesday he was carried to Evergreen Cemetery with pomp and ceremony after a burial service at his house to which only his friends and relatives were invited. As he had been a thirty-second degree Mason and an Elk, a member of the board of trustees of Colorado College and the State School of Mines, these organizations sent representatives. There is no doubt why they came. An amusing story still persists of the Colorado College professors making the long trek on foot behind his hearse. One of them had a blister on his heel. At each step he chanted in a low undertone, "Hope he left us a million . . . hope he left us a million."

It was a prayerful chant, varying only by amounts hoped

for, that was echoed throughout the State. Friends, relatives, business associates and employees, members of churches, schools, social and fraternal organizations stood by with bared heads as Stratton was lowered into his grave, more concerned with what he had left behind.

There was much to think about. The jewels of the dead man consisted of two ordinary watches, a watch fob and two pearl shirt studs. And in the inventory of his real and personal property, listed as his chattel property, the curious ran into the following queer item:

Zenobia Gold M. Co., 856,928 shares at 2¢........	$17,138.52
Dillon Gold M. Co., 50,000 shares at 20¢.........	10,000.00
Two Old Horses, pensioners at pasture, no value...	0.00

Stratton's friends of the early Cripple Creek days had long forgotten the first team he had bought to replace the old gray mare he usually rented. Stratton hadn't. He had remembered how, hitched to his buckboard, they had whirled him up the steep grade to camp, showing heels to the plodding mule teams and ore wagons. Their names were Sorrel and Baldy, a piebald, his favorite, on whom he used to ride to Victor for his mail.

His curious friends now investigated. Bills of two dollars a month for pasturage at the William Bates ranch, five miles south of town, were found. The two old pensioned horses, almost twenty years old, sway-backed and half blind, were Sorrel and Baldy.

But the estate! In Denver, Stratton's holdings comprised the old Tabor property at Seventeenth and Broadway, the Coronado Building he had erected at Fifteenth and Stout Streets, the Toltec Building at Seventeenth and Stout, the property on Seventeenth and Welton, and his $650,000 mortgage on the Brown Palace Hotel—all estimated at over $2,000,000.

In Colorado Springs his estate comprised the interurban railway, Stratton Park, the Mining Exchange Building, the corner on Kiowa and Nevada occupied by the County Court House, and two other downtown corners, all probably worth $2,745,000.

His mining property in Cripple Creek consisted of over one hundred claims, with title in the name of The Stratton Cripple Creek Mining and Development Company, for which he had paid nearly $7,000,000. Besides these claims he had acquired control of eight other mining companies at a cost of over $824,000, and it was rumored he had left 560,000 shares of Portland stock which could probably be sold for $3,000,000.

An astounding estate that was estimated to be worth anything from $10,000,000 to $15,000,000.

Everyone expected something from it. Colorado College, forgetting his huff over being denied a right-of-way for his street car line through the campus, believed he would endow it with a large present. The Masonic Order hoped for a new temple, and the B.P.O.E. was sure he would not forget his brother Elks although he had joined but a short time before his death. The city needed and wanted from him a new public library, at least Stratton Park.

Mourners indeed! They might have been a band of hungry wolves who had chased him to the brink of his grave, and stood there, tongues lolling out, hungrily eyeing his mountain-cedar casket being lowered out of sight.

Thus was Winfield Scott Stratton gently laid away in his last resting place.

And hardly had he been buried before his character and life were being furiously unearthed.

PART SIX: LITTLE LONDON

" 'Tis not enough to help the feeble up, but to support him after."

The Myron Stratton Home.

Stratton's room furnishings and clothes, formerly in his quarters at Winfield, now in the

6. LITTLE LONDON

IN Denver an old man lay on a cot in the county hospital. He was slowly passing over his last range, but with the remarkable tenaciousness of an old prospector he defied death for days with a grizzled smile. His physique was magnificent. He had a huge barrel chest and horny hands, a face brown and unwrinkled, and clear blue eyes almost hidden by shaggy eyebrows bigger than most men's mustaches.

Sensing a story, a newspaper reporter stopped in the ward and was allowed to talk with him for a few moments.

The old prospector's name was John Dunn, the man who had sold Stratton his first and no-account mine, the Yretaba in the San Juan county. Old Dunn remembered an incident connected with the venture. Stratton, coming back from the mine late one afternoon, had bumped into a huge black bear as he was entering his tent. There was no time to retreat; the bear rose on his hind feet and lunged toward him. Stratton grabbed up a butcher knife, flung himself upon its chest to escape its claws, and after a terrific struggle killed it.

Remarked old Dunn: "I only cite the incident to show that Stratton's real claim to fame is as a plucky bear-fighter, whereas he is known the world over, not for his prowess in that line, but because he stumbled upon a piece of rich ore and traced it to the place it came from. Fame and life are queer things. Sometimes I think they are good things and then again I do not."

This is a commentary on Stratton that can bear much reflection. He was not a great man as one who leaves the undying impress of his character upon succeeding generations. One of hundreds of thousands caught in the flow of westward expansion, Stratton derived all his power from the discovery of the Independence. One year, ten years later, Cripple Creek would have been founded by someone else. But it was Stratton, and he became more powerful than could have been believed. His test and the judgment upon him must rest on how he used this power.

For this reason alone, the story of Stratton does not end with his death. Always enigmatic and little known, he was the figurehead at the crest of a mighty wave that swept on forward.

On the morning of September 21st, a week after his death, Stratton's will was read. It was simple, and concisely stated. To his favorite nephew, Carl S. Chamberlin from Brooklyn, New York, he left his house and furnishings and $50,000. To Earl and Harry Hamlin, sons of his sister Harriet who had helped him during his first days in Colorado, he left $50,000 each. Elma Pearl Chamberlin, his niece, Mrs. Jennie S. Cobb and her two daughters also received $50,000 apiece. His son, Isaac Henry Stratton, was to be paid $50,000. His old boyhood chum Byron Logan, a blacksmith in Indianapolis, received a bequest of $10,000; and $25,000 was directed to be paid to the State Institution for the Mute and Blind, "the interest on which shall be given annually to the pupils as a reward for excellence in Scholarship or demeanor or both." All the rest of the estate was to be placed in a trust fund for the home for the aged poor and dependent children which was to be built and named in memory of his father, the Myron Stratton Home.

Chagrin and disappointment rose like a wave and splashed

the front pages of the newspapers. Hardly had the ink dried on the headlines screaming his death before they began to publish derogatory attacks on the disposition he had made of his wealth.

"Whatever sorrow was caused by the death of Mr. Stratton the first day or two after the event has been very largely dissipated by general anxiety to learn what disposition is to be made of his great mining interests."

The *Cripple Creek Times* was the most vindictive. In long furious editorials against the "Father of Cripple Creek" it shouted that "the will becomes a menace and a very grave one to the public weal" and that "not alone would the carrying out of the provisions of Stratton's will be a crime against the very beneficiaries thereof, but it would be a crime against Colorado Springs, El Paso County, and the State of Colorado."

Stratton's home town was particularly upset on learning there was to be given it no public library, no new Masonic temple, no park, and no great endowment for the College. An influential Colorado Springs citizen was quoted as saying:

It is a difficult matter to give away vast sums of money and not do greater evil than good. Richer men and better thinkers than Stratton have pondered over the subject, and none of them have built a home for paupers. . . . The moral effect upon Colorado Springs may well appal the thinking citizen. The fifty thousand population that Colorado Springs has been talking about will be quickly accomplished when the Home is ready to receive visitors. The ragtag and bobtail from the ends of the earth will arrive to take up residence here and acquire a home. . . . The disappointment and chagrin of the citizens of Colorado Springs is very great because they had built high hopes on the things Stratton would do for the place. . . . Instead, they are left bitter at heart and the city that it is supposed he was attempting to benefit is standing foolishly looking on, not knowing whether it shall accept congratulations or condolences. It is a fit finish, however, to the career of one of the most eccentric and erratic characters that was ever snatched from obscurity and endowed with a kingly fortune.

Facts, the weekly, confirmed the opinion by stating:

Winfield Scott Stratton was a man of many surprises, but his will is the greatest of them all. After several years of acting and planning for the good of Colorado Springs, he suddenly flew off on a tangent. . . . His opportunity was a rare one. To provide for the perpetuation of the street-railway and park system in its present condition, give the College an endowment that would insure its future, build a public library, sanatoriums or hospitals. . . . But to leave practically his whole fortune, conservatively estimated at $10,000,000 to found a gigantic poorhouse is certainly unwise. Its practicability is doubtful and its benefits far from certain.

The *Denver Post* gleefully finished off her sister-town's discomforture by echoing her complaint thus:

To perdition with the poorhouse! We don't want it. Hundreds of mendicants will be sitting around our beautiful avenues, mostly in plain view of the Antlers Hotel, where all our summer visitors can see them waiting for a chance to squeeze into a home, get a square meal, a comfortable room and a tailormade suit of clothes. It will be a nasty spectacle and we don't like it. Why didn't he do something that would enhance the glory of our incomparable metropolis? But a poorhouse. Bah!

The attack veered suddenly to Stratton himself when the *Post* came out with the red-letter headline:

THE MYRON STRATTON INSTITUTION WAS FOUNDED AS A DEED OF EXPIATION

Remorse Over a Youthful Attempt on His Father's Life Led Stratton to Establish a Home to the Memory of the Man Who to Him Was Dearest in Life and Death.

It had resurrected the old story of his quarrels with his father. Byron Logan the Indiana blacksmith was told of his $10,000 bequest and interviewed. He stated, "It is true that Stratton did get a little wild at Jeffersonville and did have some trouble with his father, and that was the reason he went West so soon, but it is not true he ever discredited a friend."

Within a month this had led to a derogatory attack by Richard Work on Stratton's character during boyhood. This in turn was replied to by his other chum, James Parker, and attested by his old Jeffersonville neighbor George Pfau.

Inevitably, during the probing, it was remembered that although Stratton had kept a picture of his father there were none of his mother in the house. And to the best of their recollection he had never in his known life spoken his mother's name. Indeed, nothing was known of her.

Why, if it had been his father he quarreled with, had he not dedicated the proposed Home to his mother? Why was he so apparently ashamed or reluctant to speak of her?

Then the story began to circulate. Stratton had once stated in confidence that his mother would never have her picture taken because she was so dark. Stratton himself had been growing darker. He had once asked a friend, "What the hell makes me so dark?"

"Oh, all that prospecting tanned you up."

"Hum," he had replied quietly. "Seems like in ten years that tan would have faded some."

It was believed to have been one of the reasons why he refused to mingle in society and remained a recluse. And then someone remembered one of his odd habits: he would sit looking at the heel of his hand. In a Negro's there is a visible color-line running down the flesh from the base of the little finger.

Amid this hullabaloo, the chagrin of Stratton's former friends and employees began to sound an ominous murmur. Many of them, they said, had been promised bequests which were not included in the will. They wanted to know why. And slowly from an unknown source spread an ugly rumor. . . .

Shortly after Stratton, Ramsay and Dr. Rice had returned from London, Ramsay had terminated his years of service as Stratton's confidential secretary and adviser. They had been the best of friends. It was held by some that Ramsay had been discharged because he had been discovered "knocking down" on all of Stratton's contracts after having been given a present of $50,000. Others now held a different version.

A certain group of men, they said, had schemed in every possible way to get Ramsay away from Stratton. They had succeeded so well that during the last two months of Stratton's illness, Ramsay was not allowed to see his former employer. After his death, Ramsay went to California. He was never the same again. As one of his friends wrote to his wife, "He was truly an honest and sincere man, just and upright in his business dealings and all the affairs of his life with Stratton. His was too fine a mind and heart to stand it. Mr. Ramsay died from a broken heart."

Who were these men and why did they want Ramsay out of the way?

Well, said rumor, Dr. Rice had been the other confidential friend whom Stratton had taken to London with him. When Ramsay was out of the way, Stratton had hired another secretary but made Dr. Rice his financial agent for all his vast Bowl of Gold undertakings. Then, unexpectedly, he had got rid of Rice. He no longer retained him even as a physician; he did not even allow him in the house. And he told one of his servants never to give him a drop of medicine that Rice prescribed.

Then suddenly Stratton had been stricken. Anna, worried about his religious views and anxious to banish his Christian Science practitioners, had called the first medical doctor that jumped to her mind—Dr. Rice.

Rice moved into the house and took charge of Stratton during his last illness. Stratton was ill for weeks and hardly conscious. A trained nurse was hired. Yet, in his lucid intervals, Stratton would allow no one to give him medicine but Anna.

The whispered inferences spread. Stratton had made a will appointing as trustees of his estate Dr. D. H. Rice; his attorney Tyson S. Dines; and his nephew, Carl S. Chamberlin, a college student in New York. Then, after his fuss with Rice, he had made different provisions—and of course provided for the many left out of the first. It was never signed. Stratton, in a coma, had passed away.

That these three men should be executors of his will and trustees of a vast estate dedicated to an abhorred pauper's home was bitterly resented. Plainly something had to be done—and was. City, State, newspapers, citizens and the Court began a battle for Stratton's millions.

Three new administrators for the estate were appointed by the Court: C. C. Hamlin who was Reed's old partner, H. M. Blackmer and O. P. Grimes.

For their part, the original executors insisted on their rights. They were afraid that the new administrators would attempt to gain valuable papers and to seize the street-car system. They appointed armed guards. And now, just two weeks after Stratton's death, his properties looked like armed camps. Two armed guards were on duty at his office, and others were posted at the power house and street-car barns. Even his grave resounded to the patrolling feet of two guards at night, and the clatter of hammer and nails during the erection of a small hut to shelter them.

Everyone in town concerned himself with giving advice on how the money should be spent, the *Gazette* offering $200 in prizes for the best essays on the subject. The *Pueblo Chieftain*, estimating his wealth at from $15,000,000 to $50,000,000, carried the suggestive editorial:

> The death of a Rockefeller child led to scientific investigations which are said to have proved an achievement of rare value, the discovery of the germ of the fatal "summer complaint" which carries off so many little ones. It might now be a good thing if some of the Stratton money could be used to direct a new campaign against that malady known as Bright's disease which even in the case of a millionaire was fatal.

As a matter of fact, on account of Stratton's early death and the many projects and investments he left hanging fire, his estate was worth but $6,307,166.36 though once the entanglements were straightened out it increased greatly.

This was enough to cause concern to Governor Peabody and the Attorney General, N. C. Miller. On the eve of their departure from the State Capital to Little London to ask the Court for the appointment of an appraiser, Miller stated definitely: "We are going to get that $7,000,000 for Colorado. It rightfully belongs to us and we need it bad.

The real fight for the money will begin next week. . . . We have employed the best counsel in the State."

That the State did not obtain the money on this first attempt in nowise discouraged the Attorney General or the Denver newspapers. They continued the campaign against Stratton's plans for a charitable home.

However, a certain young man had arrived in Colorado to precipitate matters. He was reported as being "about six feet tall, of dark complexion and smooth-shaven. He is unlike his father except that he is tall and slender. The most notable feature of the young man is his eyes which are large and deep black, but quick and observing. He wore a dark English worsted suit and black derby. He spoke and acted like an educated man trained in a home of refinement. When he parted from Judge Gunnell he excused himself with a courtly bend of the body, and when the three men entered the elevator he was by choice in the rear, touching the elbows of the other two as if escorting them in. When a woman rushed to the elevator he quietly and unostentatiously removed his hat and the other men followed suit."

The young man was Stratton's son, Isaac Henry Stratton.

He was seen in the company of Judge Gunnell, whose son-in-law, C. C. Hamlin, had been appointed one of the Administrators to Collect of the Stratton Estate. With him as administrators, Judge Orr of the County Court had also appointed his brother-in-law, O. P. Grimes, and H. M. Blackmer, now in Paris, a fugitive from justice because of the Teapot Dome trouble. When Isaac Henry Stratton accompanied Judge Gunnell back to Denver, rumors began to fly as to why he had returned. He aroused more talk and interest at the Brown Palace than had any visitor for years.

Stratton's bequest of $50,000 to his son stated specifically that it was to be given him provided he did not contest the will. Isaac Henry, or I. Harry Stratton as he preferred to be called, admitted that his feelings had been hurt, not because his bequest was comparatively small, but because his father had left his house and personal effects to a nephew. He had decided to risk his $50,000 and contest the will.

Everyone was for him. The *Cripple Creek Times* declared:

> One cannot be charitable when he [Stratton] is unjust to his own son, and when through misanthropic ideas or prejudice a man by his own will works such a palpable injustice the average person cannot but confess that he would be pleased to see the courts step in to set aside and make void such a will.

The *Post* was sure: "He May Not Lose the Paltry Bequest." Soon people knew why. James Doyle, one of the "three Jims" who had located the Portland and one of Stratton's old partners, had stepped in. He knew that Stratton's son was penniless, on a vacation from work, and had no money to prosecute such a suit. He knew too that for the boy $50,000 was a lot of money, too much to risk losing. So now he organized a syndicate of wealthy Colorado Springs and Cripple Creek mining men to furnish I. Harry the money to break Stratton's will. It was not a fatherly gesture: their own mining interests would be greatly enhanced if the will could be broken. It was rumored that these men had guaranteed I. Harry $50,000 should he lose the suit and his bequest, provided he made the attempt; also that he wanted only a cool million for his share should he succeed.

Among the men offered a share in the syndicate was Stratton's old secretary, Ramsay. But despite his quarrel with Stratton and the injustices he had reputedly suffered, Ramsay indignantly declined—to his eternal credit.

So, said the *Gazette:*

Now that the contest of the Stratton will is under a full head of steam with a large and well equipped crew of Administrators to Collect, Administrators to Expend, Administrators to Sell and Administrators to Keep, with their retinue of secretaries, clerks, agents, managers and hangers-on; with a choice assortment of Executors of all kinds; with Trustees to manage every branch of the estate; with dozens of lawyers upholding each branch of each class of Administrators, Executors, Trustees, Agents, Managers and Hangers-On—young Stratton may well take a long breath, carefully scan the judicial horizon and ask himself, "Where Am I At? . . . Where Do I Come In? . . . What Do I Get?"

For six months there was a hue and cry over the impending suit. Polly Pry of the *Denver Post* interviewed the polite young man with a sympathetic demeanor which elicited the story that his mother, Zeurah Stewart, had accompanied her stepfather to Colorado because he had asthma. In the fall of '75 she met Stratton. The following March her mother died suddenly of a heart attack. Mr. Stewart wanted to return at once to Illinois. On this account she and Stratton were married a few days after her mother's death. From the beginning she was made unhappy by his violent temper and unreasonable jealousy. From the proceeds of a small piece of property from her father's estate, she turned over $3,000 to Stratton who spent it on various mining schemes. One day Stratton ordered her to pack up her clothes. He took her to Danville, Illinois, and left her there alone without means or friends. She never saw him again.

Three weeks later I. Harry Stratton was born at Cobery, Illinois, in the house of her stepfather. By the time Harry was eighteen years old, his father had struck it rich and was famous. Hearing that he was ill, I. Harry in '95 came to Colorado for a month. Stratton was kind to his son, but as he was going on a trip to California, he sent I. Harry back to Illinois. After that he sent him to Illinois University at Champaign for three years, providing him with one hundred dollars per month.

This, in short, was I. Harry's story. The simple fact that his mother and father had been married on July 26, 1876, instead of in March, and that he had been born the following January, together with Stratton's repeated denials that the son was his, was the only evidence offered against it.

The matter came to court early in April, 1903. So widespread was the story of Stratton that it was necessary to call forty-two men in the original jury panel. Of these, twenty were selected as the group from which the final eight were to be drawn. Among them was a man named Bateman who on the morning of the trial stated that something during the night had come to his knowledge which made him unfit for jury duty. A young woman had visited him, declaring that she had received a vision from God and had been told that the will of Stratton was not to be disturbed. Bateman was excused, but thereafter the jurors were kept locked up.

That the case was sensational is a mild statement. It was more like a riot. The contestants attacked Stratton's character and charged him with over-indulgence in drugs and liquors. They maintained that when he had made his will he was a mental wreck, haunted by insane delusions, and a monomaniac on the subject of his son. It was claimed he had always regarded I. Harry Stratton as his son; that, in fact, forty-eight hours after his marriage Stratton was seeking a physician to save his yet unborn son, and two months afterward was seeking a doctor to prevent miscarriage, his only desire being to preserve his son and heir. Ex-Senator Wolcott, attorney, attempted to prove that Stratton was a morphine fiend, a drunkard and a man without principle.

The court was in an uproar. He was thrice overruled, but persisted in his claims that Stratton used morphine and as much as a quart of whiskey a day, and that he had been treated for acute alcoholism at the time he made his will.

The executors of Stratton's estate, in answer to these charges, maintained silence. They stated that in view of the dead millionaire's noble and philanthropic nature they would not trespass on his private and domestic affairs. They left it to his son to lift the curtain.

It soon became evident that a deadlock was reached. The attorneys were in the midst of a bitter battle over the admission of evidence relating to Stratton's mental balance and physical condition, and in a few hours it was apparent that the Court would have to be called upon to decide whether his whole life should be laid bare or only that portion of it at the time of his signing his will. Then, on the threshold of one of the bitterest legal contests ever waged in a Colorado court, something happened to prove that Stratton's luck still held. In death as in life he was to retain the secrecy which enshrouded him.

The attorneys on both sides, returning after an adjournment, began a friendly banter which turned into a serious discussion. The Court on opening was asked to approve a compromise. When it was settled, I. Harry Stratton received $350,000. Of this he paid his lawyers $175,000 and $3,000 for the costs of the trial.

The Estate went ahead with its plans to carry out the terms of Stratton's will.

For I. Harry Stratton, however, it was the beginning of many troubles. As he was ready to step on a train to Oshkosh, Wisconsin, he was handed a summons notifying him of a suit for $35,000 brought against him by Joseph B. Donovan. This was Stratton's old friend Joe Donovan, whom he had known in Iowa and Nebraska and who had helped him get his first job in Colorado. Donovan was now living on a ranch south of town and had always been friendly to Stratton's son. It was he who had kept I. Harry informed of Stratton's movements and had telegraphed him that Stratton was dying. During the suit he had been the chief witness for the contestants and the only one called to testify regarding Stratton's sanity.

It now developed that I. Harry Stratton had agreed to pay him 10 percent of all money recovered in return for his testimony. I. Harry Stratton had apparently forgotten the matter, as he had forgotten the $504 Donovan had given him for personal expenses, besides providing him with shelter at his ranch.

The case dragged on to October 5, 1903, when I. Harry Stratton was given the verdict. Donovan appealed the case, and three more suits aggregating $13,000 more were brought against young Stratton by others who claimed he had agreed to pay them for their testimony. I. Harry left for Pasadena, California, lost all his money in real-estate ventures, and became a bank clerk.

2

The compromise seemed a precedent, at least a signal for everyone else to try his luck. . . .

Stratton's aversion to lawyers was well known. One day on a street corner he had indignantly exclaimed, "I wish I were worth $10,000,000 and I would spend every cent of it putting every lawyer in Colorado in jail."

It is an amusing contradiction that now when his estate was worth almost that much, it was owing only to the efforts of the best lawyers in the State that it was maintained for the purpose he had desired. Or perhaps it was a subtle revenge that almost landed them in jail and the madhouse too!

For now began a period of almost fifteen years of spectacular litigation. Suits of every possible kind were instituted. Every person who had known Stratton seemed to be rushing into the courts hoping to cut a slice off his golden melon. Old prospectors remembered having discovered the Independence with him and dug up old location stakes still bearing their names. Business associates brought in old unfulfilled contracts to prove he had promised to buy interests in a hundred wildcat schemes. Women especially thronged in with old sorrows and grievances which could only be assuaged with cold cash.

A Miss Bonnie Ethel Steele discovered a musty memorandum book in the bottom of an old trunk in Kansas City. In it her father had once scrawled, "I am the owner this date of eighty thousand shares of stock in the Amazon Mine" (merged later into the Portland). On this she brought suit for $250,000.

A few years later a Rose Ellen Stratton appeared from Missouri to seek her share of wealth as Stratton's "sister." When asked the simple question why she had waited almost thirteen years after his death before claiming him as a brother, she replied that she had always been subject to lapses of memory and had just remembered to connect her long lost brother with the rich Mr. Stratton.

One of the suits, brought by a man named E. A. Meredith, was for $77,600. He claimed that Stratton early in 1900 had been desirous of obtaining for his Bowl of Gold some mining property in Cripple Creek belonging to the Mars Consolidated Gold Mining Company. He authorized Meredith to buy the stock control of the company, for which service he would be paid $10,000. Stratton was then to buy through Meredith all the stock of that company for $90,000. Meredith accordingly bought on the open market under his own name the stock control of Mars for $10,000 only to discover that Stratton had changed his mind. The value of the million shares of capital stock then dropped and left Meredith holding the sack. He was now suing for his original $10,000 loss for services, $50,000 loss due to depreciation of the stock since, and $17,600 interest—a total of $77,600.

The case passed through four courts. On technical grounds the County Court held that it was proper to sue for the $10,000 but not the $50,000. The District Court affirmed that neither was proper. The State Supreme Court held that the $50,000 was proper but not the $10,000 and remanded the case to the District Court for further trial. The case was again tried and appealed.

The case was finally lost by Meredith because of two letters he had written Stratton. One stated, "I write to ask you if there is any chance of making a deal on Mars yet? I went flat broke holding that thing together, and had to get out on location again. Hoping that we may be able to get some kind of trade, I remain . . ." The other also showed that no agreement had been drawn with Stratton, and that Meredith was simply trying to peddle his stock: "I do not wish to bore you to death with Mars, but would like to hold it together until I can make some deal with you or someone else."

It was clearly a case of trying to cash in on some of Stratton's millions while there was still plenty to spare.

There were no less than twelve women who swore they were Stratton's forgotten widows. On one day alone thirty-five suits were dismissed in the local courts because they were ostensibly "blood money" demands. And at one time the

Estate was confronted with claims and alleged debts amounting to about $35,000,000 when it had in assets scarcely more than $6,000,000.

The history of these numerous lawsuits together with their briefs and abstracts of record would not only make a book, but almost a library to which one could turn at will for humor and history, pathos, tragedy and chicanery. They are dry and dusty, but in them is found perhaps better than any place else the character of the slim, inconspicuous and enigmatic Stratton.

Of the many, there were two which gained national and international notoriety. In turn they revealed for the first time Stratton's business acumen and the extent of his mining projects, and a part of his personal life heretofore hidden. Both are chapters of his life that cannot lightly be passed over, and they read like the wildest fiction.

The first of these carried forward the old squabble over the Independence. It brought out three men of worldwide fame, and it created a stir on both sides of the Atlantic. The case was known simply as No. 2083 in the United States Court of Appeals and No. 589 in the Supreme Court of the United States: Stratton's Independence, Ltd., versus Tyson S. Dines, *et al*, Executors of Stratton's will.

A more apt name might have been "London versus Little London."

The legal counsel for Stratton's Independence, Limited, of London was numerous and formidable. It consisted of seven attorneys directed by the famous Samuel Untermeyer.

The four attorneys defending the Stratton executors were headed by Little London's erstwhile herdboy who each summer had led all of the town cows back and forth from pasture. Stratton would have remembered the first time he had seen the boy: that early January morning of '74 when he was walking down the street after the furious chinook windstorm and met Major McAllister fully dressed and holding his child in arms, ready to flee when his house collapsed. This child in arms, then herdboy, and now lawyer Henry McAllister, had the job of keeping $6,000,000 of Stratton's money in the estate.

Untermeyer's charges for Stratton's Independence, Limited, were simple. He claimed that Stratton had salted the Independence mine in order to sell it for $10,000,000.

His four expert brief-lawyers working days and nights for two years without ever appearing in court managed to state it better and to list ten specific charges. They stated in detail that Stratton's Independence, Limited, had been made a corporation under the laws of England on April 29, 1899, for the purpose of buying Stratton's mining claims, and that Stratton was one of the promoters and incorporators. Stratton had then represented that the property had exposed and in sight ore bodies worth $7,000,000 and was thereby reasonably worth $10,000,000. These representations were false; the mine had been salted; there was but $2,000,000 in sight and the property was worth only $4,000,000.

They were therefore seeking to recover the difference of $6,000,000.

McAllister's defense for Stratton's executors might reasonably have been expected to lead into a legal tangle that only the seven opposing lawyers could figure out. It happened to be appallingly simple—as simple and direct as a town herdboy defending a Hoosier carpenter against the best legal talent on both sides of the Atlantic. He picked out one point in the case to stick to as he used to pick out an obstreperous cow. (And today he can still name the characteristics of every cow in his charge.) His defense was simply that Stratton did not receive a plugged nickel from Stratton's Independence, Limited, and that he did not sell his mine to them.

To comprehend this astounding statement of fact, it is necessary to remember what Stratton, Reed and Ramsay had been doing in London. It shows at least that McAllister was not the only one who could use his head. A Jeffersonville carpenter in London among the bigwigs and world capitalists had also used his.

It will be recalled that Stratton as payment for his mine accepted 1,000,000 shares of stock in Stratton's Independence, Limited. The other 100,000 shares of the total capital stock were retained by the corporation to develop the mine.

Then Stratton had entered into an agreement with a second company, the Venture Corporation of London, giving it the right to sell the shares on the market after it had bought Reed's option for $1,000,000 as his commission. For the first 666,666 shares Stratton was to receive £1.19 each, and for the next 333,333 shares he was to receive £2.10 each.

The plan was approximately carried out. The stock was issued with almost instant success. Despite the Boer War and Hammond's gloomy predictions, the price of the stock trebled its par value—reaching £3—as $500,000 was taken out of the mine in one month. By April, 1900, 592,500 shares had been sold to the English public. Then Stratton, eager to get his money and get back into his Bowl of Gold, made an agreement whereby he sold the rest of his stock out and out to the Venture Corporation "at such a price as with the cash already received . . . to make up the total inclusive sum of $10,000,000."

On this basis McAllister made his defense that Stratton received no money from Stratton's Independence, Limited—

nothing but stock. The transaction was perfectly legal under the laws of both England and America, each permitting the issuance of capital stock in exchange for property conveyed to a corporation. Neither party was swindled or injured, and the corporation now had the property and was extracting ore from it.

Offhand it appeared like a technical point of law, an irritating obstruction lodged in the throat of the justly renowned, golden-voiced Samuel Untermeyer. His four brief-lawyers had drawn up a case of which the briefs and arguments filled 788 pages. Now with his court lawyers, Guggenheimer and Marshall, Untermeyer let loose a barrage of the oratory that has made him internationally famous. In vain he pleaded that the Court should not let a point of law interfere with justice. But McAllister stuck to his point as he would have stuck to a cranky cow. He brought out the fact that the company had not relied upon Stratton's representation, but had made its own examination of the mine and acted on the results.

And now another internationally known name was brought in, that of the great mining engineer John Hays Hammond, who had made his reputation in the gold fields of South Africa. In his report to the British stockholders of the Independence, Limited, he had said that there were but 120,000 tons in sight, worth about $2,300,000 gross and $1,000,000 net. He now tendered his resignation as consulting engineer. It was refused. McAllister pointed out that since the company had obtained possession of the Independence mine it had extracted and sold ore to the value of more than $10,198,575. And he made his opponents admit that the original purchasers of stock made money.

But he still stubbornly maintained that even if the Independence mine had not produced a dollar, the company had given Stratton for it no money, only stock. If it had been foisted on the public, then it was the final purchasers of the stock on the London market who were the ones injured and not Stratton's Independence, Limited. Stratton had sold his stock, not his mine.

He made his point stick. The Britishers took an appeal to the United States Court of Appeals, the highest and last tribunal that can hear a case, and on February 20, 1905, Judge Adams sustained the decision, saying: "The Plaintiff, therefore, cannot occupy the attitude in this case of having paid any money to Stratton. It exchanged one million shares of its capital stock for his mines. What money Stratton received came from independent investors in that stock, to whom he may or may not be under obligations."

It is of interest that the original purchasers of the stock had made money on their investments, for immediately the Venture Corporation instituted a suit for $2,040,000. This was defeated as had been that of Stratton's Independence, Limited.

Then, in August of the same year, Leslie Popejoy, the old plasterer who had grubstaked Stratton, appeared for the last time to bring suit for $8,000,000. This suit, like his previous one, was settled out of court on the advice of David P. Strickler, who had arrived to act as the Estate's attorney for over thirty years and then as trustee. The others were furious at another compromise, another damned holdup. But a start had to be made on the long delayed Home, and for the insignificant sum of $3,000 Popejoy's claims were stilled forever.

The trustees, worn out from combating rumor and litigation involving sums to the amount of $35,000,000, were almost ready to wash their hands of the whole business.

Meanwhile, the State had been continuing its fight to obtain the Stratton money.

Former Judge Robert Kerr to whom the trustees were compelled to report while he was County judge had accused them, saying:

> As administrators to collect they took for themselves $1,000 a day or $10,000 a month each. And this for services which their counsel promised would be without cost to the estate.
>
> The executors have given away $100,000 of the assets of the estate in free street-car transportation. They had no more right to do so than to give away the royalties from the Cripple Creek mines.

The Attorney General now recommended to the Governor that pressure be brought to bear on the trustees to compel them to make an immediate sale of the interurban railway at a ruinous sacrifice.

When this was defeated, the State veered to a more successful attack. According to Stratton's will $25,000 was paid to the Institution for the Education of the Dumb and Blind at Colorado Springs. On this bequest the State assessed and collected an inheritance tax of $1,600 and then refunded it by legislative action. But no refund was ever made of the $284,000 inheritance tax collected upon the like bequest to the Myron Stratton Home, although subsequent legislative enactment exempted all like bequests from such a tax. It even insisted on an inheritance tax on the $350,000 paid I. Harry Stratton. In court the executors pointed out that the Probate Court, owing to the vast amount of litigation, did not appraise the taxable value of the estate until almost four years after Stratton's death. It made no difference; interest on the inheritance tax was computed from

Stratton's death till it was paid. This had raised the sum to a total of $374,817.

Denver newspapers had long campaigned against the apparent inactivity of the trustees, although as soon as the estate had been turned over to them by the executors they had incorporated the Myron Stratton Home on November 12, 1909. This adverse publicity had its effect on State Officers who were still trying to obtain the Stratton millions for use in their own public charitable institutions.

Among the laws passed at the Nineteenth Session of the General Assembly of the State of Colorado, convened at Denver on January 1, 1913, is found Senate Joint Resolution No. 2—Stratton Estate, which reads in part:

Whereas, The said Stratton particularly specified in his will that in the event of the lapse of the bequest of the residuum of my estate . . . I direct my said executors to pay over and deliver to the State of Colorado, all of that portion of my estate included in the bequest of the residue . . . to be appropriated and applied in such manner as the Legislature of said State shall direct to the support of such charitable and benevolent institutions as are now supported at the expense of the State of Colorado, and

Whereas, The executors and trustees of said estate are, with one exception, the same persons and have had the sole control and possession of said estate for a period of 10 years and 5 months, and have under one pretense or another, failed to perform the trusts and obligations by said will and have violated the wishes of said Winfield Scott Stratton imposed upon them, therefore be it

Resolved, By the House and Senate of the Nineteenth General Assembly, that the Attorney General be, and he is hereby directed, to institute, with all diligence, such action or actions at law, suit or suits in equity as may, in his judgment, be requisite to oust said executors and trustees or either of them from possession of said estate and for the recovery, in the name and on behalf of the People of the State of Colorado of all said estate.

This suit was not brought against the Estate, nor were the trustees and executors ousted, for not two months later they executed a contract for the long delayed Myron Stratton Home.

But before Stratton's will could be followed out, there arose the most serious and spectacular obstacle of all.

3

It was the case of a woman named Sophia Gertrude Chellew versus the Stratton Estate, more familiarly known as "The Widow Case." For Sophia Gertrude was the thirteenth of the women who claimed to be Stratton's widows. This was the sole question involved, and the answer was bound to be unlucky for someone: the amount involved in the controversy was for one-half of the assets of his estate, approximately $4,000,000.

The litigation proper may be said to have begun on December 20, 1913, when the executors of the estate filed a petition asking that the woman set up her claims, although she had previously instituted and dismissed a suit in the District Court of Denver. After many demurrers, protests and showings, eight different orders for continuance and applications for jury trial, the case came up for trial on May 16, 1916.

Sophia Gertrude's story on which was based her claim read like melodrama.

She was born at Nogatoch on the Red River, Natchitoches parish, Louisiana, the daughter of a Vincent Bell who died while she was yet a baby. Her mother moved with her to Nacogdoches County, Texas; to Cherokee County where she married again; and thence to Woodville, Tyler County. Here at the home of her stepfather, Sophia Gertrude married a brickmaker and brickmason named Andrew N. Poor. They had one child, Cora, and eventually moved to Navarro County, Texas. In November, 1872, Poor died leaving her $12,000 cash, and was buried in an unmarked grave in a private burying ground on the Jameson farm near Rush Creek. For a year after his death, his wife and daughter continued to live on the Jameson farm.

In December of '73, accompanied by her daughter Cora and her cousin Alpheus, known as "Little Doc Bell," Gertrude Sophia Poor moved to the home of John Henry located a few miles south of San Augustine, Texas. On Christmas Eve a dance and party was given at the Henry cabin. In the midst of festivities a group of men came to the cabin seeking refuge from a storm, escorted by a son-in-law of John Henry named Dave Kennedy, a man who "drinked" a great deal and was then drunk. One of them was a man called Thompson, another called Russell. With them was a "Bill Scott." All names were aliases as the men had come to Texas to buy "cheap cattle."

For Bill Scott and the Widow Poor it was apparently a case of love at first sight. On December 31st, she and Bill Scott accompanied by Thompson drove to Center, Texas, to procure a marriage license. Then Bill Scott revealed his true name and the license was issued under the name of Stratton. Returning to John Henry's cabin, the couple were married the next day in the presence of their many guests.

On the following morning, January 2, 1874, the party left for Fort Worth. Stratton, Sophia Gertrude and her two-and-a-half year old child, Cora Poor, rode in a wagon, while Russell, Thompson and the others accompanied them on horseback. They reached Fort Worth on January 8th.

Twenty days later Stratton rode into Colorado Springs on a dappled gray horse (a distance of some 627 miles). During a conversation with an inquisitive friend, Stratton admitted that he had bought no "cheap cattle" but that he had "got married while he was down there" and had "got quite a bunch of his wife's money."

A year later Stratton returned to Fort Worth to find that his family had increased by the addition of twins, Frances and Winfield Scott. Living with them were Sophia Gertrude's daughter, Cora Poor, her cousin, Little Doc Bell; and her sister, Mrs. Webb. Stratton stayed but a short time. On March 5, 1874, he left for Fort Worth for the Panhandle country with Thompson and Russell, intending to purchase cattle with the money his wife had given him. Traveling by horseback, they reached Fishbaugh, Colorado, on March 30th and Russell got a job at Watson's ranch. Stratton "lit out" alone for Del Norte.

Sophia Gertrude waited for his return until the fall of 1875. Then she, Cora and the twin babies, and Little Doc Bell set out in a wagon to search for him. Upon their arrival in Northwestern Texas at Owen's Ranch, they were told that three men had been killed by Indians nearby. They believed the men had been Stratton, Thompson and Russell. Here the twins died and were buried, and here another daughter, Mary, was born. The saddened relatives returned to the home of Mrs. Webb in Navarro County, Texas, and on November 30, 1876, Sophia Gertrude married Michael Kennedy.

In the late eighties the couple moved to Colorado and in 1889 became residents of Stringtown, a fringe of Leadville. In 1895 Kennedy died and Sophia Gertrude married a Mr. Chellew. That fall she happened to overhear the conversation of two miners who were eating dinner at her house; they spoke of a mine belonging to Winfield Scott Stratton at Cripple Creek. Within a few days she went to Cripple Creek and persuaded a mining man who knew Stratton to bring him into a restaurant where she was waiting. Stratton, she said, recognized her immediately. Both confessed their marriages. Stratton told her that since they had both violated the law by remarrying, the best they could do was to say nothing about it. He gave her money and promised to visit her in Leadville. This he did, meeting Mary and saying that he would not disown her as his daughter. On a second trip he told her that if she made no trouble he would make her independent as soon as he sold his mine, the Independence at Cripple Creek. On both occasions Stratton gave her money.

A short time later she stopped in Colorado Springs on her way to Texas to see her mother, who was ill and had sent for her. Accidentally, she met Stratton who gave her $150. While still in Texas, she heard of Stratton's death from a sketch in a Dallas newspaper.

Such were the allegations, supported by testimony, on which Mrs. Chellew based her claim. Miraculously, once the news got out, witnesses appeared and depositions were taken by Mr. John T. Bottom, her attorney. Mrs. Nelson who ran a boarding-house in Colorado Springs during the seventies and eighties wrote him that she knew something which would help Mrs. Chellew. Bottom with a notary public and his stenographer drove out from Denver ninety miles to where Mrs. Nelson was then living and took her affidavit. It stated:

> I knew Winfield Scott Stratton well; he boarded at my house a good many years. Always stopped at my house when in Colorado Springs. I know when he went to Texas in the fall of

1873 and a good many others knew when he went and where he was going as he talked a good deal about the trip at the house. I know he went to Texas. He came back in the latter part of January, 1874, and came to my house before he took the horse he was riding and the one he was packing to the corral. Left most of his pack at my house. He talked a good deal about his trip to me and others. He told me he had married a widow in Texas who had a good deal of money, mostly in cash, and he had some of the money with him to invest. He said he would go back to Texas in the fall to stay awhile and maybe for good.

A man named Shaffer appeared to state:

I knew Stratton here in Denver in 1878. We were both working at the flour mills in the lower part of town. . . . The boom at Leadville was getting pretty hot and we talked a good deal about it. I told him I was going to Leadville as soon as I finished my contract, and he said he was going also and we would go together or meet there and work together, to which I agreed as I knew Stratton was a better prospector than I was and I liked the idea of going with him. This was in the spring of '78, about April I think. Well, I got away before Stratton but I met him in Leadville and we did some prospecting together but did not have any luck, so I got some burros and went packing to different camps around Leadville. Stratton was a good fellow in camp; often talked about where he had been and what he would do when he struck it big. He often spoke of his wife in Texas and once when we were in Clark's in Leadville he showed me a picture of his Texas wife. I saw it a good many times after that. . . . When the strike was made in Aspen I went there with my pack outfit and Stratton went with me. I made some locations in Aspen and stayed there pretty steady, built a cabin there and Stratton made it his home when he was around and always welcome. One time when he was in my cabin

I had a picture of my cousin, a good-looking girl, and Stratton took the picture of his wife [Mrs. Chellew] and held it up beside the picture of my cousin and asked me how I would trade girls saying he believed his wife was the best looking.

Thompson also appeared, the same Thompson who had been with Stratton when he secured his license to marry, and was present at the wedding. It now developed that Thompson "knew Stratton first in 1868 in Iowa. My first trip to Denver was in 1862. I was scout for Chivington for the Sand Creek fight when he wiped out Black Kettle's band of Indians. At that time I was known as Whistling Jack. I was all along the frontier and the Kansas, New Mexico and Texas frontiers." He confirmed Mrs. Chellew's story regarding the wedding and subsequent events in which he had taken a part, adding: "I saw Stratton in Leadville, Colorado, in 1878 at the Nicholas Hotel, run by a man named Clark. There was a young baby in the house and Stratton said he had a pair of babies about the size of the one there, when he saw them last." Clark's oldest girl "would talk to him about his twins in Texas. This girl is now married and lives within five miles of this house. . . . I saw Stratton every little while up to 1882 or '83 when I met him and asked him how Gertie and the babies were. He told me both his wife and babies were dead. I told him how sorry I was, never dreaming that he was lying. . . . I know Gertie married Stratton. I know he got a lot of money from her. I know now he beat her out of it and believe he intended to beat her out of it all the time, although I thought when he married and for several years after, he was on the square."

Thompson, finding "Gertie was alive and fighting for her share of the estate," began a search for his old partner

Russell. He found Russell at Elk City, Oregon, and persuaded him to come to Denver. He stayed about a year, expecting a quick trial, and then went to South Dakota to help his son who was running a blacksmith shop. Thompson assured all that Russell knew both "Gertie" and Stratton and would return to testify at the trial.

Such an imposing story, supported by witnesses and depositions, seemed to hold popular support and to counter the staunch denials of the Stratton trustees who thus upheld the public character of Stratton's life:

The City of Colorado Springs had its inception early in the year 1871. The following spring, Winfield Scott Stratton came here from Lincoln, Nebraska, and first found employment as a carpenter. In the latter part of '72 or the first part of '73 he formed a general contracting partnership with one Grannis, under the firm name of Grannis and Stratton, their shop being located on Pike's Peak Avenue, then and now one of the principal business streets of Colorado Springs. About the middle of April, '74, he leased his shop to Joseph Dozier and on the 24th of the following July, sold it to Dozier.

At that time Colorado Springs was a small community. Its social activities were limited. People were dependent on each other. Mr. Stratton was then a young man, a skilled workman with plenty of work, and the evidence . . . clearly shows that he entered with zest into the social and business life of the little town.

Years later he discovered the Independence Mine in the Cripple Creek district. The proceeds from this mine made millions for him, and the story of his spectacular acquisition of wealth became one of the tales that form a part of the literature of every gold camp in the West and still lures an occasional solitary prospector into the silent places. Nationwide publicity was given to his whimsical and kindly eccentricities, his very human failings and his unwavering, steadfast loyalty to those who had befriended him in the days when "pay-dirt" was still "over yonder."

Stratton, retiring and aloof, had always been an enigma. His relationship with women had been a thing of rumor and conjecture. It was again the old familiar tale of a man grown suddenly, fabulously rich and denying his old friends. Now at last his life was to be exposed and his suspected perfidies laid bare to public gaze. News of the impending trial filled all the Colorado papers and spread reports of the poor deserving widow who was suing for her share of Stratton's millions.

The *Rocky Mountain News* stated: "Romance has stalked the dead millionaire to his very grave, a deserted woman has pointed the finger of accusation at the imposing monument erected to the memory of the great mining king."

A week later a picture of Sophia Gertrude appeared. She was clad in black silk and her face was spotted with tears. Underneath was the caption, "Sorrow leaves impress on the face of the soft voiced Stratton Widow."

On September 23, 1915, the *San Augustine Tribune* carried the following story under the title "Stratton-Poor Romance":

Mr. D. P. Strickler of Colorado Springs, Colorado, was here last week looking up data in regard to the executors of Winfield Scott Stratton, deceased; and Mr. John T. Bottom of Denver, Colorado, was here in behalf of Mrs. Sophia Gertrude Poor, taking the depositions of Mr. John S. Henry and Samuel A. Henley. Judge Rufus Price of this city assisted Mr. Bottom in his work, and Mr. S. W. Blount of Nacogdoches was here working with Mr. Strickler.

This romantic lawsuit which involves $10,000,000 is drawing nearer to trial each day and much interest is being taken in it. Mr. John S. Henry, one of the witnesses who was present at the marriage, will leave for Colorado to testify in behalf of Mrs. Poor.

The nature of the case is as follows:

The man whose millions made Cripple Creek famous was at one time a day laborer in San Augustine county. He married a widow by the name of Sophia Gertrude Poor, the marriage ceremony being performed at the home of Mr. John Henry, father of John S. Henry, in San Augustine the first week of January, '74. The marriage license was issued by R. L. Parker, clerk of Shelby county, on the first day of January '74.

Subsequently they moved to Fort Worth where Mr. Stratton left his wife and went west to buy cattle with her money, amounting to $10,000. He never returned to her, and finally turned up as a mining prospector in Colorado, locating several of the richest mines in the world.

They met in after years and he acknowledged her as his legal wife and agreed to share his wealth with her and her child by him. But he died suddenly without providing for her in his will, and as he had married again, his millions were claimed by his last wife.

Now Mrs. S. G. Stratton (or Kennedy, as she has also married again) wants to prove her legal marriage with Stratton while they lived in San Augustine county.

R. L. Parker remembers issuing them the license, but the Shelby county records were destroyed by fire and hence it is a matter that demands living witnesses to the marriage at the Henry home in order to establish her legal right to one-half of these millions. Mr. John S. Henry and Mr. Samuel A. Henley are the only two living witnesses that Mr. Bottom was able to find who were at the marriage.

Anyone who has copies of the *Tribune* dated Friday, June 25, 1909, and Friday, July 16, 1909, will please notify the *Tribune* of this fact and they will pay for same.

Copies of these two papers were found, one headlined:

WHO KNOWS THIS MAN?

W. S. STRATTON, WORTH $10,000,000, FORMERLY LIVED IN SAN AUGUSTINE COUNTY AND MARRIED HERE IN 1874—WHO REMEMBERS HIM?

The other was an appeal for help toward "Unraveling the Marriage Mystery":

SECOND CHAPTER IN THE STORY WHICH INVOLVES MANY MILLIONS OF DOLLARS

Somewhere in San Augustine or Shelby County, we believe, there is living a man who would be as important a factor in solving the problem of the marriage of Winfield Scott Stratton and Sophia Gertrude Poor as Darwin's "missing link" would have been in proving the connection between man and monkey.

The *Tribune* has undertaken to unravel the mystery of this marriage and we again call upon all the first settlers of this section to aid us in the investigation.

There are over $10,000,000 involved in the case, and if the *Tribune* is successful in establishing the claim of the lonely woman, who says that it was her own money that Stratton used in prospecting and later in developing the fabulously rich gold mines of Cripple Creek, then some part of this vast wealth will be brought to San Augustine.

The facts are few, the facts that we want to establish—indeed, there is but one main fact. This is it: On the first or second day of January, 1874, W. S. Stratton and Mrs. S. G. Poor were married at the home of a citizen of either San Augustine or Shelby County. The marriage evidently occurred near the county line, probably in the Ironosa community. The name of the citizen was Henry, and the name of the minister who performed the ceremony was Proffitt, or Prophet (it is thought).

Question: Was there ever a preacher by this name in this section?

Question: Have the different denominations in this section complete records of all their churches, and have the ministers always kept records of the marriages, deaths and baptisms where they have officiated? If so, possibly there is in the minutes of one of the various churches the one entry that would prove to be the missing link in this absorbing story. Will the ministers of this section please look up their church records and report to the *Tribune?*

Maybe it was not a preacher that married them, after all, but a justice of the peace. If so, will the various justices of the peace please come forward and disclose their records? Strange things are contained in those documents, no doubt, and we should be glad to review them on general principles.

The *Tribune* has found several men who remember a Mr. Stratton that lived here about that time, and one man says he remembers both Stratton and Mrs. Poor.

This man Henry was a renter who moved from farm to farm and never owned land. Question: What landowner in this section rented to Henry in 1873-4? What became of Henry?

Is there someone now living who knew W. S. Stratton in 1873, and who was with him at a dance Christmas night of 1873?

Any information leading to the establishment of the fact of this marriage will be paid for liberally. This one fact is all that is wanted in this interesting case; when it is proven the widow of the adventurous Stratton will be able to file her petition for the recovery of the fortune that she undoubtedly should have.

A portion of a letter from a law firm in Denver, Colorado, is as follows: "We believe the woman's story, but unless we can find at least one witness to substantiate it we are afraid to file a petition alleging that she was married to W. S. Stratton in your State in 1874. If, however, witnesses could be found who would testify as to the marriage we would then feel warranted in filing a petition, setting forth the facts of this marriage relation and feel confident that the result would be beneficial not only to the widow, but to all who assist us in establishing this relationship. She is willing to pay liberally those who assist her in recovering what she thinks she is beyond doubt entitled to from this estate.

The *Tribune* trusts that someone will come forward very soon and establish the wanted fact. The estate will soon be settled and then it will be too late for any one to render this service to a needy and honorable woman and her orphan child.

The Mr. David P. Strickler of Colorado Springs mentioned in the first of the articles above, was a partner of the law firm of Chinn and Strickler retained by the Stratton trustees. Few men have had such a discouraging array of facts and allegations to untangle as did he when he left for Texas to investigate Sophia Gertrude Chellew's story. Upon his arrival he confirmed a few facts of her story: there had been "a sketch in a Dallas newspaper"; the Shelby County Court House which might have held a record of Stratton's marriage had burned down; and worst of all, the clerk, R. L. Parker, who had issued the license, had been interviewed by Bottom and remembered issuing it. With his investigations he began work on a case that was to make his reputation in Colorado.

4

Strickler came home satisfied that the Chellew story was not only unsound and false, but that its concoction was the most astounding piece of chicanery he had ever run into. As Judge Cunningham afterward stated, "It was necessary for those charged with the duty of protecting Stratton's will and the millions he had herein bequeathed to charity, to meet and explode the wildest, wickedest and most fantastic claims ever advanced in the state and federal courts of Colorado."

Strickler began gathering witnesses for the defense and massing facts. Stratton's life had been full of coincidences. It is peculiar that thirteen years after his death, his attorneys were to preserve his estate largely through a series of coincidences even more remarkable.

While attempting to ascertain Mary's paternity, ascribed to Stratton, Strickler investigated the school census records of Leadville and the surrounding country. In these were given the age of each scholar by the person reporting to the census taker. It showed that Mary was twelve years of age in 1890, having been born in 1878, three years after her mother, Sophia Gertrude, had last seen Stratton. This conclusive fact refuting Stratton as Mary's father could not, Strickler knew, be offered in court; the census record was unsigned, signatures not being required, thus making it legally only "hearsay evidence" unacceptable in court. He continued his search. Mary's age for four years, 1889 to 1894, was listed consecutively showing a yearly increase in age up to sixteen. Opposite the item in one of these records, by odd coincidence, was the signature of her mother, S. G. Kennedy, which had not been required and was entered for no apparent reason.

Another peculiarly unaccountable coincidence occurred when Strickler was searching for documentary evidence that Stratton was in Colorado Springs at the time he was alleged to have been in Texas. In the vault in the cellar of the El Paso National Bank at Colorado Springs was found a dusty packet of old checks and deposit slips. They were all Stratton's and concerned his transactions through the old El Paso

County Bank. The deposit slips, written in Stratton's handwriting, began with the date, November 8, 1873, and ran thence almost daily to January 4, 1874—the very period during which he was alleged to have married Mrs. Chellew and gone to Fort Worth with her. There was also a check dated January 2, 1874, payable to W. S. Stratton, signed by him and paid on the same date without endorsement, the cashier asserting that no one could cash such a check except the drawer in person. This date was the day after the alleged marriage when Stratton was alleged to have left the Henry cabin with the Chellew party for Fort Worth. Why, for this significant period alone, these old records of the bank had been kept when it was the custom to return such canceled checks to clients remains a mystery.

Sure of their suspicions of chicanery on the part of Mrs. Chellew, Chinn and Strickler engaged Burns detectives. One of the operatives, an inconspicuous, down-at-the-heels appearing man, was sent to Leadville. He was instructed to rent a certain room in a boarding-house, make friends with one of Mrs. Chellew's friends and ascertain if she had money to fight the case and where she was obtaining it. The operative did so. One day in a casual conversation he remarked that it would take a lot of money to fight such a rich estate and offered to supply some if he were rewarded. The answer given him was that Mrs. Chellew already had a contract amounting to the same thing.

Upon receiving this report from his operative in Leadville, Strickler summoned to his office an old fellow, B. T. Thomas by name, whom he had used before. He was thoroughly reliable, shrewd, and had an excellent blind, being ostensibly an old peddler of homemade pain-killers. In this capacity he had been working as a street-car checker for the Denver Tramway Company. Incidentally, he was a brother of the principal owners of the Woolworth stores. Thomas was instructed to take his time, establish himself in town, and eventually make contact with the Chellew principals for the purpose of confirming the existence of the contract.

The old peddler set out with his tray of homemade pain-killers, going from house to house and to many of the downtown office buildings. After a short time he began dropping in to see R. L. Parker, the former clerk of Shelby County, Texas, who supposedly remembered issuing the marriage license to Stratton and Mrs. Chellew. Parker apparently was interested in pain-killers; the peddler was agreeable and shrewd. The conversation swung to the impending trial.

"You sure are giving this Mrs. Chellew a lot of valuable help," the old peddler remarked. "If I were you I'd get me a contract with her so I'd be paid when she gets them millions of dollars."

"Don't worry. I got me one already. I'm lookin' out for Number One, old fellow!" laughed Parker.

"I used to be a good hand makin' out contracts," went on the old peddler, gathering up his bottles. "Any time you want me to look it over—to see that it's made out tight and proper—I'll be glad to. I'd hate to see a smart man like you get stung. Why, your testimony is the most important she's got to go on."

"Oh, it's made out all right," Parker replied. "Two witnesses and acknowledged by a notary public. Tol Smith, cashier of the First National Bank, wrote it."

Meanwhile, Strickler was gathering witnesses to prove that Stratton was in Colorado Springs all the time that he was allegedly in Texas. There were J. D. Raymond, Stratton's old friend and employer; F. L. Rouse, who had been with him during the Grannis trouble; W. H. Macomber—

the same Billy Macomber who had sung his famous song at the Christmas party on December 27, 1873; Joseph Dozier, to whom he had sold his shop before leaving for the San Juan county; and men like Major Henry McAllister, Charles Cavender, now judge of the District Court at Leadville, and many others—all men of unquestionable veracity and exceptional standing in the town.

The case came up for trial after three years of preparation by both sides on May 16, 1916. Seven days' time was consumed in the introduction of evidence. The Answer Brief of the Defendants in Error consisted of 74 printed pages, and the Supplemental Abstract of Record filled 280 more.

Strickler's summation of the "Inconsistencies In and Improbability of the Claimant's Story" was devastating and convincing, and it contained a dry sarcastic humor that was irresistible.

He is the type of man who in the midst of an eloquent plea before the Court suddenly loses his plate of false teeth. The courtroom is deathly still. Strickler calmly turns to the judge.

"Your Honor. I crave the indulgence of the Court. I should like to retrieve my Goddamned teeth."

And before the Court has ceased blinking its silent astonishment, he has thrust his plate down his trousers pocket and has resumed his plea without stopping to split an infinitive.

He stated:

It is certainly true that a married person is incapable of contracting another marriage while such marriage relation exists. Hence, having married Poor in 1870, Claimant was confronted with the necessity of making some disposition of him before the date of her alleged marriage to Stratton, to-wit: January 1, 1874. There are only two known ways by which a married woman may dispose of her husband, namely, death and divorce. As courts have an amazing way of preserving the record of any divorce decree they may grant, the consequent inability of Claimant herein to produce such record would demand an explanation which claimant was unprepared to make. Claimant therefore chose death rather than divorce as the method with which she would exterminate Poor. It may be urged that Claimant was unwise in making such a selection as a story that the court house containing the record of her divorce decree from Poor had burned would be plausible, as in her herein story that the court house containing record of her alleged marriage to Stratton was burned. But it may be that Claimant thought that two court houses would be too many to burn in one case.

He went on to prove that while Mrs. Chellew testified that Poor's death occurred in 1872, four other witnesses testified that Poor did not die until the winter of '74 and '75. These witnesses included her brother, Joseph Bell, who testified Poor was alive in November 1873, and her brother-in-law, Dennis Lynch, who testified that from the time of Poor's death until her marriage to Kennedy on November 30, 1876, Mrs. Poor lived with him and married no one during that time.

Mr. Strickler, in presenting the School Census Records proving that Mary was born in 1878, pointed out that Mrs. Chellew was married to Poor in 1870 and claimed to have married Stratton January 1, 1874, by whom she gave birth to twins and later to her daughter Mary. Also that she claimed she never saw Stratton after his leaving her in Fort Worth in the spring of 1875 until her marriage to Chellew in September, 1895, and admitted having married Kennedy November 30, 1876. His deductions were thus presented:

While we do not claim any scientific knowledge of the laws of nature, we boldly assert that if a woman gave birth to a child in 1878, sired by a man she had not even seen since the spring of 1875, such an incident would be out of harmony with what we understand to be nature's general custom in such manners.

But the record discloses that the foregoing is not the only remarkable feat performed by this claimant for, according to her story, within six years she had married three men and given birth to six children. . . . This record of marriage and fecundity we think without parallel.

The rapidity with which claimant claims the male sex succumbed to her charm is also interesting, for we find that she claims she first met Stratton on Christmas Eve, 1873, and by New Year's night he was her husband. Presumably the claimant would have made better time had she not been handicapped by the delay caused by Stratton and Thompson foolishly failing to stop at San Augustine for the marriage license instead of going on to Center for such purpose, thereby compelling Mr. Stratton to wait seven days instead of six before he could call the claimant "his very own."

He then pointed out that John Henry's home is eight miles due south of San Augustine, the county seat, and that Center lies twenty-one miles north of San Augustine and is the county seat of Shelby County. It was entirely unreasonable for the party in quest of a marriage license to pass through the first county seat to another and return through the first county seat to the point where they intended the marriage to occur. That way they would have had to travel fifty-eight miles in their round trip, when by getting the marriage license at the county seat of the county wherein they intended to be married they needed to travel but sixteen miles in making the round trip.

Little Doc Bell, Mrs. Chellew's cousin, further testified that he "never made any such trips, never saw any marriage performed at John Henry's house . . . and knew nothing about any of the things that were talked about in this case." Her own brother-in-law testified that at the time of Poor's death Poor was "pretty hard up" and that he "drank a good deal and therefore didn't have but very little means," and was in such destitute circumstances when he died that it was necessary for his neighbors to contribute to the support of the family. It was thus obvious that his wife's $12,000 inheritance was also part of a fabricated myth.

After pointing out these inconsistencies and improbabilities in the claimant's story, the attorneys for the defendants attacked the integrity of her witnesses. Thompson was found to have been known as Kelly in Texas, as Smith in Wyoming, and as Howard in the Colorado penitentiary where he served a term from 1885 to 1891. Shaffer's character was brought out in his testimony that he "hung around the gambling dens in Leadville." Mrs. Gordon was the ex-wife of the proprietor of the Pioneer Saloon and gambling-house at Leadville. Ambrose testified that he was town marshal in Colorado Springs in 1874 when in fact there was no such office in existence at that time. Mrs. Nelson, proprietor of the rooming-house where Stratton lived, the one who had written Bottom, now testified that Stratton said " 'my wife is poor' and I thought he meant she didn't have any money and when I read about her being 'Poor' I tumbled to what he had in mind."

One of the dramatic incidents of the trial occurred at the time R. L. Parker's evidence was offered. Knowing from the old peddler's story of the existence of a contract with Mrs. Chellew, Mr. Strickler asked him on the witness stand if any such contract had been executed to him by Mrs. Chellew. Under oath, he assented. Mr. Strickler then asked if he had that contract. At this point an old Negro janitor jumped to his feet and exclaimed that it was in his desk. The contract was presented. It read in part:

> . . . and to procure for us such other testimony as he may be able to procure touching the matter in controversy at his own expense . . . and as for said services performed I hereby sell and convey unto the said R. L. Parker one-fourth of the amount recovered by virtue of any proceedings against said Stratton Estate, let the same be in money, or property of any description.

There was also a second contract, one between Parker and a Judge Rufus Price of Texas who was to help supply money and evidence. It read:

> For value received, in cash and legal services rendered in behalf of Mrs. S. G. Kennedy, at my instance, I do hereby transfer and convey unto Rufus Price of San Augustine County, Texas, one undivided half-interest in and to the within contract and one-half the proceeds arising from same.

These contracts proved that Parker was an interested party and hence legally incompetent to testify.

The executors' defense, in addition to the vast amount of documentary evidence such as the old checks and deposit slips found, vouchers to Stratton for serving upon the jury in the old Root and Reef case, and so on, was built upon the testimony of the many old pioneers gathered for the purpose. One of the amusing incidents of the trial occurred when the old composer, Billy Macomber, was introduced on the witness stand to testify regarding the party in the old Wanless Hall the night of December 27, 1873. He is remembered for those songs which mostly "were able to stand alone but one or two of them, maybe, would fall down once in awhile." When asked if he remembered the occasion and the song, old Macomber turned to the presiding judge and with a curt preamble of "if it please the Court" unhesitatingly in a deep voice began to boom out to the delight of the audience the verses of "That is the Opinion of Your Friend Billy Macomber"—sung forty-three years before.

That the testimony of these old pioneers was irrefutable and overwhelming is borne out in the words of Judge Kinney in his findings:

On the other hand, the witnesses for Mr. Stratton's Estate are men who have been identified with Colorado Springs for many years and whose character and integrity are beyond question. Among them are such men as Irving Howbert, Channing Sweet, E. J. Eaton, F. L. Rouse, J. D. Raymond, Joseph Dozier, Chas. M. White, Sebastian Greenway, W. H. Macomber, Major Henry McAllister and Charles Cavender, now judge of the District Court at Leadville. They are all pioneers and their minds filled with distinct recollections of all important facts of the early days. It is rare that there is in any case such a number of witnesses of such exceptional standing and whose testimony is so clear and convincing. The weight of the testimony is clearly on the side of these witnesses.

On June 1, 1916, the case ended with a verdict for the Stratton Estate. The Findings of the Court were as follows:

From the vast preponderance of the evidence in this case the court finds the following facts:

1. That at all times from December 21, 1873, to January 2, 1874, Mr. Winfield Scott Stratton was in Colorado Springs, El Paso County, Colorado, and not in San Augustine County, Texas, as claimed by Mrs. Chellew and her witnesses, and that A. N. Poor, the first husband of the claimant, did not die until the year 1875.

2. That the claimant and Winfield Scott Stratton were not united in marriage on January 1, 1874, as alleged.

Statue of Stratton executed in 1906 by Nellie V. Walker, a student of Lorado Taft, which was first placed on a bluff in Stratton Park, then moved to the corners of Nevada and Pueblo Avenues in Colorado Springs; and now on the grounds of The Myron Stratton Home.

And as a conclusion of law based on said facts, the Court unhesitatingly finds that the claimant, Sophia Gertrude Kennedy, or Sophia Gertrude Chellew, is not the widow of Winfield Scott Stratton.

5

On December 18, 1913, two days before the opening of the Chellew Case, three aged men ranging from eighty to eighty-seven years quietly moved out from town to be received as the first residents of the Myron Stratton Home. The opening of the Home was marked with the simplicity and disregard for worldly show which characterized the life of their benefactor. There was no address of welcome, no speeches of dedication, no display of the sentiment, and the names of the new residents were not made public. The inmates were merely shown to their rooms in the cottages and the rules of the institution explained to them, and they proceeded to make themselves at home in the most unique institution of its kind in the world.

In contrast to this appeared the effusive oratory of a reporter in the day's newspaper:

> Winfield Scott Stratton! What a light of recognition the name brings to the faces of the good people of Colorado Springs! Stratton, the man of mines and millions; the man of simple demeanor and great heart; philanthropist and friend of the poor and aged! The dream of this man! That is the thing which will spread itself throughout the generations and proclaim to them the spirit of the man that dreamed it. For the vision of Winfield Scott Stratton, the psychic, intangible thing that once formed itself in the brain of this man long dead, has lived and become a reality.
>
> . . . In London he was taken ill. Then a great loneliness overcame him. His millions did not bring him friends. . . . The

man of the Colorado hills longed for the region of his youth. . . . It was while on this sickbed in London that the dream which was to become the one burning desire of his remaining days came to him. During his illness he learned the feeling which the world in general holds toward a stranger, and he resolved that should he live he would see that provision was made for homeless and infirm people.

He lived! Later he wrote in his will the greatest wish of his life—the inspiration of a dream. . . . His wish has been carried out. Today the citizens of Colorado Springs may turn their eyes to the southward and see far out on the plains a group of fair buildings. Behold! It is the dream of Winfield Scott Stratton. Nay, not a dream, not a phantom, but a material, existing thing. It is the Myron Stratton Memorial Home. The dream of the dead is a reality!

As a prologue to this, the now famous Damon Runyon, then a reporter on the *Denver Post*, had written, "The Gods gave him money to bitter excess, and he dreamed a wonderful dream, which today, years after he had inherited the earth, is taking tangible form."

This opening of the Home which had been Stratton's second "dream" was the goal toward which the trustees and attorneys of the estate had struggled for many years. Whatever Stratton's character was, or theirs, the Home proved now a worthy objective for the men who had proved faithful to the trust. No men ever had a harder fight.

The contract for the construction of the first unit of the Home, costing $147,895, had been executed. Four years previously the site had been acquired from the holdings of the Broadmoor Land Company, formerly bought by a Scottish syndicate of Edinburgh, for $350,000. It consisted of about 3,000 acres adjoining Stratton Park, making an unbroken body of land sloping from the mountains to the plains of exclusive Broadmoor, south of Colorado Springs, and all the water flowing from North and South Cheyenne Cañons. Meanwhile a reservoir was built at a cost of $38,000 and the trustees investigated other institutions for the purpose of planning one to fulfill Stratton's peculiar desires regarding it.

Among those investigated were the Stephen Girard College for boys, situated in Philadelphia—probably the best known benevolent institution in the United States, the Boston Training School for Girls, and the Rice Institution of Houston, Texas. As Girard College was not opened until sixteen years after Mr. Girard's death, and the Rice institution twenty-one years after the initial steps were taken, the Stratton Trustees offered few excuses for their delay in opening the Myron Stratton Home eleven years after Stratton's death.

The first unit, opened December 18, 1913, consisted of two dormitories accommodating twenty-five children each; the Washington for girls and the Independence for boys, the buildings named after Stratton's first two claims in Cripple Creek. For aged people there were ten bungalow-type cottages, each containing a living-room, bedrooms, dining-room and kitchen, completely furnished and equipped. There was also an administration building and a residence for the superintendent. The architecture of all the buildings was Colonial and Mission with red tile roofs.

As usual, the *Denver Post*, one of the chief obstacles to its founding, modestly took all credit for the Home in the following story:

In September, 1902, a rich man died. . . . That man, though dead, now becomes a vital force in the world of the living through the praise and thanksgiving on the lips of the aged poor and dependent children who are at last enjoying the benefits of his generosity.

. . . On June 26, 1912, ten years after Stratton's death, the *Post* knocked on the door of his lordly trustees and in behalf of a homeless woman asked where she could find the Myron Stratton Home.

Day after day the *Post*, in its front-page columns, asked that question of the men Stratton had entrusted to carry out his humane command. Day after day the evidence of their unworthiness and their disregard of a dead man's will became more and more apparent. "Tomorrow" was their motto, tossed with arrogance into the faces of the poor.

The *Post* appealed to the legislature to call the trustees to time. . . . The *Post* was not dismayed by the Attorney General's mildness. Right was on our side—right and justice.

. . . During its history the *Post* has written down in its credit columns many superb achievements. . . . But no work done by the *Post* is regarded with greater satisfaction than that which has resulted in the building of the Myron Stratton Home for the aged poor and dependent children.

The Home grew rapidly under the supervision of such men as Carl S. Chamberlin, superintendent from 1922 to 1934, the son of Stratton's favorite sister, Anna; William Lennox, vice-president of the board of trustees, himself a Cripple Creek millionaire; William Lloyd, president, Stratton's old secretary; and David P. Strickler who has been trustee and chief legal counsel for the Estate since 1906. Shortly after Stratton's old employer, J. D. Raymond, testified at the Chellew trial, he was employed at the Home as assistant storekeeper and died there some years later. They were all men whose main concern was to interpret and carry out as liberally as possible that provision of Stratton's will, which reads:

It is my especial desire and command that the inmates of said home shall not be clothed and fed as paupers usually are at public expense, but that they shall be decently and comfortably clothed and amply provided with good and wholesome food and with the necessary medical attendance, care and nursing to protect their health and insure their comfort.

Mr. Strickler as a boy had ridden with his father to many of the "poor farms" of the day; his interpretation of the above therefore, and the results obtained, differs widely from the dreary buildings, meager unwholesome food and squalid surroundings he had seen in childhood.

By 1928 the building operations ceased, after the total amount of $1,041,825.27 had been expended for the purpose. This was in accord with the clause in Stratton's will reading:

A suitable sum, not exceeding the sum of One Million Dollars ($1,000,000) out of this bequest shall be expended in purchasing suitable grounds and a site for said Home within the County of El Paso and State of Colorado and in erecting, furnishing and equipping the necessary buildings for the use of the inmates of said Home and for the maintenance of careful supervision over the erection of said buildings and improvements and beautification of said grounds.

Today in the children's department there are the Washington dormitory for girls and the Independence and Lincoln dormitories for boys, each a complete unit with kitchen, dining, living and study rooms. In the aged department there are ten housekeeping cottages for old people, and fifteen five-room cottages for single persons, completely furnished and equipped to electric refrigerators. The Stratton Building opened in 1923 at a cost of $90,000 is a completely equipped infirmary with isolation wards and nurses' quarters. It was found possible to move from Stratton Park the large steel amusement pavilion which now serves the Home as a community and administration building, with a gymnasium, manual-training room, theater and auditorium seating 716. Outside there is a large swimming pool. There is a service building with kitchen, dining-rooms, laundry and employees' quarters; a steam plant with carpenter and machine-shops; and the superintendent's house. Nearby is Stratton Farm with a dairy barn, creamery, greenhouse, hay barn, stable and silos. This farm provides the inmates with all the milk wanted, and maintains a herd of purebred Holstein cattle. In addition there is a herd of over 350 Hereford beef cattle which for one day topped the United States market and has often led the Denver market.

The grounds of the Home proper consist of 98 acres situated within the estate of now 5,000 acres. They have been set with lawns, trees and shrubbery, and the inmates have built a rock garden and lily pond for which for two successive years they were awarded by the Colorado Springs Garden Club, Landscape Division, the first place for the most beautiful grounds in the town and vicinity. In walking through them, past acres of lawn and along shrub and tree-lined walks, and seeing the red-tiled roofs of the many buildings, one can easily imagine he is on the campus of a state college instead of the grounds of a benevolent institution.

Like a college, however, it is not the grounds or the buildings which distinguish the institution; it is the people themselves. All seem happy and contented. The old people are generally left to themselves and regularly attend the free picture shows—four films usually—given each Friday night. All the aged are given opportunity to earn money if they so desire. The work consists of caring for lawns or for poultry, helping in the store room and cafeteria, and sewing. Several have strawberry patches and sell their fruit in town. One man builds toy sailing-boats. For the children there is a troop of Boy Scouts and Girl Scouts, and each makes use of the mountain cabin provided for them. Manual training and music lessons are given each Saturday morning, and from time to time special courses in domestic science, millinery and dressmaking. The Home has both a band and an orchestra. During summer vacations and spare time the children are encouraged to work. Unlike the aged who use their money as they wish, the children are required to deposit one-half of their earnings in a savings account in order that they may have a sum of money on leaving the Home. Instead of buying clothes for the older boys and girls, the Home now credits to them a weekly allowance and they go to town and make their own purchases, watching for sales and bargains.

When the Home was first opened, it had its own private school under the charge of certified teachers. But it was found that upon entering the public high school the children showed signs of inferiority complexes. This was probably owing to their having been segregated for so long; also to their encountering snobbishness among the town people—a common attitude in Colorado Springs. The Home school was therefore given up. The younger children now go to the Ivywild grade school, and the older children attend the Cheyenne high school. Here, in a school located in the so-called exclusive Broadmoor section and attended by many sons and daughters of millionaires, they are accepted as a matter of fact—an interesting contrast to the snobbishness of the downtown schools.

When the land in Broadmoor was first purchased as a site for the Home, the wealthy residents protested wildly, on the grounds that it would bring in orphans, riff-raff and other undesirables and lower their property values. It was offered to convey to the Home without cost a large tract of land near Fountain, further south, for its site. One of the arguments offered was that it was more desirable for the Home to be located where it was wanted rather than where it was not wanted. Last winter, at the occasion of the Home's annual New Year's party, a young couple from Broadmoor attempted to "crash the gate" and join in the frolic. Both were of prominent families and it was found that the young lady's father was one of those who had led the fight against locating the Home. This is a story told with great relish by one of the trustees of the Home.

Everything possible is being done to enable the children, upon leaving, to take their place in the world with no sense of inferiority and with only pride in their Home. As this is being written it is contemplated choosing a board of advisers from the alumni to meet with the trustees in discussing the Home's problems. This is patterned after a custom followed in Harvard and Leland Stanford Universities.

Miss Lucy A. Lloyd, now superintendent, tells the incident of a little girl who on passing Stratton's statue on a Colorado Springs street-corner exclaimed loudly, "That's our pal!"

Another of her interesting stories has to do with the proverbial "bad boy" of the institution who was everlastingly running away. After a great deal of effort, his father was located in the southern part of the State and persuaded to care for the boy. The father was a part-time barber and evidently an unsatisfactory parent. A few weeks after the boy had been sent to join him a letter was received from him at the Home stating that he had walked to another nearby town and was hitch-hiking the long way "back home." The crowning mark of sincerity was found on the inside flap of the envelope—a penciled heart with an arrow sticking through it. The boy is now one of the best in the institution and is working after school hours for a town employer who has taken a great deal of interest in him. It is hoped that on hearing his story repeated, he will never be embarrassed by his honest and well-directed shaft of appreciation.

Such stories tend to show that the Home is fulfilling its benefactor's wishes. No benevolent institution can or will ever equal a home. But the Myron Stratton Home has earned its reputation as the most unique institution of its kind in the United States. Among its "alumni" it has had no suicides or criminals, nor has it produced men and women who astounded the world by their brilliance. But consistently it puts out young men and women eager and resolute to make the transition into the world of society, and equipped to stand on their own feet. Many have worked their way through several years of college, and the trustees in rare instances lend help to the deserving for this purpose. Among the men who were once boys in the Home is one who is now field manager of a large West Coast gas company and another who is an official of a large hay-growers association. Among the former girls are school nurses, bookkeepers and employees of large banks—a typical cross-section of American society.

Perhaps no other institution cares for such a wide spread of people in regard to age. Today the oldest resident is ninety-four years old and the youngest five years. Since its opening in 1913 it has admitted 607 residents. As of January 1, 1937, it had a capacity of 185: 99 men and women, and 86 children. The cost per person per year of other institutions running $200, the amount of $250 was estimated and provided for by the trustees when the Myron

Stratton Home opened. By 1922 the cost had increased to $502.30 and was met by building up the real-estate property of the Stratton estate to the point where it was paying into the Home treasury from $100,000 to $125,000 per year in dividends. By 1924 the cost per capita was $595.43 and it is now running close to $900. Statistically the service rendered by the Home is expressed in years: thus, one person who has been taken care of for one year, has been rendered a service of one year. This service has increased from 2 months, 1 day for the first year, 1913, until as of January 1, 1937, the Home had rendered a total service of 3,196 years, 7 months and 16 days.

Over three thousand years! . . . but it means so little in figures. One thinks only of a single cold winter day and an old man in his room there with the steam radiators turned on full blast. A chance visitor happening in inquired if he knew how to regulate the heaters and if he weren't afraid of suffocating. The old man turned around slowly and answered in a quiet voice, "Yes, I know how but I like it this way. It seems so long since I been warm."

It is but one of the countless tributes to an institution dedicated to the sentiment engraved on its founder's monument: " 'Tis not enough to help the feeble up, but to support him after."

AFTERWORD*

SO Stratton's "dream-home," built from the proceeds of his "dream-mine," is today one of the proudest assets of the town which once abhorred the thought of its presence. In "Little London" it has spent over $28,000,000 and spends each year almost $500,000 more in taxes, wages, materials and supplies.

In 1932 operation of the Colorado Springs and Interurban Railway was discontinued. The road was dismantled, all movable property sold, and title to the real property transferred to the Home. The power-house, shops and car-barns have been gradually converted to rental buildings, leases negotiated with the new bus company and other business companies, the block named the "Winfield Scott Block," and a new business center formed in town. The other town real-estate properties have also been converted into paying rental properties.

Of the Denver properties left by Stratton, the old Tabor property was sold and the others have been leased for ninety-nine years. One of these properties is now occupied by the First National Bank Building, a twelve-story, modern office building. At the expiration of these leases, the properties with all improvements revert to the Home without cost.

After years of litigation the Stratton executors succeeded in bringing the Brown Palace Hotel to a sheriff's sale in August, 1907. No other purchaser offering, they

*1949 Stratton Centennial Edition

were forced under Stratton's contract to bid it in for $850,000 continuing to lease it to Maxey Tabor. On January 1, 1910, they took over the management of the hotel and spent $180,000 in alterations, finally selling it for $1,260,000.

The Stratton Estate is now legally incorporated as the Myron Stratton Home, embracing not only the Home itself but several controlled or affiliated companies: The Brookside Water Company, the Matoa Gold Mining Company, The Sacramento Gold Mining and Milling Company, and The Stratton Cripple Creek Mining and Development Company. With total assets of $6,592,710 as of January 1, 1947, they are operated for the purpose of maintaining the Home in accordance with Stratton's wishes.

The trustees are still William Lloyd, Stratton's secretary; Carl W. Chamberlin, Stratton's grand-nephew; and David P. Strickler, legal counsel since 1906. And to Lucy A. Lloyd, superintendent of the Home since 1934, belongs credit for the warm and wise guidance with which its young graduates are sent out into the world to carry on the traditions of the most remarkable Alma Mater in the country.

But what of the Bowl of Gold theory, stunted suddenly by Stratton's death?

John Hays Hammond had claimed that the Independence had petered out and was worth only about $4,000,000. Look at its production record:

1898-1908 by the first English company operating on Company account	$11,049,030
1904-1908 by the same company operating by lessees	$ 4,015,290

1908-1915 by the Argall company operating............................$ 4,571,968

A total production to June 30, 1915, of at least $23,-621,728, when it was sold to the Portland Gold Mining Company. Since then it has produced another $3,000,000: a grand total production of $26,591,644 up to 1935, when production was curtailed in its stupendous aggregate of eighteen miles of underground workings.

It seems appropriate that the old "King of the District" should have been merged with the "Queen." They are both in the same pool of eruption and on the same mountain. The Portland alone has produced over $62,000,000; and combined with the Independence, this single treasure box has yielded roughly $90,000,000 in gold.

Throughout the District other great mines are still adding to the $450,000,000 in gold already taken out of Cripple Creek. A total of some 500,000 tons per year are treated at the Golden Cycle Mill, the largest custom mill for gold ore in the United States.

Among these are the 23 mines of the Stratton Cripple Creek Mining and Development Company, including the familiar names of the American Eagles, highest in the district and 2100 feet deep, the Longfellow, the Proper, John A. Logan, Favorite, War Eagle and Orphe Mae. From Stratton's death till the present time (1948) they have produced 706,013 net tons with a gross value of $10,830,593—all for the benefit of the inmates of the Myron Stratton Home.

How long will Cripple Creek's gold hold out? The question is as pertinent now as it was in Stratton's time. And its answer still depends upon his remarkable theory that at depth would be found the richest ore bodies in the district.

To prove his theory one of the most novel engineering projects in the world has been undertaken.

It will be remembered that at the time of Stratton's death the depth-limit of all the mines was restricted by the underground water encountered—water that filled the shafts faster than it could be pumped out. Five years later, A. E. Carlton, head of the Golden Cycle Mill and a prominent entrepreneur of the region, solved the difficulty. Under his direction in 1907 a lateral drainage tunnel was driven into the side of Pike's Peak at about 8,000 feet altitude. This Roosevelt Tunnel drained off all the water above the 2,100-foot depth reached by the deepest mines, and allowed such famous producers as the Vindicator, Ajax and Cresson to sink their shafts still deeper. Still the ore held out, confirming Stratton's theory; the drainage was permanent, and proved much cheaper during the following years than pumping.

By 1939 when a new bottom was reached only one conclusion was evident. There was more gold at still greater depth, if a new drainage tunnel could be provided to make it available.

The Golden Cycle Corporation set aside $1,000,000 for the purpose of driving the new Carlton Drainage Tunnel. Under the direction of its vice-president in charge of mining, Alfred H. Bebee, a graduate of the Colorado School of Mines, plans were drawn. Placed in charge of driving it was "Long" John Austin, 6 feet, 8 inches tall. One of the most famous tunnel builders in the world, he had driven the Jones Pass tunnel near Empire, Colorado, and had superintended the construction of the Coachella aqueduct in California, part of the famous Colorado River Project.

In July, 1939, work began. The portal of the Carlton Tunnel was located about 9 miles south of Cripple Creek.

The tunnel was driven laterally into the side of Pike's Peak at an altitude of 6,800 feet—1,100 feet below the area drained by the Roosevelt Tunnel, and 3,200 feet below the surface. The tunnel was 8 feet high, 8 feet wide and over 6 miles long. At an average cost per foot of $32.18 it was driven through solid rock at a speed that broke the world's record, reaching 78 feet in one day. Two years later, in 1941, it was completed at a cost of $1,250,000; and out of it began pouring as high as 25,000 gallons of water a minute into the Arkansas River, eventually used to irrigate sugar beets.

The first property to be drained was the Ajax. At 28,215 feet a vein of ore with assays running up to 3.28 ounces per ton ($114.80) was cut. The discovery of this rich vein showed beyond question that values continued at great depth. Now being drained are other famous old mines, each driving down like the Portland to the astounding depth of 3,200 feet below the surface. What will they find?

There is every reason to believe that the ore will hold out as long as man's ingenuity to mine it, giving new life to Cripple Creek for generations to come.

The tantalizing possibility of Stratton's dream still exists: that in the depths of Pike's Peak, below the granite floor of his Bowl of Gold, will be found "more riches than those of Indostan and Malabar, or the golden coast of Guinea, or the mines of Peru."

And now, nearly fifty years after his death, what appraisal can be made of Stratton as a man? For while "Cripple Creek" is now a movement from Stringfield's musical suite "Southern Mountains," Stratton's character has never been so harmoniously resolved.

A boy possessed by a terrible temper, who tried to kill

his father and had to leave home. A young man so distorted that he abandoned his wife and disclaimed his son. A man so shrewd and penurious that he tricked out of his bonanza the partner who grubstaked him, then sold it by careful financial manipulation for millions more than it was worth; who hid from the world to give himself up to secretive pleasure and sinful folly which left a string of ruined people along his path and which finally killed him. This is the proper scoundrel seen by his many enemies.

His friends are equally positive in their assertions that he was a plaster saint. A sensitive man suffering in silence from misfortune and unjust accusations who yet returned good for evil; generous to a fault and living always for others; inspired by the divine with which he was in constant touch; a misunderstood prophet crying from his wilderness of solitude and sickness to the unheeding material world about him.

It was these unresolved contradictions which first stimulated his biography. They also determined its factual rather than fictional form; for no novelized character could possibly embrace, with any plausibility, so many opposite facets of character.

The temptation to interlard the narrative with personal family incidents was also difficult to resist. It was my grandfather who bought Stratton's contracting shop, providing him with the stake for his first unfortunate prospecting venture. Thereafter for seventeen years grandfather intermittently hired him as a journeyman carpenter while he continued his fruitless search. Then suddenly their positions were reversed. Grandfather, too, got the gold fever and indomitably sank his contracting business and town property into Cripple Creek. One of his unproductive shafts was that of the American

Eagles, an undeveloped claim which he leased from Stratton. After three years of work he gave it up, stone broke, leaving scrawled on the rafters of its shaft house the penciled record of his drivings through unproductive granite.

A short time later Stratton struck the vein. The American Eagles became the highest portal, one of the deepest shafts and most productive mines in the District. Stratton, strolling by the house with his dog every evening, promptly gave his old friend a blank check to fill out as reimbursement for the amount he had spent on developing the mine. Grandfather, as touchy as Stratton, promptly laid it away unused in one of his books where it stayed for years after Stratton's death. During the confusion at the time of grandfather's death his whole library was donated to Colorado College. And here, somewhere in the basement among hundreds of old books, Stratton's blank check may still be found . . .

With these personal family reminiscences many others have come in since the book was first published . . . From a family of boat-builders who worked for Myron Stratton in Jeffersonville . . . A woman whose family Stratton visited in Denver when she was twelve years old . . . Mrs. F. E. Vernia of Wellsville, Ohio, who knew Stratton's sister, Jenny, and had thought Stratton "was a sort of a millionaire tramp and had dissipated the greater part of his fortune instead of doing the wonderful thing for the destitute as you tell in your book". . . A man born on the island of Bornholm, in the Baltic Sea, whose four brothers worked in Cripple Creek for Stratton and who wrote, "Germany had its Grimm brothers; Denmark, the grim enough Hans Christian Anderson; England, Charles Kingsley's impossible 'Water Babies,' but

Heaven be praised America has romance and wonder enough in its history to crowd elves, leprechauns and sprites into the dim and distant past!"

None of them, interesting as they are, materially add to Stratton's character or change the facts about him. In perspective it is these facts which reveal him ever more clearly.

It has been exactly one hundred years since he was born. In this century the whole western half of a continent has been transformed from an almost virgin wilderness into a country whose technological achievements have ushered in the Atomic Age.

Born on the threshold of this frontier in the very year in which the great westward exodus began, Stratton was but one of hundreds of thousands caught in the flow. The towns and cities mushroomed along their trails are full of street-corner effigies of such as he; every section boasts its empire builder; in hundreds of mining camps linger myths of men transformed into Midases over night.

Theirs are interesting stories; they were interesting men. But they were not great men: these Tom Walshes, Silver Dollar Tabors, Nat Creedes, Ed Schieffelins and Henry Wickensburgs who labored through the desert to Tombstone and Tonopah; among the Black Hills to Deadwood Gulch; and up Mosquito and Ute Pass to Leadville and Cripple Creek. They were men at once blessed and cursed by a great unrest, the mark of their time and breed. But their courage, independence and heroic endeavors served only to attest their selfish greed, their uncontrolled individualism, and to turn them into a common type. They are dimly remembered only for the mineral districts they happened upon, the folly and tragedy of sudden wealth which warped their simple lives.

Among them Stratton takes his place. He had their faults and virtues, a prospector who would have died unknown save that by chance he struck it rich. Yet he alone stands out by the strange paradox that permeated his every act.

While others were gutting mountains, uprooting forests, despoiling hundreds of thousands of square miles of virgin earth to grow rich by cattle, grain, lumber, silver and gold, Stratton was scientifically conserving his vast body of ore. With untrammeled selfishness they indulged in orgies of spending; Stratton withdrew his wealth only as he could use it constructively. Little London, like every town, has had its plethora of wealthy patrons. But with few exceptions their gifts have been less attentive to the town's needs than to the more pressing need of glorifying their donors. Even today they are appalled by the incomprehensible idea that their vast fortunes wrung from the earth might be used to benefit the region they had helped to despoil. Little wonder then that they were infuriated by Stratton's gifts of a new City Hall, County Court House, Federal Post Office, community park and Mining Exchange; and that city, county, the State of Colorado and the public press fought eleven years against the founding of the Myron Stratton Home. Founding the first corporation and street railway in the United States to take out group life insurance on its employees, and financing a plan whereby they could buy their own homes, Stratton indeed proved himself a visionary who correctly foresaw a new pattern of socialized living replacing the uncontrolled individualism of his time.

As a mining man he had no peer. He discovered the Independence by nothing less scientific than a mere dream. But there was nothing dream-like about his development of it as the best managed mine ever inspected by the Colorado Scientific Society, American Institute of Mechanical Engineers and the U. S. Department of Mines. It was John Hays Hammond, director of the South African mines for Cecil Rhodes, and probably the world's most eminent mining engineer, who publicly proclaimed after due investigation that the rich ore bodies of the Independence had petered out—and this before it had produced $11,000,000 for the company which hired him, and $12,000,000 later. But it was Stratton, a mere ex-carpenter, rather than the world's finest geologists and mining engineers, who originated the daring Bowl of Gold theory which is proving to be the solution to the middle of America's greatest gold camp.

Nor does Stratton's acumen as a business man seem to stem directly from the poverty-stricken, debt-ridden man remembered by many who knew him "when." For no reason at all he seems to have got the best of the bargain at every turn. Against the world-famous Samuel Untermeyer and his corps of attorneys, in a case carried to the United States Court of Appeals, Stratton's sale of his mine proved a transaction as complicated and unbreakable as any deal ever engineered by international financiers. Nor could the finest legal talent employed break Stratton's astounding will.

There is no doubt that Stratton had an almost seismatic feeling for the earth, a compassion for people and a nose for business. What makes these diversified talents all the more remarkable is that after lying dormant for so long they could bloom so suddenly and fully and with such harmony in a man so inwardly tortured and discordant. In this lies the key to his character.

The real story of Stratton is the story of his psychological search for the means to integrate his complex personality. A search for a lodestone of life by which to set his compass of endeavor. A search for the truth that makes all men brothers and links them to the solidarity of the eternal universe. By this alone we can trace his trail through solitude and poverty, riches and success; through rages of frustration and fits of remorseful kindness; through cases of Bourbon and text-books of religion.

That Stratton found gold in Pike's Peak was inconsequential. But that he devoted it exclusively to the betterment of his fellow men shows how valid was his search. The worst of tales about him may be true; it should matter little. That he was human and susceptible to folly should rather be a reminder that even virtue needs a rich and hardy soil in which to flourish. Long after the last reminders of the boom days have passed with all the other bonanza kings, Stratton will still be remembered. Not alone for the gold he wrung from Pike's Peak, but for the modicum of kindly truth refined from the granite of men's unheeding and pitiless greed.

ACKNOWLEDGMENTS*

NO book belongs less to its writer. To the forty-six persons interviewed I gratefully acknowledge their generous contributions which fill its pages. Among the most helpful were members of my own family who were well acquainted with Stratton over a thirty-year period. To the additional few who declined to speak of him through some fear or prejudice I am also indebted; their silence helped to substantiate rumors of stories and were an incentive to unearth others.

Attorneys who handled the vast amount of litigation in connection with Stratton's affairs have been invariably kind in lending me their briefs and abstracts of records of the cases involved, and making available source material that could not have been obtained otherwise. Mr. Henry McAllister and Judge Young of Denver; Mr. Norman Campbell and Judge Cunningham of Colorado Springs; and Mr. Orville Dines of Denver, who gave me access to Mr. V. Z. Reed's files, have been particularly kind.

Mr. T. W. Ross, Mr. E. D. Woodworth, Mr. Bill Mulligan and Miss Ellen O'Connor of the *Colorado Springs Gazette*, Mr. and Mrs. Kyner and Miss Ingham of the *Cripple Creek Times-Record* have all aided me materially by their help and interest.

My work in gathering source material has been lightened by my friends Mr. Charles Hathaway and Miss Louise Kampff of Colorado College. To Mr. Leroy R.

*Stratton Centennial Edition

Hafen of the State Historical Society, Denver, and to Mr. Edgar R. Harlan of the Historical, Memorial and Art Department of Iowa, I also owe thanks. Both Miss Kampff, librarian of Colorado College, and Miss Ina T. Aulls, head of the Western History Department, Denver Public Library, have allowed and helped me to select the best of their valuable collection of photographs of early Colorado. Miss Lucy A. Lloyd, superintendent of The Myron Stratton Home, has contributed both pictures and data, and has extended to me on many occasions the hospitality of the Home.

Supplementing my own acquaintance over many years with the Cripple Creek district, Mr. M. H. Salsbury, superintendent of the Portland and Independence mines; Mr. Keener, superintendent of the Stratton Cripple Creek Mining and Development Company; Mr. Willard Banks, old faro dealer; Mrs. Roy Grater; numerous engineers, miners and dozens of unknown muckers have taken me down old mines, explained prints, supplied data and trudged with me over old trails.

Letters from Mr. Louis Persinger, Mrs. Addie A. Ramsay, Mrs. Sophronia Schwarz and others have given me valuable information.

My fortunate acquaintance with Miss Anna Hellmark, Mrs. Eliza Dunlap and Miss Mary Riley, old housekeepers for Stratton, and with Mrs. Leversage, Stratton's maid and wife of his old coachman, has been productive of information so pertinent that it cannot be acknowledged with the gratitude it deserves.

Above all I am deeply grateful to the two men who have made this book possible: Mr. H. K. Ellingson's reading of the manuscript as the literary reviewer of the *Gazette* is the least of the help which he has given me.

And the book itself derives from the sustaining interest of Mr. D. P. Strickler, trustee of the Myron Stratton Home and legal counselor for the Estate for over thirty years. He has made available data that could have been obtained from no other source; he has been instrumental in securing appointments, papers and all other possible leads. As an official of the Stratton Home Estate, as an attorney-at-law, and as a personal friend, his unstinting aid, advice and interest have made the writing of this book an enjoyable task.

In bringing the present edition up to date thanks are given Miss Lucy A. Lloyd, superintendent, and Herbert L. Stubbs, secretary of the Myron Stratton Home, for supplying new photographs, statistical and mining data.

To Mr. W. A. Kyner, formerly editor of the *Cripple Creek Times-Record* and a director of The Golden Cycle Corporation, I am indebted for information on the new Carleton Drainage Tunnel. His insistence, with that of Mr. and Mrs. Ericksen, in serializing the book in *The Independent* has helped to point the necessity for this present edition.

I wish to thank here also our old school friend, Mrs. Helen Sewell Caldwell, for the countless clippings she has sent during the last few years. It is through such generous interest and loyalty as hers that I have been able to keep abreast of recent developments.

Lastly an appreciative acknowledgment is made of the hundreds of letters sent me since the first appearance of the book and the later publication of *The Colorado* containing reference to it. They have both confirmed the information included and the necessity for the book itself. Such letters as these have given back to me the poignant beauty of those bare, frost-shattered hills which formed my first horizon. Better than I could express it, Mrs. Evelyn A. Calhoon, now of Cortez, Colorado, has fittingly written the feeling still held by us all:

. . ."The way those hills get to possess you in time, so that you cling to them like a child to its mother's skirts, afraid to face the competition of the outside. The way you react to the lucky escapees from that mountain spell—either a bitter, frustrated envy, or a smug prognosis that they'll be back before the snow flies. Even the doctor seems to think it a sort of treason to admit the altitude doesn't agree with some people.

"You always leave a part of you there, wherever you wander, which like an amputated limb twitches for years afterward, so that you can't forget it, ever. No matter where you go you bump into people who went to Cripple Creek once in their lives, and who inquire eagerly about men and women or the children they went to school with who are dead now or scattered from Cerro de Pasco to Baguio and the Rand. It's a fraternity with its own signs and passwords which will last until the last crumbling gallows-frame on Battle Mountain falls into a water-filled shaft."

The printed source material used has necessarily been, for the most part, generally unavailable. The most important includes:

STRATTON'S INDEPENDENCE LIMITED, CASE NO. 2083 in the U. S. Circuit Court of Appeals and No. 589 in the Supreme Court of the United States—Records, Briefs and Opinions.

LESLIE W. POPEJOY VS. TYSON S. DINES ET AL, NO. 7589, District Court, El Paso County, Colorado.

CASE NO. 9222 in the Supreme Court of the State of Colorado [Chellew Case]—Answer Brief and Supplemental Abstract of Record.

SESSION LAWS OF THE STATE OF COLORADO—NINETEENTH ASSEMBLY.

THE MYRON STRATTON HOME REPORTS—1913 to 1936 inclusive.

THE FORTUNES OF A DECADE, published in Colorado Springs, 1900.

CRIPPLE CREEK AND COLORADO SPRINGS ILLUSTRATED, published in Colorado Springs, 1896.

A HISTORICAL, DESCRIPTIVE, PICTORIAL AND BIOGRAPHICAL WORK ON THE RESOURCES OF THE GREATEST GOLD CAMP ON EARTH, by J. F. Manning.

YELLOW GOLD OF CRIPPLE CREEK, by Harry J. Newton. Denver: Nelson Publishing Co.

GENERAL WILLIAM J. PALMER, A DECADE OF COLORADO RAILROAD BUILDING 1870-1880, by George L. Anderson. Colo. College Publication, General Series No. 209.

THE BOOK OF COLORADO SPRINGS, by M. D. and E. R. Ormes. Colorado Springs: Dentan Printing Co., 1933.

FACTS, AN ILLUSTRATED WEEKLY REVIEW, published in Colorado Springs, 1900 to 1902.

A BOOK OF STRATTONS, Vol. 1, by Harriet Russell Stratton. The Grafton Press 1908, N. Y.

A BOOK OF STRATTONS, Vol. 2, by Harriet Russell Stratton. Frederick H. Hitchcock 1918, N. Y.

TRAIL MAGAZINE, 19:7 and the T. F. DAWSON SCRAP BOOKS, Vol. 23 and 24. Denver: State Historical Society.

In addition to old files of the *Rocky Mountain News*, *Denver Post*, *Colorado Springs Gazette*, *Pueblo Chieftain* and *Cripple Creek Times-Record*, I have found helpful the following published books:

HISTORIC INDIANA, by Julia Henderson Levering. N. Y.: G. P. Putnam's Sons.

THE AUTOBIOGRAPHY OF JOHN HAYS HAMMOND. N. Y.: Farrar and Rinehart.

COLORADO, by Leroy R. Hafen. Denver: Peerless Pub. Co.

ENCYCLOPEDIA OF BIOGRAPHY OF COLORADO, by William N. Buyers.

THEY BUILT THE WEST AND PAY DIRT, by Glenn Chesney Quiett. N. Y.: Appleton Company.

HERE THEY DUG THE GOLD, by George F. Willison. N. Y.: Brentano's—Publishers.

SILVER DOLLAR, by David Karsner. N. Y.: Covici•Friede.

TIMBER LINE, by Gene Fowler. N. Y.: Covici•Friede.

FATHER STRUCK IT RICH, by Evalyn Walsh McLean. Boston: Little Brown and Co.